Nordin Dechicha

Beef Wellington à la Mustafa

The Babuba Family In Stockholm

Part 1

Translated by
Anton Zetterman

Nurabook
www.nordindechicha.se
© Nordin Dechicha 2012

Cover (photo: stefan@swmedia.org):
At the moment this comedy only exists in the form of a book. Let us hope that it may also come out as a sitcom on television and then onthe cover of the next edition we can have a picture of Mustafa without a mask.

Proof-read by Jonathan Howard

Distributed by Amazon

ISBN 978-91-980603-2-4

To Adam and Meryam Dechicha

Riddarholmen (Henrik Trygg/imagebank.sweden)

Kastellholmen (Ola Ericson/imagebank.sweden)

STOCKHOLM UNIVERSITY 12
   Beef Wellington à la George Bush spiced with fear 47
   Beef Wellington à la Patrícia Gaztañaga 53
   Beef Wellington à la Jim Carrey 64
   Beef Wellington à la Lagerfeld 78
   Beef Wellington à la rape spiced with sexologists 93

STOCKHOLM, JE T'AIME 106
   Beef Wellington à la Qatar 130
   Beef Wellington à la David Letterman spiced with the
      Emir of Qatar and his prime minister 166
   Beef Wellington à la Bob Geldorf and U2-Bono 191
   Beef Wellington à la Swedish Prostitution Law 209
   Beef Wellington à la Jacques Chirac spiced with
      ex-foreign minister de Villepin 237

SWEDEN IS FANTASTIC 268
   Beef Wellington à la Vásia Trifili 286
   Beef Wellington à la Volvo 292
   Beef Wellington à la three musketeers of al-Jazeera:
      Faisal al Kasim, Ahmed Mansour and Sami Haddad,
      among the best debaters of the Arab world 302
   Beef Wellington à la John Cleese 303
   Beef Wellington à la Cameron Diaz 314
   Beef Wellington à la Mel Gibson 327
   Beef Wellington à la Parkinson 334

Sergels torg (Ola Ericson /imagebank.sweden)

PREFACE

HUMOUR WITHOUT BORDERS "BEEF WELLINGTON À LA MUSTAFA" IS THE NEW POLITICS

In preparing this book I have had friends read the drafts, I have recounted the story even more times, and above all: I have talked of the bearing metaphor, which is also the title of the book – Beef Wellington. Everyone has looked at me as if I were from Mars. Beef Wellington, what's that? Few knew the dish, even fewer had eaten it.

Therefore, I shall attempt to give a brief explanation. However, I recommend a visit to the Internet to get a picture of what Beef Wellington is. Try googling "Beef Wellington", or perhaps even better, "Beef Wellington + recipes." One can google for images too. Or maybe simply find a cookbook.

Beef tenderloin is luxury food, the most expensive meat you can buy.

There are several recipes for Beef Wellington. You can make it with mushroom stew, smoked ham, minced liver, or minced veal.

Recipe (with mushroom stew):

1. Flavour a beef tenderloin with salt and pepper and fry till browned. Place on a plate and let it cool.

2. Chop onion and mushrooms and fry together on medium heat until it's dry. Add tomato purée and minced garlic while stirring. Take it off the heat and add the yolk of an egg while stirring. Flavour with salt and pepper.

3. Add crème fraiche, if desired.

4. Roll out the puff pastry. Put the fried mushroom mix on the pastry, cover the fillet and spread the rest of the mushrooms on it. Brush the pastry with the beaten yolk of an egg and FOLD IT INTO A LOAF.

5. Put it in the oven at 200°C for 30-35 minutes.

6. Let it rest for a minute and slice it into 2 cm thick slices.

When Mustafa bakes his Beef Wellington, it looks appetizing and promising on the surface, just like a real Beef Wellington. With many spices, it smells good from a long distance, but in reality there is only rubbish inside, chickpeas, potato and tomato purée, Tunisian harissa. And above all, not a MILLIGRAMME of beef tenderloin. He folds it into a nice-looking loaf. Beef Wellington à la Mustafa is a trick, to serve people something different than they think they are served.

Mustafa is a comedian. He can neither read nor write, but he cooks a special dish to solve any problem that may confront him. Recently such Mustafa-special dishes have become fashionable everywhere: on the internet and on Wall Street, or with head-waiters in smart restaurants or with George Bush when he was President. His special dish then was an Irak supposed to be full of weapons of mass destruction, when really it was just full of oil.

There is no specific recipe for "Beef Wellington à la Mustafa". He can use celebrities like Letterman, George Bush, Mel Gibson, Lagerfeld, Bob Geldof and U2-Bono with the aid of humour, religion, history, and politics; anything and everything to convince and manipulate.

How does Mustafa's Beef Wellington work? Mustafa himself would say that it works much like a car:

1. The coachwork is the concepts of history.
2. The engine is humour.
3. The gearbox is the tempo. Tempo, tempo, tempo!
4. The battery is tension.
5. The four wheels are facial expression and voice.
6. The headlights are the timing.
7. The fuel is imitation.

And voilà!

Mustafa drives around Stockholm on his delivery bike, in the hope of seeing "the walking cash machine, Mademoiselle Nordea" (Nordea is a bank in Sweden), who could produce his comedy.

Welcome to Mustafa's two so-different worlds! In one world he is selling jasmine on a beach in Tunisia. In another he is at home around Stureplan, Stockholm's most sophisticated neighbourhood. Visit the suburb of Skärholmen and meet the Babuba family – an unusual family, who sometimes prefer to hack a hole through a concrete wall, instead of using the doorway beside it.

The family consists of Mother Merjam, Ali, Fatima,

the donkey Besbussa and, last but not least, Mustafa, the comedian who doesn't know how to read or write.

Now I am going to find a restaurant that can serve me a proper Beef Wellington. It will taste nice.

Nourddine Dechicha, Stockholm in March 2012

"OK, Mustafa Nyponros, may I ask you, why did you bring a lantern, don't you find it bright enough in here?"
"Yeah sure it is, but you know, I'm looking for a girl that is beautiful and has curves!"

"Is this the bottom you've been hunting high and low for?"
Mustafa looked up at Åsa.
"Is it! Caroline's curves are so sexy that if I had a camel's tail I would be waving it like crazy now."

CHAPTER 1

STOCKHOLM UNIVERSITY

It was Monday morning and Mustafa was standing in front of the bathroom mirror, pouring oil onto his hair and trying desperately to get that bedroom look that would make his hair look sexy and untidy, as if he had just stepped out of bed.

His sister Fatima woke up, stepped out of bed and headed for the toilet. The bathroom door was closed but not locked. She opened it and found her brother there doing his hair.

"If you're going to the toilet, lock the toilet door", she told him.

Mustafa barely noticed her and continued to work on his hairdo.

"Well, I don't want my sister to stare through the keyhole", he said after a while.

"You with your smart-talk. Why aren't you at work?"

"I start at ten o'clock today."

Fatima returned to her room. She waited for a couple of minutes and then went back to the toilet. Mustafa was still there working on that hairdo.

"Mustafa Ben Metrosexual", she said condescendingly. How long have you been in there? For one hour? For two?"

"Just a minute, I'll be finished soon."

"Guys who stand in front of the mirror for hours, it's sooo ridiculous."

"It's important to take care of your appearance. Everybody appreciates a nice, clean person, no one likes a bum. Remember that, Fatima!"

"But isn't a shower enough for that? You don't have to put two pounds of wax in your hair to become nice and clean. You use more hair care products than I do!"

"Dear sister, I happen to know that men also want to look good, and I also happen to know that women appreciate guys who smell as good as a Swedish nyponros (Dogrose)!

Fatima shook her head.

"I'm wetting my pants here, but hey, keep going, get that hair style right first", she said sarcastically.

Mustafa put on his big glasses and turned towards Fatima.

"Voilà!" he shouted.

"Please Mustafa, you just look ridiculous, such big glasses on such a small head."

"Well, that's a matter of taste, dear sister. Taste is like the bottom, split!"

Mustafa took his glasses off.

"Can you breathe on the lenses, please? I've caught a cold and my nose is stuffed", he said. Fatima looked at him with a questioning look.

"Are you going to check if I'm in good shape or something?"

"No, I just want to polish my glasses."

"I don't have time for your stupid games, Mustafa, I have to pee!"

Fatima grabbed hold of Mustafa and tried to pull him out of the bathroom.

"OK, Fatima, OK, cool it down a bit, let me walk out myself, nice and easy, OK?"

At Södertörn college

Mustafa got dressed and walked out. He took his delivery bike and cycled to Södertörn College. Mustafa worked as a cleaner for the cleaning company "Keep

Stockholm Clean". The company had contracts throughout Stockholm and for the past three months Mustafa had been assigned to clean at Södertörn College, a couple of miles south of the centre of Stockholm. It took him about thirty minutes with his delivery bike to get to the college.

He looked a bit funny, Mustafa, riding his delivery bike. He was short like Charlie Chaplin, with a long moustache like Salvador Dalí. His face was somewhat asymmetric. He had a striking potato nose, unusually big ears that stuck out and big, beautiful, kind reindeer-eyes. Everything in his face was big compared to his relatively small head. This, however, didn't stop him from attracting the opposite sex. Mustafa was constantly entertaining himself with various "pick-up projects" and he had just found a new one, Lisa Gustavsson, a secretary for one of the more well-known professors at the college. Mustafa had had his eyes on her ever since he started working at Södertörn. While he cycled he thought of Lisa. He knew he was going to see her today and so it was going to be an exciting day at work.

Mustafa parked his delivery bike outside the college's main entrance and walked in. At the reception desk he found his mate and boss Pedro, who was originally from Brazil.

"Ey, Mustafa, my man! You are here on time, man, what happened to you, are you ill?" Pedro put his hand on Mustafa's forehead.

"Hey, Pedro, easy, I put soap and washing powder in every single toilet in the campus yesterday, I worked two hours overtime, so don't come here and …."

"OK, OK, Mustafa, that's good, brilliant in fact. You can start at the lab today."

Mustafa put his arm around Pedro's shoulder.

"Pedro, my Brazilian brother. Listen, we're friends right? We're there for each other, no matter what?"

"Sure, Mustafa, sure. What do you want me to do for

you ? Isn't the lab OK?

"Well, you know I've been working on that girl at the Institute of Literature, right?"

"Yeah. And?"

"Well, that means that I have to work there! You know, I have her hooked, now I just have to use the landing net to reel her in, but to do that I have to get a seat in the boat!"

"I understand your problem, Mustafa, but…"

Suddenly Lisa Gustavsson came walking in the boys' direction.

"Speak of the devil" Pedro whispered.

"The devil? You are not exactly God's gift to mankind yourself! This is pure beauty, nature's perfection", Mustafa whispered back.

Mustafa and Pedro just stood there with their mouths open as Lisa came closer. She looked better than ever today, walking in high-heeled shoes as if it were the easiest thing in the world. She was wearing a tight miniskirt that brought out the best of her perfectly rounded pear shaped bottom (the shape that Mustafa preferred) and wore just enough make-up. She looked confidently into the eyes of every person she met, well aware of her beauty. Just before she passed them, she noticed the two staring cleaners.

"Oh, hi, Mustafa! You've made my room look so nice!"

"Oh, thank you, Lisa! But I assure you, the pleasure was mine, really."

Lisa smiled at Mustafa and turned to the right down a corridor, elegantly wiggling her bottom.

"I HAVE to work over there! That girl's bottom can make grown men cry, can't you see that?!"

"You have to remain in the lab, Mustafa, I'm going to give myself a cleaning job at the Institute of Literature today. That woman really makes me cry happy tears."

"You power tripper, you knew that I was after this

girl first. I'm on the final stretch now, you can't just come here and trip me at the finish line, Pedro, you can't!"

Mustafa turned to Pedro. He folded his hands, went down on his knees and began to beg, theatrically.

"Oh, great Pedro, I promise I'll always work for you, I'll do anything for you, until the day I die…"

"Hey, Mustafa, look over there instead…"

Mustafa turned around. Lisa came back from the corridor and walked straight in his and Pedro's direction.

"Listen, Mustafa, I thought of something. We have this cabinet in the office that we don't really need, and I was wondering, well, I know you're not in the moving business but maybe if…"

"I'll fix it!"

"Oh thanks, really nice of you Mustafa, great, really. We need to get rid of that cabinet."

"But of course, I'll take care of that. Let's go to office right now!"

Mustafa and Lisa headed for the Institute of Literature. On the way Mustafa turned his head and waved triumphantly at Pedro. When they arrived at the office, Mustafa dismantled the cabinet. He took out the drawers, one by one of course, and put them on the floor outside in the corridor. While he did that, he chatted away with Lisa.

"Mustafa, I've been wondering something. Since you're an expert on cleaning agents… what's the name of that thing you kill ants with? You know, I've had all these ants in my summer house lately."

Mustafa turned towards her, wrinkled his forehead and went through all the facial expressions of an educated man.

"You can't just kill animals, they teach people so much", he said with a home-made French-Arabic accent. "The birds, for instance, taught us to fly!"

Lisa laughed at Mustafa's accent. She wanted to hear more of it, so she asked: "What about the ants, what have they been teaching us?"

"You might not believe this Lisa, but the fact is that the ants were pioneers in many different areas. Adultery, for instance, which animal is the pioneer of adultery? Yes, that's correct, it's the ant!"

" I don't believe you" said Lisa.

"It's the truth, really! They stab each other in the back all the time, those little creeps. Betrayal, lies, marriage problems… it's everywhere, all the time, in every anthill. And much else, too."

"What else is that?"

"The ants have taught us group sex! They do it all the time, always have. Three, four, five, you know, they outnumber us all when it comes to making love".

"I don't believe that, Mustafa!"

"It's the truth!" Mustafa assured her. "Group sex all the time! The anthills are like orgy houses!"

"How do you know all this?"

"At home I have a miniature house that I use to study ant behaviour", Mustafa said. "They're really special, interesting animals to study."

"What makes them so special?" asked Lisa.

"They're special in many ways, apart from the sex thing. They're probably the only animals, apart from us, that are religious. For example, did you know that the prophet Solomon could speak with ants?"

"No, I had no idea. Unbelievable!"

"I'm not joking. He really could understand ants. There are many stories about his meetings with ants. There is s story about a strictly Catholic ant who got a visit from her two daughters. The first of the two daughters said, 'I live a good life eating from the garbage pile, I'm so satisfied with my life'. The other daughter said, 'Mom, I'm a prostitute'. The ant-mom fainted from the shock. When she woke up again she asked her daughter: 'What did you say you were?' 'A prostitute' her daughter answered. 'Oh thank God, I thought you said Protestant!'"

Lisa laughed and then she looked at Mustafa.

"And what is your goal with all this ant research?"

"I want to understand what adultery is all about. Why are we unfaithful to each other? I'm sure the answer is to be found in the ants' behaviour. I'm going to launch a website, www.mustafasants.com. Then people can mail me questions about adultery and group sex, and I deliver answers based on my ant research. So you see, Lisa, ants have taught us a lot."

"Sounds like a brilliant idea! I'm pretty sure the domain name is up for grabs, too".

Mustafa looked at her, satisfied. He felt he really had Lisa hooked now, it was just the landing-net part that remained. He took a deep breath and looked straight into her eyes, ready to make the last move, when suddenly someone knocked on the door. It was Rebecka, an administrator at the college, working in the office next door to Lisa's.

"Hey, Lisa, I think we have to go to Stockholm University, the meeting starts in an hour's time!"

"Oh, that meeting, I had totally forgotten! Well, then we have to run immediately!"

"You're such an advanced planner, Lisa! Well, let's go then!"

Rebecka turned to Mustafa.

"Hi! Does your mom work at Stockholm University?"

Mustafa became terrified. How did this woman know about that?

"Yeah."

"Does she work as a factotum?"

"Yeah!"

"Is her name Merjam Babuba?"

"Yeah, exactly. How do you know this?"

"I just spoke with her on the phone, and she said she

had two sons working as cleaners here at Södertörn."

"I'll be damned. And you're going there now? In that case, maybe you could deliver this to her?"

Mustafa picked out a box of dark chocolate from one of the pockets in his work trousers.

"I got these yesterday, but I don't really like dark chocolate."

"Oh, that's sweet of you, giving chocolate to your mom! Sure, we'll give it to her. Come on now, Lisa!"

The ladies walked away. Lisa turned around and smiled at Mustafa, who was standing at the door opening. As she disappeared around the corner he returned to her office and continued with the cabinet. The door to Lisa's office remained open when Ali came walking by with his cleaning wagon in the corridor.

Ali at Södertörn college

Ali was Mustafa's big brother. 25 years old, tall but at the same time chubby, shy and insecure, especially when it came to girls. What made things worse were Ali's tics. Sometimes his head started moving from side to side, as camels do. When he was a kid, the tics haunted him all the time; nowadays it was just when he became nervous. When it came to football it was a different matter. Ali loved football, and really blossomed whenever he got a chance to talk about it. He could go on and on. Except for being a little overweight, he looked ordinary and the only thing that stood out was his well defined potato nose.

Ali wanted to work as a pastry chef and had a degree in this speciality back in Tunisia, but he hadn't managed to find work as a pastry chef in Stockholm. Until then he made his living at "Keep Stockholm Clean".

Ali passed the open door and saw Mustafa.
"Oh, there you are!"
"Yep. Working hard as usual, you know me,

brother!"

"You missed a hell of a game yesterday."

"I did? Who played?"

"Hammarby-Gothenburg, 2-1. The atmosphere in the north stand... amazing!"

"I'll be damned."

"Next game is away, against Gävle. Pedro and I are going to take the supporter coach up there. It costs 350 crowns for the trip and game ticket.

"It's going to be freezing. I might as well watch the game at the sports bar. For 350 crowns, I could have a lot of beer and see the game on TV!"

"They have bars in Gävle as well! You can drink there."

"Oh, they have? I had no idea."

"Gävle is fantastic, a totally unique city in Sweden!"

"In what way?"

"The population hasn't changed in the last fifty years! Every time a child is born, a man escapes from Gävle!"

"Wow", Mustafa said, "so there's just women left there now?"

"Exactly! The town is just full of blondes, blondes, blondes..."

"Maybe it isn't such a bad thing after all. I'll think about it", Mustafa said.

"By the way, I hope you haven't forgotten that it's your turn to take the donkey out today?"

"Fatima said she had no school today; she'll take care of it."

"I'll believe that when I hear it from her! I'm going to call her now. Go back to work."

Ali continued to the next empty office and called Fatima on his cell phone.

"Hi, Ali."

"Mustafa says you're going to take the donkey out

today, is that right?"

"Yeah, I'm out with her now, actually."

"OK, just checking, you never know with Mustafa, you know. See you later!"

"OK see you, brother!"

Fatima was the youngest in the Babuba family, a 21-year old girl with the future ahead of her. She had a high school degree from Tunisia and now wanted to study political science at Stockholm University - a happy, outgoing girl who laughed a lot and was almost always in a good mood. She was also very cute, with big brown eyes and long raven-black hair cut in a trendy haircut with a razor-sharp fringe. To get the Swedish high school degree and to be accepted at the university, she studied Swedish and English at the adult school in the evenings and worked part-time in the kitchen of a day care centre. It was a hectic life, but today Fatima had an unusual day off.

It had been almost three years since the Babuba family, mother Merjam and her three kids, Ali, Mustafa and Fatima, had moved from their home country Tunisia to Sweden, specifically to Stockholm and its suburb Skärholmen. The Babubas were a unique family in Sweden. Unique not because the family consisted of a single mother with children, but because they had a somewhat unconventional pet, at least in Sweden: a donkey named Besbussa.

Fatima and her donkey

The family lived in a four-room apartment on the ground floor of a block of flats in Skärholmen. The apartment was a former office, rebuilt as an apartment. Besbussa was beautiful, an old donkey with a grey coat and big black eyes. She lived in a stable in the forest about 75 meters behind the apartment building. For Besbussa the best part of the day was to come in to the apartment for one or two hours. The Babuba family had settled down well in Skärholmen. They liked it very much, mostly because it reminded them of home. Skärholmen was Sweden, but at the same time a very continental place where people from all across the globe had gathered. You had the big square where you could buy all kinds of fruits and vegetables and the salesmen shouted out the prices, just like back home in Tunisia. Skärholmen also had a big shopping centre with all kinds of exciting shops. But the best thing about the place was that it was so close to the water, just a ten-minute walk down to Lake Mälaren, the gorgeous Stockholm lake.

Fatima knew how to spend her day off. She went to the stable and took the beautiful grey donkey out for a walk down to the shore of Lake Mälaren. Besbussa needed to go out every day to stay calm and not make a noise all the time. Fatima didn't mind taking a walk. On the contrary,, she loved it. She loved taking Besbussa down to the lake, finding a seat somewhere and sitting there contemplating, while Besbussa chewed the grass. Fatima found it peaceful, almost like meditation.

She dressed Besbussa in a pink scarf and four long pink leg warmers, one for each leg. In Besbussa's ears she put pink, flower-shaped earrings. She continued with a pink velvet costume which she threw around Besbussa's back and tied around her belly. To top things off, she put a beautiful imitation-gold necklace around the donkey's neck. Besbussa now looked marvelous, the beautiful grey nuance against all the pink and the gold-coloured necklace. Fatima and Besbussa got a lot of stares as they walked through Skärholmen. When they reached Lake Mälaren and the water, the donkey started braying and jumping up and down from pure happiness. This was her time of the day. The old donkey loved just to stare at all the water, just as she had done at home in the small island of Djerba in

Tunisia. But now the olive trees from Djerba had been replaced by leafless birches and the water was more grey-blue than green-blue. Besbussa took a bite of the green grass while Fatima patted and tickled her. Every now and then small boats passed. Fatima squinted at the water, smiled and stroked Besbussa across the muzzle. A pre-school class passed by on an outing. All the small kids went crazy when they saw the donkey and started running towards her. Fatima had been through this before and had nothing against it. Patiently she let all of the kids take a ride on Besbussa, one by one. They all loved it, of course. At last the teachers called the kids in. It was time to go back to school. Fatima and Besbussa stayed a little longer, watching the lake.

At Stockholm university

Lisa and Rebecka arrived at Stockholm University. As they walked through the corridor leading to the meeting room, they saw a woman they both knew. She was 49 years old, sturdy, had short hair and a beautiful smile. It was Merjam Babuba, factotum at the University library and the mother of Ali, Mustafa and Fatima. Merjam was a strong person with a warm heart. One of the things she cared most about was her work at the non-profit organisation "Help Africa", which took up a lot of her time outside of work. She had the simple nickname "Mother Merjam" , which not just her kids called her but everyone close to her. Rebecka and Lisa had not come so far in their relationship with Merjam, but they were glad to see her. You always became glad in some way when you saw Merjam, unless you happened to run into her when her sons, especially Mustafa, had done something stupid.

"Merjam!" Rebecka shouted.
Merjam stopped.
"Oh, hi, Rebecka, hi, Lisa! What are you doing

here?"

"We have a meeting with the administrator at Stockholm University in just a few minutes."

"Oh, how nice!"

"By the way, Merjam, your son Mustafa - we met him today. He asked me to give these to you."

Rebecka gave Merjam the chocolate box.

"Oh, that's generous of him."

Merjam took a further look at the box.

"Ah, I think I've found the explanation for his generosity. This is dark chocolate! Had it been light chocolate he would never have let anyone get hold of it!"

"Really?" Rebecka said. "We have to move on. Nice to see you, Merjam!"

"OK, have a nice time here, girls!"

Merjam continued to the library, where the librarians Lotta and Karin stood by the information counter, talking to the student organisation's chairman, Åsa.

Merjam handed over printing paper to Karin.

"Thanks Merjam!" she said.

"No problem."

"You've got eyes everywhere, Merjam. You see what is missing", Karin went on.

"That's kind of you… Can I do something illegal here at Stockholm University?" Merjam said with a twinkle in her eye.

"Are you going to shoot a professor?"

"No, but as you know, the Help Africa collection container has been empty for a week now. Can I borrow the microphone and tell the students?"

Karin was silent for a moment.

"OK, we can make an exception for Africa and Merjam", Karin said, "here you are!"

Merjam took the microphone to the public address system. She looked out in the library, where some of the students were dreamingly looking out the window. She smiled at Karin.

"Dear students!" she began. "We're closing the library in half an hour. If you want to borrow some books you must come to the issuing counter now!"

Hundreds of heads turned around and looked at their watches. A buzz went through the library.

"OK, OK, take it easy, just kidding", Merjam said. "Just wanted to get everyone's attention! I just want to tell you that we've put up a container outside, and it'll be here for a month. During that time you can throw clothes that you don't use or need into that container. We're thankful for all the help we can get."

Merjam put the microphone down and turned around. Suddenly she came to think of something else.

"Excuse me, there's something on my mind. Dear friends, all you do is study, from morning until evening. If I were the top dog at this university I'd introduce 'cuddle-breaks'. Every student has to turn to her left and start cuddling with whomever is sitting there. But notice! Cuddling, and nothing more than that! Don't take it to the next level in here! I'm sure this would push up your test results, what do you think?" Merjam joked.

"Brilliant", shouted one guy with a baseball cap on his head.

"Great idea!" shouted a girl and started applauding. More students joined her.

Merjam smiled and interrupted the cheering.

"Sweden's future and upcoming Nobel prize winners! You understand me ?"

"Are you finished now?" Karin said.

"There's one more thing", Merjam went on. "This cuddling thing has to stay between me and you! Don't tell the rector, or he'll fire me and make me tread sand in the Sahara for the rest of my life! Now I'm done, go back to whatever it is you're studying!"

Merjam gave the microphone to Karin.

"Merci beaucoup!" she said.

Merjam left the library together with Lotta.

"Good idea, this 'cuddling'. I think that can make immigrants come to the universities and get an academic degree", Lotta said.

Merjam was well aware that most of the immigrants in Sweden stepped right into Unemployment Land after they finished studying.

"Absolutely, so that the immigrants have something to think back on when they are kneading the pizza dough and have several hundred thousand crowns in study loan debt."

Lotta laughed.

"You're absolutely right. But it's hard for *everyone* to find work nowadays", Lotta said.

Merjam looked at her watch.

"Oh, my break started ten minutes ago! You forget time and space when you get a chance to shine with the mic!"

"You certainly do."

"I have to go to the restaurant and give this book to the chef. See you later, Lotta!"

In the kitchen the chef was beating omelettes.

"Hi, Gunnar! Voilà, gastronomy in seven languages!"

"Thanks, Merjam!" Gunnar replied. "You're an angel. Now I know how to say salmon with Béarnaise sauce in different languages."

"Yes, it's an interesting book. You can borrow it for four weeks."

"Thanks, I'll check it out... But, Merjam. The law students are organising a party on Saturday night."

"That's nice."

"Yeah, it's going to be really fun..."

"Are they going to give all the students a weekly allowance so that they can go and buy Swedish vodka on

Saturdays?"

Gunnar laughed.

"No, Merjam, they have their student loans, that'll be enough. No, we're going to throw a party with the message 'Find new friends and love' - a dating party!'"

"Great! Good idea!" Merjam said enthusiastically. "It's a good thing that the law students organise parties like that. There are companies that charge money and exploit lonely guys, without result."

"Merjam, we need some extra staff in the kitchen. Can you help us out on Saturday?"

"Of course! That'd be fun!"

"Thanks, Gunnar! Bye, see you!"

At Södertörn college

The next day Mustafa and his cleaning wagon had, funnily enough, found their way to Lisa Gustavsson's office again. Just as he arrived at her office to empty the waste paper basket, he heard a familiar voice in the corridor.

"Mustafa, Mustafa, are you there?"

"I'm here!" Mustafa shouted.

He turned to Lisa, shrugged and left the office. In the corridor, he saw an exhausted Ali come running with a crazy look on his face.

"What's the matter?" Mustafa asked and looked at Ali, who was soaking wet.

"You have to come with me to the men's toilet now! The water's running!"

"The water's running? Is someone having a baby?"

"No, just come with me!"

Ali took Mustafa by the arm and pulled him along. Mustafa followed him with a reluctant look on his face. They ran through the corridor down to the men's room.

"Why do we have to do this now? I'm on my way with Lisa! I was trying a new technique, which would…"

"Bah, technique! Your hook-up techniques have the same effect as spitting in the Sahara! She has a boyfriend, I've seen them walking hand in hand on campus!"

"No, come on, don't tell me that!"

"Promise, and it's a handsome one as well. I think he's a professor in journalism. You have no chance, brother!"

Mustafa put his hand on his forehead to show how disappointed he was.

"My bad luck, always my bad luck!"

They reached the men's room at the end of the corridor. Ali opened the door.

There was a water inferno in there. Water was squirting straight out into the room from a tap on the wall. Mustafa threw himself at the tap, trying to stop the water flow. It didn't work. The water pressure was too strong. He was pushed back again and landing seated on the floor in the middle of the room, under the shower. He looked up on Ali with a mad look on his face.

"What the heck have you done, Ali?" he shouted.

Ali wasn't paying attention. He was busy trying to close the tap.

"Unbelievable, I had no idea you could have so much fun without laughing", he said.

Mustafa glared at him. He didn't find Ali's joke a bit funny.

"Idiot! Why did you play with the tap?"

"There was too little water in the closet and I wanted to increase the flow."

"Really?"

Neither of the two brothers had noticed it, but Pedro had entered the men's room.

He looked around the room and then walked over to the main tap at the top left corner of the room. He knocked on the pipe with a hammer. Immediately the water flow stopped. Ali and Mustafa turned around in surprise. Pedro looked at them and clapped his hands.

"Pedro! Our guardian angel!" Mustafa cheered. Pedro shook his head.

"How did you do that?" Ali asked.

"I just knocked with the hammer", Pedro replied.

"But I knocked too, with my hand; it didn't work."

"Let me tell you a story, Ali. Back home in Brazil, I used to repair sewing machines. One day I was at a workshop to take a look at a sewing machine that didn't work. I looked at it, then knocked carefully with the hammer. It started working straight away. I turned to the owner and said that I wanted 30 real for the job (thirty Brazilian real is about a hundred Swedish kronor). He thought that 30 real for just one knock with a hammer was too much. I said to him 'The knock cost just 1 real, it's the knowing where to knock that costs you 29 real, so it's 30 for you, mister!"

"Wow, what a clever guy!" Mustafa said.

"Seriously, boys, what are you doing? Do I have to follow your every step like some pre-school teacher?"

Mustafa looked at Pedro with a look that seemed to say, "My brother is so stupid I don't know what to do."

"Don't drag me into this", Mustafa said, "it was Ali. I was just trying to clean up his mess."

"That's what I'm saying, you pre-school kids. Well, I don't know about you two, but I came here to take a piss, not to save your sorry arses . But I guess that comes with this job… It's a good thing that the dating party is on Saturday so I can forget all the trouble at work."

"Yeah, but Pedro, what is a dating party?"

"OK, Mustafa, sit down and daddy Pedro will tell you. A dating party is simply a way of keeping girls from loneliness and boredom, and boys from fights and devilment. If there were no dating parties, the mental hospitals would be full of lunatics."

Mustafa watched Pedro, contemplating.

"Interesting. If they could hold dating-parties in Iraq, maybe they could keep people from fighting a war and that kind of devilment."

"Yeah! It's going to be a cool party with my favourite girls, 4You!"

"Who are 4You?"

"They are four girls from Russia, Poland, the Czech Republic and the Ukraine. They sing a cool song, 'If you're a man, then we're looking for you!'"

"Absolutely wicked! Hey, Pedro, you must get me into this dating-party!"

"So you really want to go?"

"Do I want to go? I'm the man they're looking for!"

Mustafa, overwhelmed by the message, started dancing Arab dances, using his cleaning wagon as a dance partner. A couple of students entered the bathroom, looked at Mustafa and started laughing at the dancing cleaner.

"Stop it, Mustafa, you're embarrassing us!" Ali hissed.

"I know I am, but I just can't stop!"

"Are you freezing, Mustafa?" Pedro wondered.

"No, but I have ants in my pants!"

"You're crazy, Mustafa!" Ali said.

"I have to go now, can't be standing here soaking wet in the middle of the working day, can I?" Mustafa said. Ali took his cleaning wagon and left the men's room. Pedro followed him.

At café-bar Bux-Biou

Mustafa wanted to be seen; he loved being the everyday clown. During his first two years in Sweden he wore a jacket and jeans and blended into the Stockholm crowd, but he had difficulty contacting girls. He realised that he had to do something drastic with his appearance in order to solve this, a big problem in his own opinion. He decided to do a total makeover. He started to grow long moustaches in the same style as the artist Salvador Dalí, whose face Mustafa had painted many times on big Arabian plates during his spell as a potter's apprentice on the island of Djerba, Tunisia.

He started to mix Western European-style clothes with more traditional Arab clothes. "Sinbad-pants" with wide legs were mixed with shirts and jackets from famous designers like Jean Paul Gaultier, Dior and Armani. As headgear he started to wear a bandana, which he tied on his forehead. Nowadays Mustafa was recognised when walking along the Stockholm streets. His style was hip and, combined with his sharp humour, this made him popular with the girls.

It was Monday afternoon on October the 25th, and that meant payday. It had been a week since Mustafa, Ali and Pedro first heard the message about the dating party. Mustafa wanted to get into the party at any price, and he wanted to make a big impression when there. He quit work at two o'clock and threw himself onto the first commuter train into central Stockholm. When he reached Stockholm's Central Station he jumped off the train and walked towards the hippest spot in Stockholm, Stureplan, where the rich and the famous party all night long. On the fashionable street Birger Jarlsgatan Mustafa had his favourite beauty salon, "Mona and Sara". Today's "beauty investment" was to dye his moustache, this time blue, white and red, like the French flag. After the colouring he took a full body wax treatment. To his own despair Mustafa had quite a lot of hair growing on his upper body, stomach, arms, chest and back… He screamed like a pig when the cosmetologist ripped the wax strips off his body, but it was worth all the pain. Afterwards, he felt young and happy. He left "Mona and Sara" and headed for a clothing shop on Biblioteksgatan, where he bought a Gaultier shirt. Then he took the underground to Slussen and his favourite drinking spot in Stockholm, "Bux-Biou" (Buxom is beautiful), a very exotic place. The whole place was arranged around a big swimming pool, but it was not like a public swimming pool. Everything was very green, like at the Mediterranean or in Los Angeles. There were little palm trees and bushes and all the decor gave the place a Southern feeling. The huge swimming pool was shaped like a lagoon, with artificial rocks climbing up the walls. The pool was divided in the middle, where there was a big cave, popularly called "The love grotto" after the infamous love-cave at the Playboy Mansion. Along one of the pool sides, there was a long pool bar, with everything liquid you might need for a good evening. Mellow salsa music played in the bar and gave the place an even more "southern" atmosphere. Mustafa changed into bathing clothes and headed for the pool area. He felt right at home at Bux-Biou. It was quite expensive but the drinks were heavenly. Mustafa had decided to meet Ali in the bar, but his brother was nowhere to be found. Mustafa shrugged and ordered a Piña Colada. Mustafa had pissed in his own territory at Bux-Biou and he was well on his way to a reputation as a regular, especially as he had got to know Lasse, the owner. Mustafa hung out in the bar, checked out the girls and sipped on his Piña. He lit up when he saw Lasse enter the bar.

"Hello, Mustafa! So you're here sneak-peeking again? Don't you have a job or something?"

"No, I sneek-peek full time, I thought you knew that?"

Lasse laughed and shook Mustafa's hand.

"You look sharp today, Lasse", said Mustafa.

"I'm always sharp when Hammarby wins, you know."

Mustafa laughed.

"My brother was there watching. He said they played well."

"Yeah, they did really well. So your brother supports Hammarby?" Lasse asked.

"Yeah, he's become a real fanatic lately, going to away games and stuff like that", Mustafa replied.

"I'll be damned. I think I'm starting to like Ali, I'm going to give him a croque-monsieur next time he comes."

"He's on his way, I'm waiting for him", Mustafa said.

"Great, I'll tell Tia to get one for him."

"Hey, Lasse?"

"Yes Mustafa?"

"How did you come up with this idea?"

"With Bux-Biou?" Lasse asked.

"Yeah! I mean, this is freaking good, sitting here in October and it feels like summer. That's just brilliant!"

"Well, I've run a number of bars over the years, mostly just regular bars. But I always felt I wanted to do something different. I watched TV one day and it was something about that guy Hugh Hefner, do you know who that is?"

"You're kidding? I know more about him than I do about Ali! But I wish I knew his Playmates a little better."

"He leads a good life, sheik Hefner", said Lasse. Yeah, he's still going strong, believe me. Anyway, there was some documentary about Hefner and the Playboy Mansion, and they showed this 'Love Grotto'. There must have been a whole lot of action going on there over the years. Did you know, they say that Hugh Hefner has magnetic hands that can make women with a headache or a back pain healthy again. That's why so many women want him."

"Really?" Mustafa asked. "I thought he could only make women sick! You know, my ex-girlfriend was crazy about him. All she ever did was nag about Hugh Hefner, every day, every night. You know, I couldn't sleep! I went to the doctor to get sleeping pills. Those were finished pretty quickly, so I had to go back to the doctor to get more."

"But isn't that dangerous? I mean, taking many sleeping pills over short time…"

"But they weren't for me, they were for my girlfriend!"

Mustafa and Lasse both laughed.

"Good story, Mustafa, good story. Anyway, about this place, after seeing that TV programme I just ripped the whole thing off. Pool bars, palm trees, the grotto, you know, everything. I sold off my other businesses and invested all I had in this."

"You did right, Lasse."

"I'm not complaining."

"Nor am I", Mustafa chuckled and took another sip of his Piña Colada.

"Mustafa, how long have you been here in Sweden, just a few years, right?"

"Yeah, three years, just about."

"You speak good Swedish, you have that Södermalm slang (Södermalm is a district in southern Stockholm) and it's even more distinct that mine! How have you been able to pick it up so fast?"

"Well, I just go out a lot, drinking beers, talking with people, you know, you pick things up."

"You really are a social bastard, aren't you, Mustafa? By the way, why did you come to Sweden?"

"For medical reasons."

"Yeah, problems with your liver or what?"

"No, my schoolteacher back home in Tunisia, he used to grab my ears and pull really hard, you can see my ears, here, don't they stand out a bit?"

"Yeah."

"What a mean teacher!"

"He used to pull my hair as well, and you know, after a while there was no hair left to pull! He pulled so hard the hair stopped growing back."

"Damn, there are some schoolteachers in this world…"

"Yeah, it's insane. So you know I started skipping school. When I was 18 I met a Norwegian tourist and I explained to him why my ears were standing out and why I had almost no hair. He didn't believe me, he had this theory that it was due to low blood pressure, and the only thing that could get my blood pressure up again was Scandinavian blondes! So here I am!"

"Did you come to Sweden riding on a donkey?" Lasse joked.

"Yes, what do you think?" Mustafa joked back.

Lasse started laughing out loud and gave Mustafa a friendly pat on the back.

"Nowadays my problems are of the opposite character," Mustafa went on. "I've got hair everywhere! On my back, my stomach, my shoulders, soon it will start growing out of my ears!"

"See it from the positive angle Mustafa, you could have nice pigtails, maybe even put some curlers there."

"Very funny, Lasse. No, I think I'll stick to waxing."

Lasse's cell phone rang.

"Yes? OK, I'll be there", he said and hung up. "Hey Mustafa, I've got to go, nice seeing you, tell Ali he's got a free croque-monsieur in the bar, OK?"

"Sure thing, Lasse."

"And next time you'll tell me the true story about why you came here, OK?"

"Sure thing, Lasse."

"Yeah, and you know what? We're running the first round of the 'mini-bikini contest' tomorrow."

"Finally! I've been waiting for so long!"

"Bring Fatima too, there's an underwear contest as well. We're promoting new Swedish designers every month."

The dating party

Lasse left. Five minutes later Ali strolled into the bar. Mustafa glared at him.

"Where have you been?" Ali was not upset by his brother's angry question but instead he looked amused at Mustafa's new moustaches.

"Oh, you've coloured your moustache again?"

"Yeah, but where have you been?"

"I'll tell you, but you have to tell about the moustache first. I see you're going French!"

"Well yeah, you know, I'm in a French period, sort of. I also bought a Gaultier shirt and a jacket, they're stunning. And it's all just to honour France!"

"I see, I see."

"My moustache has to go along with the rest of my appearance. It is one of my accessories; just as Paris Hilton has her little dog in the Gucci bag, so I have my moustache."

"You're such a fashion boy, Mustafa."

"You know I am, Ali. You have a free croquet-monsieur in the bar by the way. I saw Lasse before."

"OK, nice."

"Now, tell me where you've been."

"OK, this is what I've been doing: I've been around every broom cupboard in the entire Södertörn campus to see if I put the bag with dates in any of them." Ali had brought to work a bag of Tunisian dates that he had planned to give Pedro.

"That's odd", Mustafa said, "have you checked in your cleaning wagon?"

"Yeah, sure. But it's just nowhere to be found!"

"Hmm, weird. But hey, do you have the list of girls going to the dating party?"

"Yeah, that I do have! I would never lose that list."

"Great! Tell me about this dating party, how does it

work?"

"Hmm… it's sort of three parties in one! The first one is called 'Y', because everyone going there gets a yellow note…"

"What Y? Stop blabbering and tell me straight, I'm an illiterate for God's sake!"

That really was true. Mustafa had never learned to read or write. This, of course, made everyday life a bit complicated, but Mustafa would never have admitted that. On the contrary, he was proud to be illiterate and thought that he did well in life without knowing how to read and write.

"OK, Mustafa, stay calm, I'll try to explain. The people going to this 'Y' party, they've contacted one another before on the Internet and so everyone has an idea about whom they want to date. All these people with yellow notes gather around the bar, and just start dating. The party can begin!"

"Oh, that party's not for me, I don't chat on the net a lot. Tell me about the next party instead!"

"OK, the next one is called 'E', it stands for exhibitionists…"

"What's an exhibitionist?"

"It's someone who likes to be seen a lot by other people, for example on a stage. Ring any bells?"

"Not a single one."

Ali sighed.

Mustafa exhorted him. "Go on!"

"OK, brother, these people going to the 'E' party, they don't have time for the Internet, they want eye-to-eye contact straight away!" Mustafa lit up.

"That's my style! Brother Ali, check the list and look for a rich girl, I want 'the walking cash machine, Mademoiselle Nordea'!" (Nordea is one of the biggest Swedish banks.) Ali sighed even louder. Mustafa picked up the list of girls who had signed up for the 'E' party and gave it to Ali - upside down.

"Hmm... it's turned upside down, brother Mustafa."

"It's not the list, stupid. It's the world that is turned upside down!"

Ali, ignoring his brother's remarks, started going through the list.

"There's this girl here, might suit you well. Number 105, a mature lady, works as boss for the ladies' department at NK (a big department store in Stockholm). Oh, wait, what's this?" Mustafa looked at him, puzzled.

"'Sado' wants to meet 'Maso'. You have to like sadomasochism."

"Sadomaschosch... what? I don't understand... Who's 'sado' and who's 'maso' then?"

Ali had gone to primary school in Tunisia for six years and then trained as a pastry chef, but like his brother, he was not particularly well educated

"I have no idea, Mustafa."

"These upper-class ladies always have strange ideas, sign me up as 'interested'."

Ali did what his brother told him.

"The third party then, what about the third party?" Mustafa asked.

"The third party is called 'R', because everyone going there gets a red ticket. Those going to this party want to be anonymous and they want a partner who doesn't think that looks are the most important thing. They will all be masked and are seeking a serious partner, for a serious relationship."

"That's even better! Look in the list, see if any of the ladies is loaded!"

Ali started going through the list. Mustafa turned around, checking out the pool and saw a girl swimming really fast. He was impressed and turned to Ali.

"Have you found something?"

"Hold on", Ali said, just as he discovered an

interesting name on the list, 'Eva Goldberg'.

Ali often reads the Swedish tabloid newspapers, Aftonbladet and Expressen. He thought this Eva Goldberg was related to the famous businessman and billionaire, Martin Goldberg, who often appeared in the tabloids. Ali put Mustafa to the test and played along with his brother's 'gold-digger dreams'.

"Well, I think we've struck gold! Here's your 'sugar mama', Mustafa! Number 80, a gold mine named Eva Goldberg! Great name, huh? Some sort of eye-doctor, expert on 'iris diagnosis', but most important, known as the daughter of Martin Goldberg, the billionaire!"

"Bingo! She's the one! The one who will produce my comedy show! Write her name down, brother."

Ali looked despondently at Mustafa.

"Now I'm starting to understand why everyone in Tunisia called you 'Le Saharien Imagineux', the Imaginative Saharian. Did you catch mad cow disease or something?"

"What, why?"

"You can't be serious when you're saying that this Goldberg girl would in the first place be interested in you and in the second place be interested in producing your comedy show".

"Yes to both questions. Of course she'll be interested and after meeting me she won't think of anything else!"

Ali filled his cheeks with air and blew it out, just to show how he despaired of his brother and his inability to face up to reality.

"OK, Mustafa, you do what you like!"

"By the way Ali, what's 'iris diagnosis'? I don't understand."

"It means 'I know what your eyes mean, but I don't know the rest of you!"

Mustafa saw the fast-swimming girl coming up from the pool. She walked past him and sat down at the next table. Mustafa turned to her.

"Excuse me, lady, do you know what 'iris diagnosis' is?"

"Yes, it's when you can diagnose someone just by watching his or her eyes. By doing that you can tell exactly what illness someone has."

"So that's what it is, huh? OK, thanks for the answer. By the way, I don't know much about swimming, but aren't you on the Swedish Olympic team?"

"How come?" the swimming girl asked, smiling beautifully.

"You're a sensation, Haven't you won medals in the Olympics?"

The girl smiled.

"No, I'm not on any Olympic team."

"Where did you learn to swim that fast?"

"Well, I worked as an escort in Venice for a few years!"

"Are you allowed to swim in the canals?"

"Of course not, but what do you do when the police are after you? You just have to jump in!"

"Interesting", Mustafa hummed and then turned to Ali. "And don't forget brother, my name isn't going to be Babuba at that party."

"What's it going to be then? James Bond?"

"Better than that!"

Ali sighed again. "Come on Mustafa, tell me, I'm dying to hear this."

"OK, buckle up now, it's Mustafa Ibrahamidozlanisulsielbouzouritunisiauchouri."

"Oh dear. I'm not going to write that down, I have the weekend off and I want to enjoy it, not sit and write 'Ibrablblabla'. Why must I write all that down?"

"Excitement, brother, excitement and drama! I promise, when I take the ladies by storm using my new name, you can follow in my footsteps and pick up the leftovers. And there are going to be ladies wherever I go!" Mustafa's plan with the long name was to hit the main stage at the party long before the host had finished pronouncing his name.

"OK, OK, I'll write it down. But only for that reason! Say it again…"

"Ibrahamidozlanisulsielbouzouritunisiauchouri."

When Ali had at last finished writing down the name, he continued to fill in Mustafa's facts.

"What are you writing now, Ali?"

"Age: 23, occupation: cleaner…"

Mustafa exploded: "Idiot! Do you think any of these girls is going to be interested in a cleaner?"

Ali lifted his head and looked surprised at Mustafa.

"Write 'exchange student'!"

Ali shook his head and did what his brother had told him.

"OK, here on question four, they want you to describe the girl of your dreams…"

"Easiest question I've ever heard! OK, first and foremost, she has to have a bottom on the size scale going from Jennifer Lopez to Queen Latifah. She must be beautiful, well rounded and hungry for sex. And she must have the money to produce my comedy show!"

"Not bad, monsieur Le Saharien Imagineux! OK, I'll write it down. You're looking for mademoiselle Nordea, a living cash machine with beautiful curves".

"Are you mad? Just write that I want someone who's nice, funny and spontaneous. And decisive."

Ali sighed heavily. "Sure, Mustafa, sure."

"What about you, brother Ali, what have you chosen?"

"Chosen? Are you mad? At five o'clock it's Hammarby-Malmö on Channel Four, then at eight it's Milan-Lazio on Canal+, then at ten, Real Madrid-Barcelona on Channel Four! I'll have my orgy in front of the TV!"

"Look here Ali, you have to start seeing people, outside, in the real world! We've been here in Sweden for three years now. You know I love football too, but life isn't just work and watching football. You must start integrating into Swedish society!"

"What do you mean integrate?"

"Go out, have a beer, meet some Swedes, talk some shit. If you meet a supporter of Hammarby, talk bad about AIK, if you meet an AIK supporter, talk bad about Hammarby. Easy! You'll be popular in no time, it's called 'shooting some shit' and getting to know your fellow citizens!"

"I don't want to shoot shit and I don't want to drink beer. I'm a teetotaler and I love football."

"OK, have a coke then, but you have to learn how to meet the ladies, pump the tires, become a womaniser"

"I don't think any girl wants a fat cleaner."

Ali felt bad about being overweight and about his way of speaking. He was very insecure as a person, talked slowly and gently. Mustafa on the other hand was confidence personified. He did his best to encourage Ali, though he was well aware that his brother's starting point wasn't the best.

"Of course there's someone for you too. There are lots of women who like fat guys!"

"But maybe they're not my type. I'm obsessed with big ladies, with a bottom on the size scale going from Queen Latifah, Kirstie Alley and upwards! I'm sure there won't be one single girl at the party who looks like that."

"How can you be so sure? You never know, do you?"

"Yes, you do know. Those girls would rather hide at home than go to a party and feel let down by mean people, idiots who stare and judge. You can read about it in the newspapers every day!"

"Try to be positive! Don't just sit around reading

about all the misery in the world in Aftonbladet and Expressen."

"You don't know anything about this, Mustafa, there's discrimination everywhere! Axel and George and I went to this restaurant in Södermalm last week, and my, did they stare at us, as if we were from outer space or something".

"Please, brother, George IS from outer space!"

"Don't destroy my story here, my message. George is a little chubby, that's it, and Axel too, good blokes, like to eat a little too much, as I do. Anyway, they served us lousy pyttipanna (fried hash), just so that we wouldn't come back! Man, were they relieved when we left! What did they think we would do, break the chairs by just sitting on them or something?"

"So you didn't break any chairs?"

"You really are a great brother, Mustafa, such a great support. Do you want me to help you with writing this or not?"

"Easy, Ali, calm down, I was just joking! Of course you didn't break any chairs. You know what, I think what you need is a good old Swedish blonde. Well, not old, but you know, just a blonde! Swedish blondes hold the key to the solution of many problems in this country! They give you joy in life, make you positive, might even make you fall in love!"

"I don't know about that."

"Please, Ali, come with me!"

"OK, I'll go with you, but I won't fill in any of these forms!"

Mustafa shone up like the sun.

"That's my brother! Keep filling in my form. Tomorrow's the last day to send them in!"

Ali went back to filling in Mustafa's registration form. Mustafa drummed with his fingers on the table while Ali's pen worked hard. After a while he was finished.

"OK, write your name here!" Mustafa spat on his thumb and put it on the paper.

"Voilà!"

"Do you have a photo as well", Ali asked.

"Yeah, voilà Monsieur." Mustafa held out the photo. "What do you think?"

"It's fantastic, really fantastic. Just think what might happen if you looked like that in real life."

"Oh, come on, Ali, I really am that good looking!"

Mustafa leaned back and took a sip from his drink, looking satisfied. Then suddenly his mood shifted. His expression turned from satisfied to tormented. Ali looked at him, surprised.

"What's the matter, Mustafa?"

"Oh, how I regret eating all the dates you were going to give to Pedro!"

"What do you mean by that?"

"I ate them all…"

"Did you just get a stroke of guilty conscience or what?"

"No, but a stroke of stomach ache!"

Ali was in a weak position towards his brother. He was too kind and let himself be run over time after time. Now he just sighed.

"OK, but then you'd better go to the pharmacy and buy some medicine."

"No, I'll have a whisky in the bar instead. That'll clear my stomach."

"But it's so expensive, Mustafa! You know we're going to Tunisia on vacation soon. Put your money in the bank instead!"

"No way! In one year I would get eight per cent from the bank; from whisky I get forty percent immediately. By the way, I'm not coming with you to Tunisia, I won't go back there until I am a successful comedian. Then 'Le Saharien Imagineux' will show them!"

Ali shook his head.

Mustafa took from his briefcase a white plastic bag, six centimeters square, full of parsley.

He put a bunch of parsley behind one of his ears.

Mustafa headed for the bar. "Hello, Tia, can I have a whisky?"

"Sure! That'll be 60 crowns!"

Tia poured the whisky.

"Here you are."

"Thanks."

She looked funnily at him.

"Is this the new fashion, to have parsley behind the ears?" she asked.

"No, my friend, it's a reminder to take it after I have been drinking alcohol."

"How funny. Why?"

"Because, dear Tia, my mother is a dictator."

"Oh", Tia said.

"She doesn't allow me to drink alcohol, but I love her above everything else on earth. When I chew parsley like chewing gum and then swallow it and gargle my mouth with two kinds of mouth wash, then she doesn't notice any smell."

"Interesting."

"Thank you, Tia."

Mustafa returned to the table with a triumphant smile on his face, as if he had just won some big prize. This was his night. He could feel it in his entire body. He sat down, leaned back and looked lovingly at Ali.

"Shouldn't you go for a swim, Ali? I and my whisky will be here."

"No, I don't feel like it."

"But we're at Bux-Biou! Are you afraid of water or what? You must at least take a shower, Ali, Saturday afternoon at the latest. Girls want a Mr Nyponros, a man who smells as good as a dog rose."

"No, they want a really sweaty, fat guy."

"Ha, ha, very funny. Take a shower at home then. I'll get you into some shower, you'll see."

The boys stayed at Bux-Biou for a little while before going home to Skärholmen.

At home in Skärholmen

Fatima was cooking lasagne. There was a wonderful smell in the apartment. When Mustafa and Ali came in, they felt the smell, noticed what was going on in the kitchen and broke out in a spontaneous homage to Fatima, with made-up lyrics to the melody of "Viva España."

"What would we do without you?
Viva Fatima!
What could we possibly do?
Viva Fatima!
Fatima por favor!
Fatima por favor!"

After the song was finished, Ali and Mustafa both hugged Fatima, who was really touched by their little homage.

"You're so cute! You must try and qualify for 'Pop Idol' on Channel Four, promise me that!"

All three laughed. Ali knew his limitations as a singer.

"If we went on like this our neighbours would move out", Ali said.

They laughed again. Mustafa looked at the oven.

"How much time left before it's ready?" he asked.

"Maybe half an hour. It has to cool off a little too."

Suddenly someone called Fatima on her cell phone. She walked into her room to take the call. Mustafa walked into his room and started to iron his Arabian trousers. After a little while Ali knocked on Fatima's door.

"Hey, Fatima, do you have a pair of nail clippers that I can borrow?"

"I'll be out soon", Fatima answered from the room. Ali sat down in the kitchen waiting. Fatima put on make-up and then came out to Ali in the kitchen.

"Here you are, the nail clippers!"

"Thanks! You look great in that make-up! Going somewhere?"

"Yeah, I'm going to this dating-party at the university." Ali almost fell off his chair.

"You can't do that! Absolutely not! Fatima, we have a different culture. We care about you, we don't want you to get into trouble. You have to understand that." Fatima froze. She hadn't expected this.

"What do you mean? So you won't let me go to the party?"

Ali interrupted her, repeated and tried to make himself clear:

"But please, Fatima, we have a different culture."

"What kind of culture doesn't let a girl go out to meet a nice guy to fall in love with, maybe even marry, while you guys are out meeting girls and having fun. We're in Europe now, we're on equal terms. Vive l'Europe!"

Mustafa had finished ironing his trousers. He had the door open, so he heard the kitchen discussion. Now he couldn't help but interrupt. He entered the kitchen.

"Ali, stop the fuss about culture, go and take a shower! I agree with you, Fatima, vive l' Europe! This knobhead doesn't know how to express himself."

Beef Wellington à la George Bush spiced with fear

Fatima was furious for having her night out questioned by Ali. To calm down she took a glass of juice and sat down at the kitchen table. Mustafa smiled at her and stroked her hair in the protective way that big brothers have.

"Of course you can go out, Fatima, but just not tonight!"

"Why not tonight?"

"Fatima, did I ever stop you from going out, back home in Tunisia? Did I ever stop you from hitting the bars with your friends until one, two in the night?"

"No."

"Why didn't I stop you? Because in Tunisia a rapist gets five, six years in jail. The cops will beat them up and in court the judge will believe the woman. It's not like that here in Sweden where you have to have DNA and a videotape showing the rape to 'prove' it happened. One rapist in twenty is found guilty in Swedish courts."

"And where are you heading with this little monologue?"

"Fatima, haven't you heard the commercial they are running on the radio?"

"No", Fatima said. She didn't know about the party but Bibbi had called her and ask her to come along.

"It's going to be a disaster!" Mustafa replied. "Just think, with the message 'If you're a man, then we're looking for you!' it's going to be chaos at the university tonight! All of Stockholm, including suburbs, will go straight there."

"Wonderful!" Fatima said. "The girls will feel like queens, they will be able to pick and choose among the guys."

"Of course! The girl have a right to chat up guys, just like guys chat up girls! Vive la Suède, land of equal opportunities!"

"Thanks!" Fatima said and hugged him "It's good to have such a smart brother."

"But you have to understand, Fatima, these ads on the radio about the party, 'If you're a man, if you're a man…', have messed up the heads of the rapists and the psychopaths."

"Really?"

"You know, Fatima, there are some convicted rapists out there on leave from prison tonight and they want to get laid!" Mustafa said.

"How do you know that?"

"Please, dear Fatima. Where do all the immigrants in Sweden work? In the service sector; in restaurants, hospitals, prisons… The person who came up with that phrase 'Are you a man…', he or she should get an Oscar for best line!"

"Why should he or she get an Oscar?"

"The person who starts a psycho wave all across the country just with one single line deserves an Oscar, don't you think? There are other examples, too."

"Like?"

"I have a friend from Morocco who works at a hospital in north Stockholm. He told me that he has two patients there, real lunatics. They had really long moustaches, but when they heard the commercial they cut off their moustaches, shoved them up their nostrils and escaped from the hospital."

"Why would they do this?"

"They hoped to find a Swedish match at Stockholm University!"

"You mean Swedish blondes, the ones that can set all the guys on fire?"

"Yeah, just imagine if you ran into one of those lunatics tonight, you never know!"

Fatima looked at Mustafa, surprised.

"And not only that! I have another friend, Usama from Somalia, he works at Huddinge hospital in southern Stockholm and he says it will be like Christmas for the crazy tonight! An American exchange student from Dallas ended up in the psychiatric clinic at Huddinge when he heard Swedish girls sing 'Are you a man…' on Radio Stockholm. He told Usama to go and buy him eight packages of laxative. He gave almost 300 crowns in tips! After Usama gave them to him he had a couple of busy days, running to the toilet and back all the time. Usama discovered that he had a colander with him. Usama told him: 'Brother, you can't go on eating this shit everyday, you're fucking up your stomach! And why do you bring a colander'? The lunatic told Usama he had swallowed his student identity card! 'How could you do that? When?' Usama asked him. Apparently, he had swallowed it six months ago, he was afraid he'd lose it otherwise, and it was an important item to him, so he dipped it in wine to make it soft, rolled it into a nice ball and swallowed it! Usama asked him why he suddenly wanted it back out again and he said: 'Come on, Usama, haven't you heard the commercial on the radio? Nice young Swedish girls want to date men, it's a dating party, they'll ask for ID!' Usama tried to calm him, said he knew someone at the University who could get him in through the back door. The crazy man went nuts when he heard that! And then when the chief shrink came in, the lunatic complained about his stomach pain. The chief shrink gave him permission to leave the hospital for five days, saying he'd be better off taking it easy outside over the weekend, getting some rest. What do you think about that, isn't it crazy?"

"Absolutely! Completely wacky!"

"I'm afraid something might happen to you, hundreds of psychopaths are on their way to Stockholm!"

"How do you know that?"

Mustafa imitated the newsreader on Fox News.

"The police say they've been informed that there's a rape-wave coming. They don't know where and when it's going to strike but they say they have a plan for how to react if something happens. The Stockholm police force is ready. The barometer reading for the rape threat is on red, that's the highest level!"

"What do you mean?"

"You know, Fatima", Mustafa said and used the war propaganda technique of the American media, "the police use this scale to measure just how threatened we are by rapists and other crazy people. It goes from green, which means little threat, to red, which means 'Alarm, alarm, the rapists are coming!' Green means you can go out and have as much fun as you want, red means you'd better stay inside, be very careful."

Fatima looked at Mustafa, worried.

"You know, Fatima, I love you and I don't want anything bad to happen to you. I want to protect you, keep you safe."

"Thank you for telling me this, Mustafa."

"Oh, that's nothing. We have to help each other out in this family, right?"

Mustafa looked into Fatima's eyes and saw the fear. He realised that his fear rhetoric, George Bush style, had convinced her.

They hugged each other. After the hug Mustafa walked towards his room. Fatima looked at him as he was walking.

"So what are you doing tonight, my brother?"

Mustafa stopped, turned around and put on a charming smile.

"Ali and I are going to meet some friends from work. Just talk, maybe play some cards, it'll be fun."

He turned around, entered his room and found Ali standing there. Mustafa looked angrily at him, walked up to him and stood close, looking sinister. He lowered his voice and whispered: "What are you doing? Are you going to prevent Fatima from going out? Here, in Sweden? Women here have exactly the same rights as men. Mom would make our lives a living hell if she found out."

Ali was staring right back into Mustafa's eyes.

"So you think it's better if our sister is attacked by some crazy guy tonight?"

"Of course I don't want that to happen. But you can tell her in a good way, scare her, use the 'Beef Wellington à la Bush, spiced up with fear'."

Ali gave Mustafa a sceptical look.

"But if Fatima finds out tomorrow that no one escaped from any prison or hospital? She will be able to find out from the newspapers, you know."

Mustafa had an answer.

"Then we just go for the Bush technique. He blames the CIA. We just blame my friends for giving me false information."

Mustafa's answer satisfied Ali.

"Ali, for every problem there's a 'Beef Wellington' solution. You just have to serve it with humour and warmth to make it a success. 'Beef Wellington' is the new politics! Everyone's using it, from the politicians to the businessmen to the bouncer at the little bar in town. It's everywhere nowadays."

"I'll be damned."

"You know what? I'm going over to Fatima and give her a surprise just to cheer her up a little." Ali gave his brother a surprised look.

"And how are you going to do that?"

"You know that book you found at Södertörn. Where is it?"

"What book?"

"The one you read to me, about what a woman should do to get a man."

"Oh, that one, it's over here."

Ali picked up a book from the bookcase on the wall and gave it to Mustafa who took out a pair of scissors from his pocket and started cutting in the book; the cover and

the first pages, where the title and author's name was written. Ali didn't stop him until he was done.
"What are you doing?"
"I'm trying to find the solution."

Beef Wellington à la Patrícia Gaztañaga

Mustafa knew that Fatima (who could speak Spanish) was a great admirer of the famous Spanish female talk show host Patricia Gaztañaga and had seen most of her shows on TV.

Mustafa reached into his pocket and picked out a photo of Patricia Gaztañaga. He stuck it onto the first page.

"Take this pen and write her name above the picture."

Ali shook his head, took the book and wrote her name in big letters on the front page. As soon as he had finished writing, Mustafa took the book and headed for the kitchen.

"Voilà! From me to you!"
"What's this?"
"Ali found it at Södertörn College!"
Fatima looked at the book, puzzled.
"Why doesn't it have any cover?"
"He who had it before must have been mad about Patricia Gaztañaga, maybe he tore it apart and put a photo of her on it instead. Anyway it's really she who has written it. It's called 'The art of meeting a nice, caring and reasonable man'."

Fatima looked at the book again, pretending to be interested.

"What an interesting title! So if I read this, I'll find the man of my dreams, Him with the capital H?"

"But of course! This isn't just any semi-celebrity pretending that she knows enough to write a book. This is Patricia Gaztañaga! She wants to share her wisdom with other women, women in all countries, that's why she wrote this book. You know, Spanish women are known to be smart. They just need five minutes with a guy to know if he's worth going for. This book will help you learn all the tricks you might need to capture Mr. Right. And you know what, Fatima, no one would be happier than I if you were to!"

Fatima showed Mustafa her cutest smile.

"This was really nice of you, Mustafa. I'll read it."

Mustafa started singing "l'Amore", the famous Julio Iglesias ballad. He gestured dramatically, sang a verse and the chorus and then calmed down.

"It's a shame she hasn't written anything about beauty tricks in the book", he went on.

"What kind of tricks?" Fatima asked.

"You know, this woman is unique! She lit up the whole of Spain with her new recipe."

'Bon Appétit!'"

"And exactly what is that?"

"When she goes to bed she lights a candle, and then she sleeps like that, with the candle on her stomach."

"Why?"

Mustafa looked triumphantly at Fatima.

"Because it flattens her skin! I mean, look at her, she still looks 20 and she's about 35, all because of this 'candle therapy'. Isn't that just fantastic? No skin cream, no surgery. You just stick a candle into your belly button and sleep all night long!"

"All night long? You have to have it in for so long?"

"Yes! Every night, light, light, light!"

"But what is it with a candle that gives the skin a face-lift?"

"Well, after a while the candle wax starts dripping down into and around the belly button. It's something with the candle wax, it stretches the skin out, makes it flat."

"So the candle wax makes the skin flat, that's a new

one for me, never heard of that", Fatima said in an ironic voice.

"It's the truth, I promise! Don't you sometimes wonder why the Spaniards are so happy and full of energy? Voilà! This is the answer! This candle therapy gives the Spaniards back their lust for life ."

Mustafa started singing the Iglesias ballad again. Fatima smiled at him.

"When will men start showering and shaving, not in the morning but in the evening? And sleep with candles in their belly buttons?"

"Well, the Spanish men are not impossible, they're quite flexible actually, and there's been some tries in the name of equality, but the results have been disastrous. One woman touched her husbands head in her sleep and asked him "Why is your arse on the pillow?' 'What do you mean', asked her husband. The woman lifted her head from the pillow and, to her dismay, she discovered that he had become bald from the candle! Since then, not even women want men to do it."

"Ah, so you say…"

Mustafa headed back to his room, proud as a rooster. Fatima leafed through the book again and shook her head.

"What does my brother think of me, really?" she quietly asked herself. She couldn't take it that her big brothers saw her as the naïve little sister that they had to protect. And now this, a torn-apart book with a pasted photo and a title written with a felt-tipped pen? That was just too much.

"And to top it all off he's trying to trick me into believing in some mumbo jumbo about sleeping with a lit candle on your stomach!" she thought while looking at the book. Then she threw it into the garbage bin.

After that she opened the oven and took out the lasagna. She let it join the 'Patricia book' in the garbage bin. She took out two cookbooks from a shelf, 'Nice and easy' and 'Food from A to Z.' Then she took a pen, deleted the authors names and wrote a new one, 'Patricia Gaztañaga.' Fatima then opened the shelf and brought out two big, deep plates. She put the books onto the plates and finished by putting Arabian lids over the plates. She laughed a little, then she cupped her hands in front of her mouth and shouted from the top of her lungs:

"Food is ready!"

Ali and Mustafa ran towards the kitchen like Olympic sprinters, both as hungry as wolves.

"Oh, what's that smell? Smells so good!" Mustafa wondered." "What kind of lasagna is it?"

"Yeah, doesn't it smell a bit different?" Fatima said." It's this new recipe I made up myself, I call it 'Lasagna Bon Appétit'!"

Mustafa started singing: "Bon Appétit, la, la, la, Bon Appétit, la, la, la…" Ali discovered the plates on the kitchen sink.

"Oh, is it gourmet food today? Lids over the plates and everything."

Fatima giggled.

"I just wanted to make it exciting for you, leave something to the imagination and not just reveal it all, like some girls do nowadays."

Fatima had laid the kitchen table with cutlery, glasses and orange juice. Mustafa was just about to open the lids on his plate.

"OK, very exciting, now I want to eat, I'm hungry as a wolf!"

"Please, Mustafa, wait! Take it easy, sit down, I'll serve you", Fatima said.

"OK, but make it quick!" Mustafa responded.

The boys sat down at the table, happy and excited. Fatima took the plates and put them on the table, one in front of each brother. They lifted the lids.

"What is this?" Mustafa exclaimed.

"It's a Spanish cookbook written by Patricia Gaztañaga, 'The art of cooking lasagna instead of dinner'."

Mustafa's face turned red from Fatima's practical joke. This wasn't something he could just shrug off, especially when he was hungry.

"What do you mean by this, then? I can feel the smell of lasagna, OK?"

Fatima looked him straight into the eyes.

"And what do you mean by giving me the-art-of-meeting-the-right-guy-book, then? Do you think I'm four years old or what? I don't fall for everything and you don't need to be Sherlock Holmes to figure out that Patricia Gaztañaga is not the author of that book." Before Mustafa could find the time to say something, Ali broke in, trying to calm things down. He was becoming nervous, and his head was moving like on a camel.

"I just want to eat immediately, I'll go crazy from this! Why can't you just bring the lasagna, Fatima?"

Fatima sighed and shook her head.

"Seek and you shall find", she said and walked towards her room. She went in and closed the door with a bang. At the same time her brothers were sniffing like dogs after the lasagna. Their well developed sense of smell took them to an unpleasant place: the garbage bin.

Fatima in Skärholmen

Fatima sat down on the sofa. She turned on Oprah on the TV. After about an hour, the phone rang.

"Babuba!"

"Ey, girl!"

"Claudia!"

Claudia was Fatima's classmate from adult school, a tough girl with a father from Venezuela and a mother from Argentina. She worked extra as a taxi driver. Fatima had got to know Claudia well in a short time and saw her as one of her best friends.

"I just have to work a little tiny bit longer, until the next-shift-guy has changed his clothes, then it's... PARTY! I've rented this really cool 'fifties dress with a hat and a veil. You know, I'm going to be incognito at this party."

"That's great", Fatima said in a low voice.

"I know, this is going to be so much fun! So what do you say, the University underground station at... half past nine?"

"Claudia, I'm not going tonight."

"WHAT???"

"You know, my brothers, they don't want me to go out, they say it's dangerous for me to be outside tonight."

"Oh, what a load of crap! Dangerous? What's not dangerous in this world? You have to live your life, don't you?"

"Seriously, Claudia. It IS dangerous outside tonight. There will be murderers, rapists, just a lot of lunatics."

"There are murderers and rapists out every night, Fatima! Everything is dangerous! But it can be fun as well! You can't let your brothers control your life!"

"But my brothers just want what's best for me."

"Fatima, how many times do I have to ask you? A hundred? Will you change your mind after a hundred times?"

"You can ask me a thousand times, Claudia. I don't feel like it. I'm sorry about this, but I'm staying home tonight."

"Fatima, you're breaking my heart! But if that's how you feel... Oh, I have a passenger here, I'll call you later, darling!"

Fatima went back to the sofa and Oprah. She tried to watch for a few minutes but felt restless, and not even Oprah could take the restlessness away. She took up her cell phone and called Bibbi. Bibbi was a cop and a friend of the Babuba family, well, almost a family member. Fatima saw her as a sister. When Fatima called, Bibbi was in a police car with a colleague. She answered after the first signal.

"Hi, Fatima!"

"Hi, Bibbi, I just wanted to tell you something."

"Yes?"

"I'm not going to the party tonight."

"Know what? I was just going to call you and say the same! A colleague got ill, so I had to fill in."

"OK."

"So what's your excuse? Claudia is going, right?"

"Mustafa has said that it's going to be the night of the lunatics tonight!"

Bibbi shook her head.

"Mustafa's full of it! What does he know about that?"

"He says a number of lunatics have escaped recently."

"No, no, Fatima, don't believe him. This smells like a 'Beef Wellington à la Mustafa' from a long distance! Are he and Ali at home?"

"No, they left. I guess that they went to the…"

Bibbi interrupted:

"… Damn, now they're calling us on the car 'phone, something's going on. Fatima, I'll call you later, OK?"

Bibbi turned on the sirens on the police car and drove away into the night.

The party at Stockholm university

Åsa, the hostess of the party, was standing on the stage presenting the evening's programme. She was excited and wanted her excitement to rub off onto the guests.

"What an audience, what a vibe we've got in here! Amazing! Good evening, ladies and gentlemen and welcome to Stockholm University's special evening, 'Find new friends and love!' L'amour, die Liebe, l'amore. As you know, there are three categories of partners to choose from. The first category is the one with the yellow cards, let's just call you the 'net-daters', OK? You'll be hanging out here, at the bar, and you want to meet your partner right now! You've already met each other and had a cosy time on the net, haven't you?"

There were cheers and applause from the audience. The loudest cheers came from the bar.

"The second group is those with a green card. You are the exhibitionists! Yeah, I think you know very well yourself just who you are! Your photos are right here on the wall! There's no escape!"

There were giggles here and there, people turned around and looked at each other.

"The third group here tonight is the red-carders - you'll be hanging out in the Gula Villan (Little Yellow House, a student's association building) and a colleague of mine, Karin, will take care of you. I mean, you're so anonymous, so you need someone to take care of you! I call you 'The unknowns'! Cowards!"

Åsa smiled slightly and continued.

"Jokes aside, you red-carders want a partner who doesn't believe that looks matter, and that's a good point, because it really is the inside that counts, right? You're masked and you're looking for serious relationships with serious partners. All of you, remember that you have the right to date as much as you want, there are no limitations here! OK, so now you know the rules... Have a great night, everybody!"

Ali meets Hermine and Debora

Ali stood outside the men's toilet waiting for Mustafa and Pedro when two slightly tipsy single girls came up to him.

"Do you speak English?" they asked him.
"A little", Ali replied.
"I'm Hermine, and she's Debora", said one of the girls. They shook hands.
"What languages do you speak?" Debora asked.
"Arabic, French, Swedish, and a little English…"
"Aha, vous parlez français!"
"Oui, oui!"
"Bonjour, bonjour. Est-ce que tu veux aller avec nous ou avec toi à la maison?"
Ali didn't understand, Hermine and Debora's French sounded weird to him.
"You know, I speak French but I have no idea of what you're talking about! Say it in Swedish instead!"
"Ah bon, c'est bien! Shall we go to your place or to ours?"
This flattered and astonished Ali at the same time. He had never got this kind of 'dirty invitation' before. He became cross-eyed and his head started shaking. The camel movements were on their way. He tried to come up with something to say but didn't find the right words.
"Amazing", he said at last, "I've never had this kind of invitation before. Is it a dream or is it real?"
"Of course it's real", Hermine said. "You don't have to stand here and argue for hours if you know what you're after, right?"
Ali laughed nervously, then he came to think about Mustafa's talk about team-playing.
"Can my brother come as well?" He asked gently.
"Sure, why not? If he's as cute as you this can be very… hot", said Hermine.
Ali didn't know where to go now, but luckily he had the toilet right next to him.
"OK, wait outside, I'm just going to the toilet quickly."
Ali entered the men's rooms. He was nervous, his

entire body was shaking. He discovered Mustafa and Pedro at the end of the room, in front of the mirrors.

"Hey, Mustafa, you know what just happened to me? Two chicks walked up to me and asked if I wanted to come to their place, just like that! Wicked!"

"You see, Ali, it's the smell, they're attracted to the smell! Haven't you found out what the expression "nyponros" means? The girls even come up to you at the toilet to pick you up, don't they, Pedro?"

"Absolutely! It's in every Swedish ladies' magazine! Nyponros, nyponros!"

Ali shook his head shyly.

"But anyway Mustafa, two hot chicks, right outside, you're coming with me, right?"

Mustafa rolled his index finger against his thumb in a 'money talks' gesture and then looked at Ali.

"I don't think so. You know I want a girl with this sort of heat!" He did the 'money talks' gesture again.

"You know, money, geld, bakchich (Arabic for 'money') is the only heat that exists for me tonight. But it's about time you hooked up with someone, and now you even have two! You've got to grasp the opportunity!"

"But I need support. What about you, Pedro? Are you coming?"

"No, you know what I'm waiting for! I hope Claudia is coming tonight. Fatima has done a good job finding such a vixen as a friend."

Mustafa and Ali smiled.

"Go by yourself, Ali", Pedro said. "Take both of them, it's called 'ménage à trois', ever heard of it?" Mustafa shook his head.

"He hasn't even pulled a 'ménage à deux'!" he shouted.

Ali didn't appreciate the joke, but he had not given up the idea of taking one of the boys with him.

"It's just not my style" he said.

"And what's your style then?" Pedro asked. "How do you want the girl of your dreams to look?"

"How shall I explain", Ali began, "she has to be beautiful and sturdy, like Queen Latifah, you know? Her size and upwards!" Pedro found this shocking.

"Wow, that big! Tunisians, Tunisians, you're crazy! How about you, Mustafa, the girl of your dreams?"

"Hey", Mustafa said, "I have taste enough for all of us! The girl of my dreams must have a really nice, well rounded butt. On a scale from Jennifer Lopez to Queen Latifah, just about!" Pedro laughed.

"Different culture, different culture. OK, I get it. For me, it has to be tight girls, like Shakira, they have to be fit." Mustafa smiled.

"OK, glad we straightened that out! But Ali, seriously, get out there, they're waiting for you! Your style or not, you have to take your chances! It's girls, chicks, ladies…"

"But they're too thin."

"Too thin… you're insane! Haven't you heard the Tunisian expression, 'Start with flip flops, soon enough you can afford real shoes!' I mean, this must be better than walking barefoot!"

Pedro found Mustafa's expression extremely funny. Ali looked doubtful. Mustafa didn't give up and continued to encourage him in his own special way.

"If you don't go soon, they will give up and move on. Go now, or I'll beat you up!"

He gave Ali a friendly push in his side. Ali shrugged.

"OK, OK, I'll go out there, see what happens."

Mustafa and Pedro cheered and did the high five. Mustafa looked proud, glad that shy Ali was trying to overcome his insecurity.

"That's my brother! Go out there and take 'em!"

Ali smiled a shy smile at his brother, turned around and walked out of the toilet, nervous as hell. Mustafa and

Pedro were left alone in the toilet. Mustafa sprayed perfume on his neck. Some of it happened to fall on Pedro, who was standing just next to Mustafa, combing his hair. .

"Ey, what are you doing, Mustafa?"

"Get away", Mustafa said, "you smell like garlic!"

Pedro shrugged and walked into one of the toilet booths.

Beef Wellington à la Jim Carrey

Mustafa loved standing in front of the mirror. As often as possible he stood in front of the mirror and trained his mimicry and his facial expressions, because Mustafa had a dream: to be a great comedian! Already as a small kid, on the little island of Djerba in Tunisia he used to practice comedy skills. Often he skipped school and went home and practised mimicry and gestures instead. He used to hang a small mirror on one of the olive trees by his house, with the Mediterranean in the background and the small donkey Besbussa as only company. He practiced and practised until his jaws hurt.

And now he was standing there again, in front of the mirror, exercising his mimicry. He looked at his eyes and at his face and thought about which muscles he had to move to make people laugh. He hesitated for a moment, thinking that he wished he had the same rubber-face as Jim Carrey. Then he wouldn't even have to open his mouth in order to make people laugh, just looking at him would be enough. A second later, his prayers were answered. Two guys came in, and when they saw Mustafa practise they started laughing.

"Nice face, man", one of them shouted and walked into one of the toilet booths.

Mustafa smiled. He decided that this was enough practice for tonight.

"Ey, Pedro, I'll wait outside, OK?"
"Sure."

After a little while Pedro came out of the men's toilet. Right outside of the toilet there were steep stairs down to the dance floor. Pedro slipped and fell down the stairs.

"Shit man!" he shouted, "there should be a freaking warning sign here!"

"There was one until three weeks ago, but when they found out there were no accidents they took it away!" Mustafa said.

Pedro laughed. He got up and wiped the dust from his clothes. At the same time, a couple of girls passed. One of them really gave Mustafa the look. Pedro looked at Mustafa with envy.

On a sign on the wall there were photos of all the girls from the 'exhibitionist' group.

"This is my favourite girl, Caroline", Mustafa said and pointed out one girl as he and Pedro were standing in front of the sign, studying the girls.

"It's one of my dates, Ali told me earlier."

"Really hot one", Pedro said.

They walked to the restaurant and sat down at one of the tables.

From the restaurant they had a good view of the dance floor. Mustafa and Pedro let their eyes scan the floor as they waited to be served. When the waitress arrived to their table Mustafa ordered beef steak with fried egg and French fries and Pedro chicken fillet with rice. They ordered Cokes to drink. The waitress came back with the food quite quickly, which made the boys delighted. She put one plate down in front of Mustafa.

"Here you go", she said with a country accent. She came from the same part of Sweden as Ingvar Kamprad, the man behind IKEA.

Mustafa looked surprised at the plate.

"Miss, I ordered beef steak with French fries and egg!"

"Sure you did."

"But where's the beef steak? There's no beef steak here!"

"Sure there is."

Mustafa looked down at his plate and then at the waitress.

"Where?"

"Right under the egg!" Mustafa lifted the egg with his fork, and there under the egg lay the beef steak, a really small one.

"Is this what you call an IKEA beef steak?" Mustafa asked.

"Why do you ask?" said the waitress.

"Because IKEA is run by stingy people from the south!"

"No, it's not an IKEA beef steak. I'm from the south, like IKEA Kamprad, but all that about us being stingy is just talk. We're smart and successful!" Mustafa didn't want to spoil the evening by starting an argument.

"OK, lady, sure, but this is the smallest beef steak I've ever seen!" The waitress smiled at Mustafa.

"Well, if you compare it to the dancing halls of Stockholm University, then… sure. In my opinion it's just about, do you know the Swedish expression 'lagom är bäst' ('everything in moderation')?

"No."

Pedro interrupted.

"That was the first expression I learned when I came to Sweden. It's a pity there isn't a similar expression in other languages."

"I think so too", the waitress said.

"I use that expression when I'm talking Portuguese to my friends."

"Bravo!" the waitress said. "We Swedes love to say

that 'lagom är bäst'"

Mustafa gave the waitress a friendly look.

"OK, lady! I admire people from Småland, they really know how to convince you!"

"Thanks", the waitress said, "enjoy your meals!"

They started to eat. Pedro leaned over towards Mustafa.

"Mustafa", he whispered, "I want to hook up with a chick, I need to cook a 'Beef Wellington'. Tell me, how do you do that?"

"Dear Pedro, there are thousands of methods. Every woman is a riddle, her own secret! You can't just know immediately how to get her, you have to listen and be open, find the special short cuts to her heart. Flatter her and give her what she wants to have, tell her what she wants to hear. You have to create your own belly dance rhythm in your dialogue with her that will make her body vibrate!"

"And what exactly do you mean by belly dance rhythm?"

"That the woman enjoys listening to you! You have to speak so beautifully that it goes straight to her heart. There are a lot of politicians that are using the belly dance rhythm to get votes."

"But that's not so easy – I can't invent a new language".

"You need to know a few things, Pedro. Girls like four kinds of guys. First, good looking, at least by their standards. Second, rich. Third, famous from the movies, TV, music or sports. Last but not least, they like real bastards. Then there's another type, a fifth category. I used use to call it 'the fifth element'."

"That sounds exciting, what is that?"

Mustafa's eyes were glowing by now.

"Those who manage the 'Beef Wellington'! And that could be anyone, normal working guys like you and me, guys who just want to live like everyone else, picking up girls and stuff, guys who…"

Caroline and Mustafa on stage

Mustafa was interrupted by Åsa, the hostess, whose voice came out loud through the sound system.

"Ladies and gentlemen. Now it's time for some great entertainment, and these girls have travelled a long way to get here, so give them a warm welcome. From Russia, Poland, Ukraine and the Czech Republic… the hottest band from the east…'4you'! You already know the song! And remember boys,these girls are NOT in any dating category so don't try anything stupid! Just looking, OK? Well, here they are… '4you'!"

The famous line from the commercial started pumping through the sound system and four hot girls came onto the stage. They sang the commercial over and over again, and the audience sang along with them. The whole place was rocking, filled with people dancing and singing. Mustafa and Pedro remained seated.

Suddenly Mustafa picked up a lantern from a plastic bag he had been carrying around.

"Pedro, do you have a match?"

"Yes, but what are you up to? You don't smoke, do you, Mustafa?"

"I'm going to light this thing up!"

"What are you going to do with a lantern, isn't there enough light in here or what? This isn't the Sahara!"

"Hello, Brazil, this is Tunisia calling! Is there a brain in there or what?"

Mustafa knocked lightly on Pedro's head.

"I have to create the comic 'field of excitement', to give my 'Beef Wellington' some breakthrough power!"

"OK, so that's what you need the lantern for?"

Pedro laughed and handed over a matchbox to Mustafa. He used to call Mustafa "The happy Saharian".

He enjoyed Mustafa's company, they usually had a good time together. Pedro found it fascinating that he, from São Paulo, Brazil, could laugh at the same thing as a Tunisian. Mustafa was really geared up by now, but once again he was interrupted by the hostess Åsa.

"All you green cards out there, pay attention!" Said the conferencière Åsa and everybody cheered.) Mustafa and Pedro looked amused at the stage.

"The first candidate tonight is Caroline Johansson, number 105. She's looking for a man and if he's an immigrant, that's a plus. Caroline seeks someone who wants to start a new life, preferably as a slave. Most importantly, he has to be religious!" People looked at each other, stunned by the somewhat unorthodox criteria.

"The first one who signed up as interested in Caroline is… and now I have to read carefully… Mustafa Ben Ibrahamidozlanisulsielbouzouritunisiauchouri!" Everyone in the audience started laughing at the ridiculous surname. Åsa looked embarrassed. Mustafa was already down by the stage. He had started walking as soon as Åsa said the first letter in his invented surname and he arrived when she said the last. When he started walking up the stairs to the stage, the audience started laughing and clapping.

"So you're Mustafa? I want to apologize, I'm not sure I got your last name right", Åsa said.

"Oh, that's OK!" Mustafa said. More clapping and cheering from the audience."I'm not going to say your last name again, but I wonder, do your near ones have any 'nick-surname' for you?"

"Nyponros! They call me Mustafa Nyponros!"

Applause from the women in the audience. Mustafa continued: "I'm looking for a girl that is beautiful and has curves!"

"Oh, that's an unusual wish, I must say. I have to ask you, Mustafa, have you met this Caroline before, I mean, here tonight?"

"No, but I saw her picture on the sign over there. And I use to say that behind every beautiful woman there's a beautiful bum!"

The audience was cheering, chanting, applauding...

Mustafa's confidence went up with the applause. He took a look around the stage and discovered a rectangular board, about a metre square, with a hole in the middle of it, just about big enough to put your head through. Mustafa wondered what the hole and the board was there for. Then he heard Åsa's voice again.

"OK, monsieur Mustafa, now that we've got to know one another, we can start the serious business. I want you to stick your head through the hole in the board over there!" Åsa pointed at the board.

Mustafa was thinking that this couldn't be that bad, it would probably be entertaining for the audience, and that would be good for him too.

"Sure, madame, of course!"

Mustafa got down on his knees and stuck his head through the hole.

"Ladies and gentlemen, may I introduce to you... Caroline Johansson!"

Caroline walked down the stairs and up to the stage. She had got a whip in her hand. Mustafa didn't notice this and kept his head down. Åsa continued.

"Caroline's 30 years old. Between 1992 to 1995 she was an economics student here at Stockholm University, earning a Master's degree. Nowadays she's the head of a department at the NK department store. Caroline wants a slave who can help her realise her dreams and fantasies."

Caroline had now almost come down to the end of the long stairs to the stage. But when Åsa said what Caroline wanted, Mustafa started hitting the stage floor with his fist with full power.

"Stop, stop, stop!" he shouted.

Caroline stopped when she had almost reached the end of the stairs. Åsa and the audience thought Mustafa was having trouble breathing or sore knees or something. Åsa, who was standing between him and Caroline, looked at him, concerned.

"What's the matter, Mustafa?"

"Hostess, please take a step back, so that this beautiful sun can shine on me!"

More cheering and applauding from the audience. Åsa stepped back, embarrassed.

Caroline really was shining with joy and continued to walk down to the stage. She stopped on the last step before the stage. Mustafa called on her.

"Caroline, I haven't seen you yet, not one part of you! This hostess had been standing in my way! Couldn't you please do your little walk up the stairs and then down again?" Caroline, exhibitionist to the bone, didn't mind Mustafa's suggestion. She turned around and walked up the stairs, with her sexy back wiggling. Just what Mustafa wanted to see. He followed her with his eyes for a while, then he turned to the audience and showed them a grimace to show what he thought of Caroline's bottom. He let his tongue hang out like a dog.

Åsa walked up to Mustafa.

"Is this the bottom you've been hunting high and low for?"

Mustafa looked up at Åsa.

"Is it! Caroline's curves are so sexy that if I had a camel's tail I would be waving it like crazy now."

The audience applauded. Mustafa spoke Swedish with a French-Tunisian accent when he wanted to make his audience laugh. His accent worked as kind of a fuel for his humour. Caroline proudly turned around and took a look at the audience and enjoyed their attention. Then she walked down the stairs and up to Mustafa on the stage and stopped right behind him.

"Are you deeply religious?" she asked Mustafa.
"Yeah."
"What religion?"
"I'm a Muslim."
"How can you prove to me that you really are religious? It's really is a must for me that you are."
"How can I prove it? I don't know, but what I do know is that I love my enemies."
"Like Catholics, Protestants, Jews, is that what you mean?"
"No, that's not what I mean. We're all brothers and sisters. We have the same God and the same prophets."
"Then who are your enemies?"
"My enemies are American whiskey and Swedish pork meat, oink oink!"

Cheer and applause from the audience. There was an electric atmosphere and Mustafa loved it.

The truth was that Mustafa also loved whisky. The pork meat part he put in just to entertain the audience.

New applause. Mustafa loved the audience's reactions.

"You're a real comedian, aren't you?" Caroline watched Mustafa with a serious look on her face.

"Why do you want to be a slave?"

"Because my love life has become like the BBC's weather reports for Great Britain." Mustafa imitated the English weathermen in an exaggerated British accent: "A lot of low pressure, rarely any high pressure!"

The audience cheered again. Caroline pointed at Mustafa's bottom with her whip and tried to make him spread his legs.

"Mustafa, do as I say! Spread your legs and relax. That's right, just like that. Have you ever been tied up?"

"No, never." Caroline started whipping Mustafa until he screamed.

"Has anyone whipped you before?"

"No, never, ouch, ouch, it hurts, ouch!"

Caroline tried to see how much pain Mustafa could take.

"Who knows, with a little whipping every now and then and you might start liking it! I want to hear you scream louder, with your lips like this." Caroline did small kisses in the air with her lips to show Mustafa how to express his pleasure. Mustafa didn't understand what she wanted him to do, he just kept on screaming.

"Mother, ouch, ouch, mother, what have I done wrong, mother, ouch!" Caroline stopped whipping him and walked past and squatted just a few meters from him.

"No, no. You've got no mother here. Look at me, Mustafa, you have to put your lips like this, 'Je t'aime, je t'aime'!"

She said the famous line from the well-known song by Serge Gainsbourg and Jane Birkin. Mustafa didn't follow her commands. His bottom was now hurting so badly that he imitated different animal sounds to express it, sheep, horse, rooster, donkey, dog: "Je t'aime, je' t'aime, ich liebe dich"... the audience of course loved it. Caroline went back to whipping. Mustafa suffered.

"Ouch, why so aggressive?"

"Because it gives me sexual pleasure."

"Do you have to use such barbaric methods? This is like the Romans when they occupied Cartage!"

Caroline didn't answer, she just went on in her sexy voice: "de Sade, de Sade."

Confused by the pain, Mustafa thought she said "sarduk", which means rooster in Tunisian. He thought Caroline just wanted to have fun and whip him in front of the audience. Maybe she would stop if he screamed louder, but that just made Caroline go on whipping harder and harder.

"Mustafa, you have to cure me, you have to cure me! Can you do that?"

"Yeah, drink 15 litres of water a day for a month! It's the ration of a camel."

A roar of laughter from the audience. Caroline got mad, disappointed by Mustafa's flippant answer.

"So that's your answer?" Mustafa's grimaced and screamed, sounding like a variety of animals: donkey, cow, dog…

"Ouch, do you hate men? What kind of pleasure do you get from tormenting others?" Caroline just kept on whipping and her answer surprised Mustafa.

"I enjoy it, I enjoy it!"

"You enjoy it, you enjoy it! I must have been an idiot for accepting to be your slave!"

"I was so interested in you I didn't notice that you were an idiot", Caroline replied.

"Caroline, please stop, what do you think I am, a Tunisian donkey?" Mustafa begged her.

"That's a possibility we shouldn't exclude!"

"Do you hate men?"

"No, but religious fundamentalists."

"I'm no fundamentalist!"

"You're hopeless… I don't want you!"

She stopped whipping him, left the stage and walked up the stairs. Mustafa got out of the hole, angry and disappointed. He stood up, raising his fist at Caroline.

"Thank you, thank you! I'm going to report you to the police for assaulting a poor religious immigrant!"

The audience started whistling and booing in discontent. Mustafa left the stage and walked towards the toilet with his head down. He couldn't understand why Caroline didn't want him. Pedro saw where Mustafa was heading and left the restaurant for the toilet. He met Mustafa just outside the toilet door.

"How could you miss this opportunity? Doing your silly animal sounds… how could you believe that would work? Your 'Beef Wellington' went off at the speed of a camel!"

Mustafa just shook his head.

"What do you mean?"

"You just thought about the audience and forgot about Caroline's wishes and needs", Pedro said.

"I had no choice. This woman thinks that all believers are fundamentalists…"

"No, no…"

"What do you mean no? She is looking for a religious immigrant just so that she can spank him!"

"No, no, Mustafa, you are mixing sex with religion."

They walked into the men's toilet.

"Didn't you understand that she was a sadomasochist, when she went 'de Sade, de Sade'?"

"Who is de Sade? Never heard of him. I'm an illiterate, I just watch al-Jazeera, and they never say anything about any de Sade!"

"Then you should report al-Jazeera to the police for disinformation! Listen and let Papa Pedro explain. de Sade was a French author who needed to humiliate and torment women in order to get sexual pleasure. Thus the name, **sad**omasochism!"

"I don't get how al-Jazeera could have missed that; their shows have everything."

Pedro looked curiously at Mustafa.

"I don't think al-Jazeera is interested in sadomasochism."

"You're right", Mustafa said. "Good thing this de Sade guy wasn't an Arab. If he had been, there would have been all kinds of experts and Islam-doctors sitting in the TV studios discussing why the Muslims have such strange ways of having sex! I can see it before my eyes; them sitting there in the morning show, stroking their bald heads, going 'Hmm, can this have something to do with the Koran?'"

Pedro looked amused.

"That's true, I've seen that since I moved to Europe, there's all this fuss about what's wrong with Muslims and the Koran", he said.

"And now there's a European guy who comes up with this sick thing! Just thinking about it makes me want to go to the toilet and piss on de Sade!"

Pedro smiled at Mustafa.

"Just go, I'll wait."

Mustafa walked into the toilet booth and locked the door. The he picked up his Lagerfeld perfume and sprayed his entire body. He looked at his watch. Not much time left until his date with a "stranger" at Gula Villan. But there were still twenty minutes to go, and they had started to play music again in the big room. Mustafa and Pedro threw themselves onto the dance floor.

Mustafa was an expert at mixing different dancing styles, to take the best from both west and east. Pedro was impressed with Mustafa's dance moves.

"You know what, Pedro, I feel like buying a whole bottle of Swedish vodka and getting drunk!"

Pedro looked at the ceiling and lifted his hand in the air.

"Allah!" he laughed. "He calls himself a religious Muslim!"

Bibbi at Stockholm University

Bibbi had plans for a girls' night out with Fatima and Claudia at the university campus in Frescati. She was not into the dating thing, just wanted to let loose with her friends, dance the night away. But nothing had turned out the way she had planned. First she had to step in for her colleague, then she heard about the "Beef Wellington" that Mustafa had pulled on Fatima. Now she had a new mission for the night. With a little arranging she managed to get two free hours from the police commissioner, from 10 to midnight. She headed home, changed clothes and drove to Frescati, dressed in a hat with a black gauze veil and an elegant 40s style dress from Chanel. She headed for the information counter, where a young girl was sitting, looking so bored she could fall asleep any minute.

"Hi", Bibbi said, "I'm looking for a guy who's registered for the party, but I have forgotten his room number."

The girl behind the counter looked indifferently at Bibbi.

"OK, what's his name?"

" _ Mustafa, Mustafa … It's so difficult to remember those immigrant names.

The girl sighed.

"OK, I'll take a look." She took her time going through the lists.

"We have a buffoon who calls himself Mustafa… and then it's some kind of world record for longest surname. I can order a weekend trip to Paris, fly there, be there and fly home before you're finished reading it."

The girl handed over a list to Bibbi, and pointed at Mustafa Ben Ibrahamidozlanisulsielbouzouritunisiauchouri. Bibbi laughed a little when she read it.

"He should be in Gula Villan right now", the girl said.

"OK, thanks for your help!"

Bibbi headed for Gula Villan. She had no trouble finding it. She studied law in her spare time and she knew her way around Stockholm University.

Bibbi took a moment to look at the little note about Kerstin Goldberg outside room number 10. All participants registered for the "R" party got a little note outside the door of the room to which they had been allotted. The note also showed whose turn it was to use the room and at what time.

Bibbi grabbed the corner of the note where Kerstin Goldberg's name was written, ripped it off and threw it into a paper basket next to the door. She walked into room number 10. The room was sparsely decorated. There was a couch, two armchairs and a small table. Bibbi stopped right in the middle of the room with her hands on her hips. After a while Mustafa came into the room, breathing heavily. He had got lost at Frescati and was ten minutes late. Bibbi introduced herself as Kerstin Goldberg in a haughty Marstrand accent. (Marstrand is a meeting spot on the Swedish west coast for high class society.) Mustafa was stunned by Kerstin Goldberg's elegant appearance. He had expected rich, but this classy…He couldn't get one word out of his mouth, just sounds: "Ahum, hum, hrm…"

"And you? Who are you?"

"I'm, I'm…"It was as if Mustafa had been struck by lightning.

"Yes, you, you?"

"I'm, I'm…"

"Who are you?"

"You're so… grand! I'm so shocked I forgot my name, oh my God!"

'Bibbi Goldberg' moved erotically on the couch.

"Shall I call you 'Monsieur Smell Good'?" It just said "click" in Mustafa's head and he came up with the ingredients for his "Beef Wellington".

Beef Wellington à la Lagerfeld

"Thanks for reminding me of my nickname! My friends call me 'Nyponros', 'Mustafa Nyponros'!"

"OK. So may I ask monsieur Nyponros what delicate perfume he uses?"

"Oh… it's my good friend, Lagerfeld!"

"Ah…interesting!"

"I happen to be a former colleague of his, I worked as a photographer", Mustafa bragged and went on, "and I must say, when I saw you in Chanel Haute Couture, it reminded me of the wonderful days with Le Grand Maestro Lagerfeld, the man who has influenced fashion world wide!"

"So… monsieur Nyponros is a photographer?"

"Eh, well… I'd rather call myself an artist. I do art, and I thank Lagerfeld for that. He gave me the inspiration to shoot artistic photos of beautiful women in beautiful clothes."

"But it says here on the information sheet that monsieur Nyponros is an exchange student…"

"Yes, and that's also true, I'm here to learn Swedish, I'm going to work here quite a lot in the time to come and I want to try to capture Swedish beauty."

"How interesting! So… monsieur Nyponros, is your art just work, or is it love?"

Mustafa was getting impatient. He wanted to see the woman behind the gauze. Did she look as sensual as she sounded?

"Work? It's passion, it's pure love! Through photographing I've learned to see the character behind the model. And when I buy her a glass of champagne after the photo session, I sometimes feel as if I understand exactly how the woman thinks, how her mind works."

"Oh… is monsieur Nyponros by any chance related to Mel Gibson?" Bibbi had seen the Mel Gibson movie in which he hears women's thoughts. Mustafa laughed.

"No, but he is one my favourites."

"Monsieur Nyponros, please have a seat", Bibbi said and pointed at an armchair facing the couch she was sitting on. Mustafa's bottom was still sore after the adventure with Caroline, and when he tried to sit down…

"Ouch!" He flew out of the armchair like a rocket.

"Oh, monsieur Nyponros, there weren't any drawing-pins on the seat, were there?" Mustafa went for a white lie.

"Oh no, you see, I'm just so fascinated by Björn Borg, you know the tennis legend. I was going to watch a tennis game on TV the other night. I'd taken a whisky or two and happened to sit down on a flowerpot with a cactus in it."

Bibbi recognised Mustafa's way of lying, that he could pull a story out of his pocket in no time, and recognised the spices in his "Beef Wellington'" She played along, pretending to believe in his story.

"Oh, how unlucky for monsieur Nyponros. I'm sorry to hear that."

"It's OK, mademoiselle, no problems. I can stand up. I've done that before. When I worked for Lagerfeld, I sometimes had to stand up for twelve hours at a stretch."

"Oh, fantastic, can monsieur Nyponros stand up straight for such a long time?"

"Oh yeah, no problem, mademoiselle! Excuse me, but we've been talking about me for long enough now. I want to know more about you. I'm curious about what you do. It says on the information sheet that you're an expert on iris diagnosis. Is there such a subject here at the university?"

Bibbi got up from the couch in order to be polite to Mustafa. She walked around the couch and stopped a few meters away from him.

"No, not here in Sweden. I studied iris diagnosis abroad. But I have studied French and German here at the university."

"You know what?" Mustafa said. "I have trouble believing that you can see people's illnesses just by looking in their eyes."

"You don't believe it works?"

"I doubt it."

"It's a way of diagnosing a patient's problems just by looking into his or her eyes."

"Yeah, I did know that actually, it's really interesting."

"I can do a little examination of monsieur Nyponros if he wants to."

"I'd love to!"

"Then I want monsieur Nyponros to stand behind the couch." Mustafa obeyed. Bibbi walked around the couch.

"Look straight ahead. Put your arms behind your back." Mustafa obeyed. Bibbi paused for a few seconds. She knew Mustafa's ailments, both the real ones and the imagined, and it was easy to make him believe that iris diagnosis worked.

"I can see here in monsieur Nyponros's right eye that he is a very kind person, but that he suffers from both gastritis and bad blood circulation."

"Fantastic", said a stunned Mustafa, "that's a hundred per cent right!"

"Of course! Iris diagnosis is a very accurate way of recognising a patient's illnesses. OK, let's take the left eye." Bibbi paused for half a minute.

"Ouch, I see that monsieur Nyponros has some problems with his love life."

"Way, way, way, what do you mean by problems?"

"I'm not sure if monsieur Nyponros is aware of this, but we Protestant women are a bit moderate when it comes to talking about love... hum... I mean sex, if monsieur knows what I mean." Mustafa wanted to show this Goldberg woman that he was a virile man with colossal sexual power, but at the same time he had to be polite and careful with his words.

"I have to protest. I have absolutely NO problems when it comes to the sexual thing. Let me tell you, madamemoiselle, that I have plenty of fuel."

"Oh... all men around the world talk like Usama bin Laden these days. I've got plenty of fuel, I've got lots of fuel' OK, that's fine, but it seems to me that they can't start their engines."

Mustafa smiled nervously.

"So what are you saying? That their engines have become rusty?"

"Not only that, but a lot of women have put their engines on monsieur Lagerfeld's shelf as French souvenirs."

Mustafa was embarrassed and said with a smile.

"You have a most delicate sense of humour, mademoiselle Goldberg. I've never heard about monsieur Lagerfeld's shelf, and I mean, he's a close friend of mine."

"Among my friends, it's called Lagerfeld's shelf, but also Coco Chanel's shelf. It's about women who have lost their appetite for love-making, well, hrm, I mean sex." Mustafa's face blushed. He was starting to realise that this Kerstin Goldberg was a very intelligent and tough woman. And he couldn't understand how she could see all his ailments just by looking into his eyes. He started to think about how to push his "Beef Wellington" into a new direction. Just as he opened his mouth, Bibbi interrupted him. She wanted to show Mustafa once and for all, give him a lesson for treating Fatima the way he did.

"So, monsieur Nyponros, describe your ideal woman to me."

"Hrm… let me think…she has to be kind, warm, have a good sense of humour, just like you mademoiselle."

Bibbi sat down on the couch and looked like a shrink.

"Hmm, interesting."

Mustafa tried to gain control of the conversation again.

"And how about you, what's your ideal man like?"

"His appearance or nationality - I couldn't care less. If he's a professor or works at a pizza place, or is a photographer for that matter, it doesn't matter to me. But it's very important that he has a tight bottom. I mean, for medical purposes."

"A tight bottom? I don't understand."

"Listen, monsieur Nyponros. A friend of my mother is American, and he's told her that a woman with sleeping problems can benefit from, how shall I put this, giving bottom massages. On tight male bottoms, that is. It can take the heat off anger and frustration, it can reveal stress and lead to... well they sleep better at night without sleeping-pills. And this method works for nervous women as well. They become calm, relaxed."

"Unbelievable! American women have visions! It's a pity that Oprah hasn't said anything about it. She talks about everything under the sun."

"Do you watch Oprah?"

"No, but mum does, and everything that Oprah says spreads fast."

"Oprah is careful, she can say anything she likes, especially about bottoms."

"This sounds fantastic. I can become famous if I whisper this to Amelia and to Veckorevyn (two Swedish women's magazines) and to Swedish Elle, it can help many women who have sleeping problems."

Mustafa sensed a spark of hope.

"You know what, mademoiselle? The bottom you're looking for is closer than you might think!" He pointed at his own backside. "The girls usually throw long looks at it when I pass them by."

"Oh, really? But then let me ask monsieur Nyponros: is his bottom firm, because that's what's most important!"

"Oh yeah, mademoiselle, firm and hard all the year round!"

"Hrm, I'm not convinced yet. May I have a look at it?"

"Avec plaisir", Mustafa said, "with pleasure!"

"OK then, lie down in the couch."

The cold Stockholm night had forced Mustafa to put

on a lot of clothes, he was still not used to the Swedish winters. Bibbi pulled his pants and underpants down, just to find another pair of underpants. And another. And another.

"I guess monsieur Nyponros isn't used to our climate. His bottom is cold as ice, despite all this underwear!"

"Yeah, you were right about bad circulation!"

"Yes, we really have to solve this problem!"

Mustafa smiled and began to understand where this was heading. Bibbi rolled the last pair of underpants between his buttocks, like on a sumo wrestler. Then she started kneading his bottom, hard.

"I have to warm it up. I don't think massage is enough, I think I have to spank it as well!" Mustafa tried to keep the conversation going as Goldberg spanked and massaged his botttom.

"By the way, what do your parents think about you dating a guy from Tunisia?"

"My mother thinks that the best relationships are those where opposites meet. Yin and Yang."

"Your mother sounds like a sensible woman! That's why I want a girl who's generous. As I said before, I'm stingy as hell!"

'Bibbi laughed and spanked harder. Mustafa yelled loudly.

"Ouch! What does your father think then?"

"My father's different. The most important thing to him is that those who are going to inherit from him are Protestants."

Mustafa lifted his left eyebrow in a funny way.

"OK. Well, I think that as long as there is warmth and love, there are no problems, only solutions."

"So monsieur Nyponros is willing to convert, then?"

"Absolutely! I'll switch, like this!"

He snapped his fingers.

"Would monsieur Nyponros want that?"

"Sure, no problem! I can't understand how people can argue about these things. We're all Abraham's children."

Bibbi, who spoke Arabic and knew that there are 99 different names for Allah, spanked Mustafa hard again.

"I have read somewhere that Allah has 99 different names. I was wandering if monsieur Nyponros would like to say 'I want to be a Protestant' 99 times? It is really important to me."

"No problem, mademoiselle, I'll start right now! 'I want to be a Protestant', 'I want to be a Protestant'..." Bibbi massaged hard and spanked. Mustafa screamed from the pain.

"Ouch, I want to be a Protestant, ouch! It really hurts!" After a while, when Mustafa's poor bottom had become so red that it resembled a Tunisian tomato. Bibbi stopped.

"Go on like that, 99 times! I will be right back, I am just going to get my mother, she is waiting outside."

"But please, mademoiselle, I can't lie here like this in front of my future mother-in-law. Even though I have a fantastic bottom, I don't want it to be the first part of me that she sees!"

"There is not much I can do about it, monsieur Nyponros. My mother demands that the man I am going to marry has a very firm and hard bottom, so that I can sleep at night." Mustafa looked up at the ceiling, his eyes filled with the joy of victory.

"So it's she who checks the incoming patients?"

"That is one way of putting it; you see, my mother is a vet."

"Fantastic, I love dogs!"

"Very good. I will go get her now, just continue: 'I want to be a Protestant'. 99 times! And if you are finished before we get back you just repeat it. OK?"

"OK, I understand. 'I want to be a Protestant...'"

"And when we get back you can't turn around until my mother has examined your bottom. If she sees your face everything will be ruined." Mustafa shook his head.

"Absolutely not, your wish is my command!"

Bibbi turned around and walked out of the room. When she closed the door behind her and looked up she saw a young couple, a guy with an elegant Armani suit and a girl with a beautiful white dress and a theatre mask. They had been standing there waiting patiently with red cards in their hands. Bibbi took a step forward.

"I know it's your turn now", she whispered, "but please, can't you just wait five more minutes?"

The guy looked impatient, giving Bibbi a doubtful look.

"OK, you get five minutes, after that we go and tell the reception."

Bibbi was in a hurry now, she had to get back to work, and she had to get Mother Merjam to room 10 in Gula Villan. On the way to her car she called Merjam.

Mother Merjam was working in the kitchen at the restaurant. She answered immediately when Bibbi called. Bibbi told her the story, fast forward version, from Mustafa's "Beef Wellington" up to now. When Merjam heard the provoking story, she dropped her work and headed for Gula Villan, room number 10.

Five minutes passed and the young couple walked to the information counter to complain. On their way to the bored girl at the information counter, they passed a foreign looking, sturdy woman in her late forties dressed in cooking clothes. She looked upset and she was walking fast in the opposite direction. To room number 10.

When Mother Merjam put her left ear to the door, she could hear Mustafa screaming about wanting to be a

Protestant. She carefully opened the door and walked into the room. She stopped a good distance from the couch and Mustafa and tried to distort her voice the best she could. She was going for the Gothenburg accent (on the Swedish west coast), just as Bibbi had told her to do.

"So this is the man who wants to be a Protestant?" Mustafa swallowed the bait.

"Mustafa, the dog whisperer." Merjam shook her head.

"Fantastic! Do you have dogs yourself?"

"Sure" Mustafa lied to "Mother Goldberg", "I love dogs. A life without a dog is no life!"

"But what if your dog gets ill and crazy and infects me, my daughter and my husband before we have drawn up the will."

Mustafa had the answer to that.

"No problems, no problems! It will take time before such a disease has spread."

"So you say."

"Yes, Mrs Goldberg, that will never happen. I'd rather let my dog bite and infect my mother than anyone in your family!"

Merjam bent over and took her shoes off.

"Sorry, I am a little deaf. Can you repeat that?" Mustafa raised his voice.

"I said I'd rather have my dog bite and kill my mother than anyone from the Goldberg family!"

Merjam couldn't hold it in any longer. She took her left shoe and hit Mustafa on his bottom with it. She dropped the Gothenburg accent and shouted in a mixture of Swedish and Arabic.

"You idiot! Do you want to trade your religion for money? You should be ashamed of yourself! You lie here with your bottom in the air for a few banknotes! But you prevent Fatima from going out and meeting someone! Idiot!"

She continued to hit Mustafa on the bottom, angry and sad at her son. Mustafa turned around, shocked and confused when he looked into his mother's eyes. He tried to put on all his underwear again. It was not easy, they had rolled up around his thighs.

"Mom, this isn't what it looks like, I didn't mean anything bad."

"You didn't mean anything bad?"

"I'll explain, you know this thing with Fatima, I just wanted to protect her from all the crazy psychos and rapists out there."

"You just bluff and lie! Nothing of what you're saying is true, you just make things up to scare her! And you're lying here on your face with your bottom in the air and shout that you want to become a convert! Who taught you all these stupid things?"

"The politicians, it's the politicians, mom! They say one thing and mean another. Allah knows I don't want to change religion."

"Allah will fry you in hell for bluffing and lying!" Merjam said, but Mustafa repaid in kind.

"Please mom, hell is fully booked, you have to wait at least a hundred years to get in. Enjoy life and be kind!"

"Who said that?"

"Monsieur Sarkozy."

"Stop kidding around. Why are you doing this?"

"I need 'the walking cash machine, Mademoiselle Nordea', so that I can finance my comedy show! I can't work as a cleaner any more, I don't have the energy to get up at five every morning."

Merjam looked sanctimonious.

"Oh, an illiterate who wants to be a celebrity! Start by learning how to read and write, then you can begin to talk about your own comedy show! Think about what you say and do! Idiot!"

She walked out of the room, furious.

On the way to the kitchen she passed the information counter again. She saw the young couple, the bored girl and Karin, whom she worked with at the library. Karin was working as a coordinator at the party. She lit up when she saw Mother Merjam.

"Merjam, glad you came! Can you walk over to room number 10 and see if everything is OK in there. These two", she pointed at the young couple, "say that there's a student in there shouting, 'Ouch, ouch, ouch, I want to be a Protestant!'"

Merjam sighed and looked dejected.

"Not only does he want to become a Protestant, he wants to do two things at the same time, kill his mother and become a Protestant for the sake of money."

"So you've been to room number 10?" Merjam nodded.

"Who's in there? What kind of an idiot says such things?"

"It's of course my son, Mustafa, who else? But don't worry, I've given him a lecture, I hit him on his bottom with my shoe, I don't think he'll be able to sit for a few months."

"Oh, I'm sorry", said Karin and looked at the list.

"But your name is Merjam Babuba! This boy's called Mustafa Ibrahamidozl… well I can't say the name, it's too long." Merjam sighed again.

"You see, Karin, my son is an expert at coming up with stupid things to do. Anyway, he's left now." Karin smiled and turned to the young couple.

"Well, I guess the room is yours. We're terribly sorry for the delay." The young couple headed for room number 10. Merjam turned to Karin.

"Karin, I have to go back to the restaurant now, but there's just one thing I have to know first. This Kerstin Goldberg, is she here tonight?"

""I'll check the list."

Karin went through the list for a while and then turned to Merjam.

"Seems like she made a late cancellation, she's not here tonight."

"OK. Thanks, Karin."

Merjam realised how it all fitted. Bibbi had hit the jackpot, Kerstin Goldberg had never turned up and Bibbi had served Mustafa her "Beef Wellington à la Swedish blondes."

Merjam smiled, thinking about Bibbi's little "extra job" as Kerstin Goldberg.

Ali in Solna with Hermine and Debora

Meanwhile, Ali had followed Hermine and Debora to their apartment in Solna north of Stockholm. He had been suspicious about these two girls from the moment he met them, there was just something about them. But this was a special opportunity for Ali, he was not used to being invited to participate in a "ménage à trois." When he came into their apartment he became even more puzzled than he was before. The apartment had a very special kind of furnishing, to say the least. The wallpapers were dark with weird patterns on them and there were symbols of the supernatural everywhere you looked. In every corner of every room there were bottles filled with some red sludge, scarily resembling blood. Ali walked into the living room, which seemed to be an arena for rituals and séances. In one corner there was an altar with weird figures on it. Ali tried to have an everyday conversation with the girls.

"So, what do you study at the university?" he asked.

"Ah, it doesn't matter. Sure, we're enrolled there, but to be honest with you, we're not there very often", Hermine answered.

"We don't have any interest in studying", Debora filled in, "we like parties, boys, wine, love…look, we have to go and change to nightgowns, just wait here."

Ali looked at the pictures hanging on the walls. They all portrayed witch symbols, distorted faces, creatures who looked like they were obsessed with Satan. Ali shivered, the place was just weird, the whole atmosphere was creepy. He was getting more and more nervous, and finally his tics started kicking in. He called for the girls.

"Hermine, Debora, where did you go?"

"I'm here in the bedroom", answered Hermine. "Come here!"

Ali again looked at the witch-pictures on the wall. He was getting really scared now, and he thought that he didn't really want to have sex with the girls.

"No, you come here instead. Maybe we can just talk, listen to some music. I'm a romantic, you know."

Debora walked from the toilet into the bedroom, wearing a sexy gown, and danced a little in front of Hermine.

"What is he yelling about?" she asked.

Hermine lay in bed and rolled her eyes.

"He's a romantic!"

"Come here, Ali!" Debora shouted in a resolute voice.

"What do you mean by 'romantic'?" Hermine continued. "Do you or don't you want it?"

"I just want to sit down and have a little chat first, kiss a little, have a little cosy-time."

"Kiss? Have a little cosy-time?" Hermine asked. "Is this how you do it in Tunisia? You offer a guy a fast car, and all he wants is one wheel?"

Ali started laughing hysterically, the laughter sounded like a mixture of fear and appreciation for Hermine's joke. He was still for a few seconds, hesitating. Then he walked to the bedroom, opened the door and walked in. Hermine and Debora lay under a big blanket in a huge bed. Ali could only see their faces. He wanted to say something but didn't find the words, just occasional sounds.

"Eh, eh…"

"Welcome in, Ali", Hermine whispered in a sensual voice.

"You know, Ali", Debora continued, "we've had some troubles with boys."

"Like what?" Ali asked.

"We simply haven't been satisfied. You know, Hermine and I, we're the kind of girls who go straight at it, we don't have time for all this stupid theatre. We have the same need for sex as you boys."

Ali's tics got worse, his head moved to the left, to the right, back and forward. He couldn't get a word out of his mouth.

"Oh, eh…"

"But we have a little suggestion here", Hermine said. "You look like a nice guy. If we're completely satisfied you can choose between three nice, expensive gifts. We have a lot of cash, I'll tell you that."

Ali regained control of himself and his head stopped moving.

"Are you so desperate you have to bribe people with gifts to get laid?"

"No, but normal, boring sex we can get any time we want, so we're not looking for that. But good, satisfying sex, that's what we want!" Hermine said in a joyful voice.

"Listen Ali, there's three different prizes here tonight", Debora continued. "If you send us to seventh heaven, a luxury cruise to Helsinki. If we're semi-satisfied, you know if we just get a little tickle in our stomachs, then you need some exercise, then we'll give you a bike. The third prize, well, it's a secret. It's up to you Ali, what's your choice?"

Ali paused for effect and kept looking at the girls, then he lit up.

"I'm aiming for the secret prize, but if I can't get that, then I'm going for Helsinki!"

"That's my boy!" Hermine cheered, delighted by Ali's sudden decisiveness.

"What IS the secret prize then?" Ali wondered.

"Can't tell you that, then it wouldn't be a secret prize, now would it?" Debora asked .

"Now get undressed, Ali!" Hermine commanded.

Ali started stripping in front of the girls. He took his jacket off, then his shirt. Hermine and Debora cheered in unison.

"Take off your trousers too!" Hermine roared, "and the T-shirt and the underpants, off with everything, off with everything!"

Ali opened his belt… he shook his bottom. The girls cheered even louder, but when he dropped his pants to the floor they got disappointed. Instead of a T-shirt he had a jellaba, a kind of long chemise, which went all the way down to his ankles.

"Going to the mosque, Ali?" Hermine asked.

"I've never been naked in front of a girl before", Ali answered.

The truth was that Ali was a virgin. He had never even been in this kind of situation before.

"Can we have the lights off?" he wondered.

"Sure, lights on, lights off, doesn't matter as long as you give us what we want", Debora said.

Ali turned the lights off and crawled into bed.

Beef Wellington à la rape spiced with sexologists

Ten minutes later Hermine and Debora jumped out of bed and immediately started getting dressed. Ali looked at them, surprised.

"What are you doing? Shouldn't we cuddle a little afterwards?"

"Get dressed you too, Ali. You'll get your prize soon", Hermine said.

Ali looked at Hermine and Debora for a while, confused. Then he started looking for his clothes. He found the underwear, the shirt, the pants...but where was the jellaba?

"Aren't you dressed yet, Ali?" Hermine said.

Ali looked around, he couldn't see the chemise anywhere. He skipped it, put on his shirt and his pants. Just as he was about to button the top button on his shirt, Hermine came up to him and pushed him down on the bed again.

"Mmm, Ali", she said.

"What are you doing, what happens now?"

"Now it's time for the second half", Debora shouted.

Then everything happened very quickly. Ali could barely react before he was tied up. Hermine and Debora lifted the bed up to a vertical position and turned it with the upside against the wall, so that Ali had his head against the wall and could not see anything else.

"What are you doing?" he asked. No answer. "You can at least tell me what I won?"

Debora smiled an evil smile. "Congratulations, Ali, you've just won the third, secret prize! Any guesses what it might be?"

"I've no idea."

"You've won..." Hermine drummed her fingers on the writing desk in the bedroom to build up the excitement.

"...At least three years in jail and deportation!"

Hermine and Debora walked around the bed so that Ali could see them. They grabbed hold of their skin, just below their chins, and pulled straight up. It turned out they had been wearing masks all the time. Underneath the masks new faces appeared, and their hair had a different colour. It turned out they were both brunettes. Ali screamed louder than a frightened camel. His tics started and his head began jerking sideways.

"Who are you people? What have I done to you? Why are you doing this?"

"You're like all men, an egoist. We haven't been satisfied. We're disappointed in you, and you're going to jail", Hermine answered.

"For what?"

"For rape! Debora shouted."

"For rape? Please, I've done my best. Can the Swedish government really afford to put all men who can't satisfy their women sexually behind bars?"

"Absolutely", Hermine said coldly and stared at Ali.

Ali was tied up and desperate and he couldn't see any way out of this dilemma.

"Where do you live, Ali?" Debora asked.

"In Skärholmen." Hermine tried to terrify him even more.

"Debora, go call the police." Ali was shivering from fear of the police and jail, and inside his head all kinds of thoughts came up. *The police are going to believe them. What a scandal! This will damage mom and Fatima. How could Mustafa persuade me into following these two lunatics home?"*

Debora walked to the toilet. She picked up her cell phone and called for a cab.

"I want a car for Bergsvägen 230, 'Larsson'."

Hermine took a pair of scissors and cut off one third of Ali's left trouser leg, and two thirds of his right.

"Please, stop, please! What have I done to deserve this?" Ali pleaded.

Claudia the taxi driver

Debora looked out the kitchen window on the street. She saw a cab stop just outside the entrance. She put on her shoes and walked out of the apartment and down the stairs.

When she got out and up to the cab she opened the door on the passenger side.

"Hi, we have a person here going to Skärholmen, how much is it from here?"

"That would be about 300 crowns, plus the fee for driving here, it'll be around 400 crowns", the taxi driver, whose name was Claudia and was Fatima's best friend, replied. Debora first gave her 500, hesitated for moment and then gave her another 200.

"You can keep the change if you're willing to do me a favour."

"Depends on what it is."

"Follow me up to my apartment. When we get up to my door, stamp on the floor hard a few times and clear your throat loudly."

"And why should I do this?"

"Well, you know guys, right? Always bragging about what sex gods they are, that kind of thing. I have this guy up in my apartment who thinks he is God's gift to women. I'm so tired of him, I want to give him a lesson."

"And this guy is from Skärholmen?"

"Yes."

"I'm from Skärholmen, I know a lot of guys there, and they're just like that. What is this guy's name, if I may ask?"

"Ali, he says it's Ali."

"Is he tall, but at the same time chubby?"

"Yeah, exactly!"

"You know what? Keep the 200, I really want to do this! I know this guy, he stopped his sister from going to a party tonight, he tricked her into staying home."

"Really?"

Debora and Claudia discussed for a while, then they walked together up to the apartment. Debora went in first.

"How's everything, Hermine?"

"Everything's fine."

About a second later the door bell rang.

"That should be the police, right?"

"Oh, so they're here already? Good they could come so fast", Hermine said.

"The cops are always fast if it's a crime against women", Debora replied.

Ali was now crying, begging for mercy. He was scared out of his life, but at the same time he oddly enough started to think rationally, about what to say to the cops to make them believe in him.

"Hi, good you could get here so fast!"

"We were in the neighbourhood."

Claudia tried to distort her voice as much as possible, her voice muffled. She looked around the apartment and started to feel bad. She immediately felt that something wasn't right. She became silent for a moment. Debora looked at her and mimed to her to continue the act, say her next line. Claudia regained composure and cleared her throat.

"Jaha, where is he then?"

Debora pointed at the bedroom. She said loudly and clearly, so that Ali could hear it:

"He raped us several times. He's right there, in the bedroom!"

To come across as an authority, a police, Claudia used the only Swedish words that she could say without an accent. "Jaha, jaha", she tried, in a throat-clearing voice.

"Go ahead, this side!" Hermine said.

"No, please, I haven't done anything!" Ali screamed in despair. Claudia recognised the voice. She stamped hard on the floor to scare the rapist. Then she and Debora walked into the bedroom. Ali heard the steps on the parquet floor. He begged, prayed, cried.

"Please, dear police! I haven't raped them. I've done my best. What am I accused of?"

"You've used us sexually", Hermine answered

quickly.

"Jaha, jaha", Claudia said.

"How could you come with us when you don't have a driving licence?" Debora said with an indignant tone in her voice. Ali opened his eyes, surprised. He now felt he had some kind of evidence to give the police, or whoever was behind him.

"Do you have to have a driving licence to make love to a girl here in Sweden?" he wondered.

"Absolutely", Debora answered quickly. "You have to have a paper that shows that you know your thing. It's a must when you follow a girl home!"

"Ah, so I have driven too fast then?" Ali asked.

Debora was having a hard time preventing herself from bursting out laughing.

"You didn't just drive too fast, you were up on the pavement driving as well!"

Ali didn't understand anything of what was going on.

"Is it that bad? Couldn't you just give me a second chance?"

"You can take a course!" Debora said.

"Absolutely! I'll do that", said Ali, who wanted to avoid prison at any cost. "I promise you, I'll take that course, whatever it costs! I'll eat porridge and save for that course, every penny. How do you register?"

"At the county administrative board. You can look it up on the Internet, at the site called www drivinglicence dot com. Look over here!"

Debora and Hermine turned the bed about a quarter of a circle, so that Ali could see the computer. The monitor showed a line of courses with sexologists to choose from, offering "girls to drive with", and they were not cheap. Hermine pushed Ali.

"Do you promise to take a course?"

"I promise, I promise! The police will be my witness!"

Hermine and Debora turned the bed a little bit more, and he suddenly saw Claudia standing right in front of him. He started screaming like a camel.

"Thank you sisters, for inspiring me with such a good idea as a 'driving licence'. I'm going to try to launch that back home in South America!" said Claudia.

"They need it there too?" Hermine asked.

"Oh yeah, as much as they need it here! I bet all men are the same, anywhere you go!"

Debora and Hermine untied the ropes and let Ali go. He got dressed and followed Claudia out of the flat and down to the cab. He was dead silent. They jumped into the cab, Ali chose the back seat. Claudia looked at him through the rear-view mirror.

"So, where are you going, little Ali?" Perhaps back home to Skärholmen?"

Ali nodded.

"Ali", Claudia continued, "there's a well-known saying: if you dig a hole for others, you often fall into it yourself. Sin will find you out. If you are unfair to your sister, sooner or later you end up in a weird flat in Solna with two crazy witches, it's an old truth! I'll give you a piece of advice: Don't talk to Fatima about culture this and that, you live in Sweden now."

Ali searched for words, arguments, something that could defend his way of treating Fatima. He couldn't come up with anything.

"Please, Claudia, don't tell Fatima what just happened here, pleeeeaaase?"

"On one condition: that you never try to stop Fatima from going out partying, or just going out for that matter. Never ever again, OK?"

"OK, Claudia, I promise."

Mustafa and Ali come home

Fatima had trouble sleeping. She sat by her computer, working on an essay in Swedish. She had spoken to Bibbi and heard all about Mustafa's adventures, but nothing about Ali's.

Mustafa got home, tottered into the apartment. He had trouble walking. He stumbled into the living room and tried to sit down on the sofa but his bottom hurt too much. Instead he went down on his knees and ended up standing like a dog on the sofa. Fatima came out from her room. She pretended she didn't know anything about what happened to Mustafa during the night.

"Hi there! How was it tonight?" She saw the strangled look on Mustafa's face.

"Has something happened? Are you hurt?"

Mustafa didn't want to reveal anything about the evening.

"Ouch, I'm in so much pain, ouch!"

"Where does it hurt?"

"My bottom!"

"But why? What happened?"

"I'd rather not talk about, but I'll tell you this: I've gotten my punishment for being unfair to you!"

"Aha, so you've been unfair to me, huh?"

Mustafa was ashamed about the whole thing. He wanted to move on, to change the topic.

"Can you please get the fan? It's up on the shelf over there."

Fatima gave him the fan.

"Fatima, could you please cool my bottom down with the fan? It burns like hell!"

"No way! You scare me out of my life with your talk about psychos, rapists and God knows what, and now you want me to cool your bottom with a fan like some kind of servant?"

"Cruel women", Mustafa mumbled.

A minute later Ali came stumbling home. He looked ridiculous, like a clown with his pants all cut up.

"What happened to you? Is that the latest fashion?" Fatima asked him.

Ali felt ashamed. He kept his head down and avoided looking into Fatima's eyes.

"No, I've been intimidated and deceived. Look, Mustafa, look what the girls did to me. And it's all your fault, you made me go with them!"

Ali stumbled away to his bedroom. Before he got through the door, Fatima stopped him.

"Ali, before you go into your room I have a little question for both you and Mustafa: will you try and decide over me in the future as well?"

"No Fatima", Ali said, "I know I won't anyway, I promise you that."

Ali went into his room. Fatima turned to Mustafa and looked him in the eye.

"And how about you?"

"Dear sister, since we live in egalitarian Sweden, I guess we have to take turns, one week I decide over you and the next week you decide over me."

"No, I won't accept that. We can overlook what happened this time, but next weekend I'm going to a party in Stockholm, in Gamla Stan (the Old Town)."

"Inshallah, Inshallah" (God willing) Mustafa answered calmly.

"Inshallah? Stop using Allah to frighten me and hold me down!"

"What's the matter with you? Don't you believe in Allah?"

"Of course I believe in Allah! But I don't believe in Mustafa, the conceited Saharian, who lies and manipulates to get what he wants. Damn you, Mustafa!"

Fatima went into her room and closed the door. Mustafa was still standing on all fours like a dog on the sofa. He took the fan and tried to cool himself off.

" What a cruel world we are living in... Are there any nice kids here, who can cool my bottom off? It's burning like hell."

There was no reply. Mustafa gave up and went to his bedroom. When he got in, Ali was already in bed, pretending to sleep.

One hour later Mother Merjam got home, still angry with her sons. She walked straight from the vestibule into Mustafa's and Ali's room and turned the lights on.

"Tomorrow you move out of here, both of you!"

"Please mom, why?" Ali begged.

"I've sacrificed so much for you, given everything I can to take you to this beautiful country! But all you do is spoil everything! You spoil everything for your sister, whom I trust one hundred per cent. She's smart, funny, sensible, you don't come near her in maturity! Still you want to hold her down and scare her."

"I've heard from my mates, and there's lots in the media every day! We just want to protect our sister", Mustafa said.

"Bullshit! This is the last time that you screw things up for Fatima. If you do it again, I'll change the lock and your bags will be packed in the staircase! Is that understood, Mustafa?"

Mustafa was dead silent.

"Can I get an answer?"

"Mom, here in Sweden it's forbidden to hit your children on the bottom so hard that they almost can't sit down properly."

"Mustafa, here in Sweden it's forbidden to discriminate against your sister just because she's a girl. Damn you, both of you!"

Merjam was a warm and caring person, but if there was something that she couldn't stand it was when people treated others unfairly. Her sons' way of treating Fatima made her furious. She stood still in the room for a while and glared at her two sons. Then at last she closed the door and went to her bedroom. Both Mustafa and Ali were quiet. Mustafa wanted to say something to break the silence which he found unbearable. He wanted to chat, just among brothers, anything just to take his mind off the dating-party and all that had happened. Ali didn't want to talk. He just wanted to sleep, but he couldn't. He had all these pictures in his head, little movies, short films being played over and over, Hermine and Debora, their scary apartment and being humiliated. He regretted deeply following Mustafa to the dating-party and falling for Mustafa's and Pedro's peer pressure. Mustafa tried to get his attention.

"How did it go with your 'ménage à trois'? Did you get any action?"

"It went straight to hell, I don't want to talk about it."

"Come on, Ali, I'm your brother, you can tell me."

Ali hesitated for a moment, then spat it out.

"These two girls, they were fundamentalists."

"I'll be damned. So there are girls here in Sweden that are fundamentalists?"

"Obviously! Or… well, not fundamentalists, it was something similar, Pedro told me about it a while ago… but it had the same meaning!"

Pedro had told Ali about radical feminism one day at work a couple of months earlier, but then he said "fanatics", not fundamentalists.

"But what does it mean? Here in Sweden, I mean?"

"That they hurt and suffocate innocent people. Like so many other fundamentalists! Because that's what the word means."

"But why would they do that?"

"I don't know, maybe men have treated them badly

before. Maybe they just go to dating-parties like tonight just to revenge themselves on men, on poor guys like me."

"But what was it that they did then?"

"I'm not going to tell you. I just can't. Oh how I regret that I went to that stupid dating-party. Watching football would have been much better."

"It can't be that bad, can it? Come on Ali, tell me!"

"I just can't, it's too much." Mustafa gave up and the room became silent again.

"Good night, Ali" Mustafa finally managed to get out of his mouth. Ali didn't respond.

"Shut up, Mustafa." The room became silent again. After about an hour, both boys were snoring loudly.

"Yep! Now listen closely, brother, and write it down on your pyjamas so that you can read it the first thing in the morning!"

Ali sighed.

"Integration", said Mustafa, "is to buy a new identity! If you don't stand out, you're nothing at Stureplan, they don't let you in anywhere, you HAVE to stand out in the crowd. That's what integration is. Buying the bouncer at Café Opera, at every sort of place. To walk past the queue with all the Swedes in it, to order first in the bar, offer a Swede a free drink, buy a new friend, THAT'S integration! Bribing the hairdressers, buy their friendship and their friends, that's integration."

"No chance in hell, I'm an abstainer!"

"No, no, Ali, you're a fanatic. And that's what's wrong with you, you don't want to integrate in Sweden."

CHAPTER 2

STOCKHOLM, JE T'AIME

Stockholm is a beautiful city, built on a collection of islets between Lake Mälaren and the Baltic archipelago, with the Baltic Sea outside. Wherever you go in the city, the water is just a few minutes away.. Stockholm has a humble elegance, just like the people that live there.

Merjam and the donkey Besbussa walked slowly down from Slussen towards Skeppsbron, heading for the Royal Dramatic Theatre, Dramaten, where Bibbi waited for them.

Bibbi didn't know where she had put the keys to her flat but she had given a spare key to Merjam. Bibbi had been working extremely hard lately, and hadn't been able to take care of her flat. Bibbi was like a daughter to Merjam, who was always willing to help her. She cleaned, washed clothes and watered the flowers. Now Bibbi had her lunch break and needed her keys back. Bibbi lived at Östermalmstorg, a couple of blocks from Dramaten.

Merjam had made lunch for herself and for Bibbi. It was Bibbi's favourite food, Tunisian tajin. Merjam had the lunch box strapped on Besbussa's back. It was late April and the weather was wonderful It was like early summer, not a cloud in the sky. Merjam and the donkey listened to the ships' signals. The cars honked after Besbussa.

Outside Dramaten Bibbi waited for them, looking like a goddess with her blue eyes, long neck and long blonde hair. The tourists sitting on the stairs leading up to the Dramaten entrance were delighted and they took pictures of her standing in her blue police uniform, with the Dramaten façade. as background. They probably thought that the beautiful blonde in police uniform had a role in one of the plays at the theatre, but that was not the case. At last Merjam and the donkey reached Dramaten.

"Oh, my saviour of the day!" Bibbi shouted when she saw Merjam.

"Always ready!" Merjam replied. Bibbi gave her a big hug.

"Where's Madame Volunteer?" Bibbi asked. Merjam looked at her with sad eyes.

Madame Volunteer's name was Elisabeth and she was responsible for Help Africa. She, Bibbi and Linnéa Blixt were called "The three musketeers".

"Elisabeth went to Nacka, her daughter Ebba is in the hospital there, she's got an eating disorder."

"Oh, how terrible! How long has she been there?"

"She was sent there the day before yesterday. I really hope it turns out all right. I'd really like to help her."

They started walking up towards Östermalmstorg and Bibbi's flat. On the way they talked about Elisabeth and her daughter. But Merjam also had problems of her own that she wanted to discuss. She opened her heart to Bibbi.

"Mustafa screwed up again", Merjam began, "he borrowed Fatima's credit card and emptied it, 8000 crowns in one week! And he's spent it on nothing, just a bunch of nightclubs on Stureplan!"

"8000? In a week? How could she agree to give her credit card to HIM of all people? I mean, he's not going to stress himself to death trying to pay back the money, is he?"

"Yes, I know, and Fatima only has a half-time job. Soon she starts studying at the university and then she will only have her student loan to live on. On top of that Mustafa is going on about getting his own credit card. He says there are people around Stureplan who have ten or fifteen credit cards."

"Not on your life! He musn't get a credit card, the way he is with money. As soon as he sees a pretty girl, he has to invite her out."

They arrived at Bibbi's apartment. Merjam heated the food in the microwave oven while Bibbi went to the toilet.

While setting the table, Merjam got a brilliant idea.

"Lunch's ready!" she shouted.

"Oh, it smells delicious, as if I were in Tunisia!"

"Yes, tajin and salade tunisienne!"

"Mmm, delicious!"

While they enjoyed the food, Merjam presented her idea.

"Suppose we give notice to the credit control authorities and tell them Mustafa is a high-risk customer?

"That sounds an excellent idea," answered Bibbi with her mouth full. "Perhaps in that way we could stop him throwing money away."

Merjam felt encouraged when she heard that Bibbi supported her. "I thought I would do like this: I pay the eight thousand out of my own pocket, so that Fatima doesn't get a bad credit record. At the same time we tell the authorities to give Mustafa the worst possible credit rating. They will start sending a lot of letters to him ... "

"Which he won't understand a word of." continued Bibbi.

Merjam really cared for her son and didn't want to harm him, but she did want to teach him a lesson and save him from financial ruin. "Exactly – we keep Fatima in the clear and we keep Musafe away from the debt trap. But I need your help, Bibbi."

Merjam knew that since Bibbi was in the police, she was in touch with all the authorities. "I want you to see that the credit control authorities give him a bad rating that lasts a long time."

Bibbi smiled and said she could arrange that. "I do

admire you," she went on, "I wish there were more mothers like you, both in Sweden and in other countries."

"Oh, I just do my best. It isn't easy being a single mum in a new country."

"You're so clever! Just remember to fight and never give up." Bibbi looked at her watch.

"Damn it, I have to get back to work."

"And I have to meet Elisabeth and Linnéa", Merjam said and got up.

"I thought Madame Volunteer was at the hospital?"

"Yeah she is, but she'll be joining us later, we're going to Danderyd (a leafy suburb in northern Stockholm) to collect some clothes. I'm sure it's good for her to get out and work and focus on something else for a while."

"That's probably true. So, shall we go?"

"What about the dishes?"

"I'll take care of that later, you can't fix everything for me! I'm a grown-up now, mum!"

"OK", Merjam said with a snobbish Östermalm accent (Östermalm is an affluent part of Stockholm), "how do you kids say… let's roll?"

Bibbi burst out laughing.

"Cool, mum, you talk the talk!"

They heard a car honk down the street.

"That must to be Linnéa", Merjam said.

"OK, let's roll!"

Linnea and Merjam collect clothes

Bibbi locked the flat, They shoved Besbussa and themselves into the elevator and went down to the ground floor. When they got out on the street they saw Linnéa Blixt, leaning against her van.

Linnéa Blixt was 35 years old. She worked as a music teacher and was very committed to "Help Africa" in her spare time. She hugged Bibbi and Merjam and gave the donkey a pat on the back.

Bibbi had to move on, they all said goodbye and Merjam and Linnéa helped each other pushing Besbussa into the van. Then they drove towards Danderyd, where they were going to collect clothes which they would redistribute to people in Africa.

When Merjam and Linnéa reached Danderyd they took the donkey with them and started their lap. A week earlier, they had handed out flyers to all the households in the area, asking for clothes and other benefits for those who needed it. They had a trolley with them to put the hoped-for clothing bags on. They looked at the first house on the street, a gigantic villa made of calcium silicate bricks, shook their heads at the luxuriance, then walked up to the door and rang the bell. Two kids, a boy and a girl, both around ten, opened the door.

"Hello, we're from an organisation called 'Help Africa'", Merjam said.

"Hello", the children replied and the boy handed over two plastic bags filled with clothes.

"Here you are", they said univocally.

"Oh, thanks a lot", Merjam said and gave the kids two lollipops.

"No thank you", said the girl, "I don't want any lollipop But I do want to ride the donkey. If not, then you're not getting any clothes!"

OK, OK", Merjam said and laughed a warm laugh.

"Yipeee!" the little girl screamed and looked at her brother. The boy and the girl put on their shoes and ran down the big vestibule terrace and down to the street in front of the house.

Merjam turned to Linnéa.

"The things you have to do for Africa's children", she said.

Linnéa smiled.

"This is a small price to pay, I mean, Besbussa can carry that slender little girl, right?"

"Sure, no problem, Besbussa's done this before, she's a donkey with a lot of experience."

Merjam helped the girl up on Besbussa's back, and then she led the donkey and the girl around the neighbourhood. When they got back it was the boy's turn. The girl turned to Linnéa.

"Thanks, it was so much fun! What are you going to do with all these clothes?"

"We wash and iron them and then we sell them", Linnéa explained. "The money we get from selling them goes to people in poor countries."

"Is that necessary?" asked the girl.

"Absolutely! Fifteen to to twenty thousand people die every day of lack of food and medicine!"

"Oh, I didn't know that."

"Yeah, there are a lot of people that need help. It was really kind of you to give us clothes, it will help a lot of people."

"Good. It was mummy who told us to give the bags to 'Help Africa', but she didn't say why. Now that I know why, it makes me happy."

Linnéa stroked the girl's hair.

"What luck that I had a chance to tell you! Say hi to your mum, tell her that the people of 'Help Africa' thank her a lot."

Merjam got back with Besbussa and the boy. She and Linnéa thanked the kids and moved on.

They continued up the road until it split in two. They decided to go separate ways, Merjam went right and Linnéa and Besbussa headed left.

Linnéa had an appointment with Jonas, an older man who used to assist "Help Africa" with gifts every now and then. He came out on the street with a bag of clothes right on schedule.

"Thanks for the clothes, Jonas," she said. "How's the training going?"

"Not that good, I feel exhausted."

"Just hold your head up high and clench your teeth."

"But how do I do that? I have a wry neck and false teeth!" Jonas asked nonplussed.

Linnéa laughed and hugged Jonas.

"You have a good sense of humour, that's the most important thing of all!"

Merjam and Samuel

Merjam moved on to Ringvägen, a street that harboured some of the richest in Danderyd. One of these was the retired businessman Samuel Johansson. He had contacted "Help Africa" and promised to give away an expensive suite of furniture which hopefully would generate some money. When Merjam reached the house, Samuel's private driver was already waiting for her.

"Hi", Merjam said.

"Hi! It's Merjam, right? Are you coming without a car?"

"Yes. But it's on its way."

"Do you want me to bring out the suite?"

"No", Merjam said. "Or you can bring out the sofa, but please wait with the table and the armchairs."

"OK, I'll just go for the sofa then", said the driver, who seemed to be a sympathetic and sensible person.

Merjam had agreed to meet a Polish salesman, Marek, who bought furniture cheap and sold it at a higher price. He arrived just minutes later with his van.

"Oh, hi, Marek! It took you so long!"

"Well, it was hell of traffic!" Marek spoke Swedish with a strong Polish accent and lisped.

Samuel's driver carried out the sofa. Marek inspected it carefully.

"Shall we do quick business?" Merjam proposed. "6000 crowns for a nice sofa."

"No way, I give you 150, not a penny more."

"Are you kidding me, Marek? Look at that house. Do you think they have low-price furniture in there? This one is imported from Italy, it's silk and teak. I'm not going under 5000."

"Then it's no deal! I can't give you more than 2500."

"Don't try, Marek, I know you can sell it for at least 5000-7000!"

"You just think that, Merjam. I work all day just to make a few quid. Look at me, I'm skinny!" Merjam knew Marek, she had done business with him before. She imitated the Polish accent.

"You just talk. When I see you with your beautiful wife Malgorzata in an expensive coat, I can see that you're making money."

"It's just what you think."

"By the way, what's the matter, monsieur Greedy? Yesterday you spoke normally, today you lisp. Have you bitten your tongue?"

The Polish purchaser let his tongue flicker like a dog...

"No, I spilled half a bottle of whisky on the floor last night!"

Merjam laughed.

"You're a funny guy, Marek! OK, give me an offer, what do you want for it?"

"2501?"

"OK, I don't have time to argue with you."

Merjam got the money straight away. They started carrying the sofa up on Marek's trailer.

When they were finished Merjam turned to Samuel's driver.

"Can you please bring out the armchair and the table too?"

"Sure!"

Marek had just finished strapping the sofa to the trailer when he saw Samuel's driver carrying an armchair in the same style as the sofa. He went mad.

"What is this? You've set me up, Merjam! Why aren't you selling the whole suite?"

"I got an order on these from a family several months ago", Merjam lied.

Merjam had a plan for how to trap the purchaser. She picked up her cell phone and called Linnéa.

"Hi, Linnéa! Can you come over here? We have two armchairs here. I promised I'd give them to a Moroccan family in Tensta (a suburb in northern Stockholm). OK, see you soon!"

Marek's face was red from anger.

"Merjam! Give me the rest of the suite right now, or give me my money back!"

"No way, a deal's a deal! You've given me the money and I've given you an Italian designer sofa for practically nothing. It's a bargain, you should be satisfied."

"I'm a loyal customer! Why don't you sell the whole suite to me? Are you a racist or something?"

"I'm not a racist, I do business and give the profit to the needy. I've already made a deal with a customer about the table and the armchairs."

"And what has the businesswoman sold them for, if I may ask?"

"6000 kronor for the armchairs and the little table."

Marek became silent, stared at the table and the armchairs. They looked as good as new.

"I'll give you 6001 for them! If you say no to that offer, you have to give me my money back right now. It's all or nothing!"

Samuel's driver observed, surprised and confused,

the salesman drama that the two immigrants were enacting.

"I don't want you to call me a racist. Take that back, and we have a deal", Merjam said.

"OK, I'll take that back. And I want a kiss on the cheek!"

"I'm sorry, can't give you any kisses, you haven't shaved and you smell of whisky. But I can give you a cry of joy. That will bring you luck in future business!"

Merjam hit the palm of her hand in front of her mouth several times to bring out her characteristic sound: "RRRA, RRRA, RRRA. RRRA…" Marek shook his head. They shook hands and lifted up the rest of the suite on Marek's trailer. They said good bye and Marek drove away. Samuel's driver smiled as he saw Marek's car disappear on the horizon.

"How are you going to explain this to that Moroccan family in Tensta?" he asked Merjam.

Merjam started making her sound again: "RRRA: RRRA: RRRA…"

"The Moroccan family is a fiction, it's as made up as the weapons of mass destruction in Iraq! But it helped to push the price up, didn't it?"

Samuel's driver laughed.

"Supreme, Merjam, supreme."

Merjam shrugged.

"You learn a trick or two over the years. You know what? I have a little thank-you gift for Samuel."

Merjam picked a painting out of a plastic bag she brought with her. Just as she picked up the painting she saw how the driver's eyes were focused on something else, something further down the road. She turned her head in the same direction and discovered a man, staggering his way up the road helped by a stick. From a distance he looked a hundred years old. A skilled doctor would probably diagnose him with rheumatism just by looking at him, and that was also the case. The driver looked at Merjam and saw that she was looking at Samuel.

"That's Samuel", he said. "He's been out on his daily walk."

"Ah, so THAT's the great Samuel Johansson", Merjam said.

"The one and only."

Samuel got closer and reached talking distance.

"I heard such a beautiful sound", he said with a rather distinct American accent. "Did you hear it too?"

Samuel stopped and caught sight of Merjam.

Merjam made the sound again: "RRRA, RRRA, RRRA…"

"Oh, was that you? Such a delightful sound! So delicate, sensual, it goes straight to your heart! Tell me, is it you who I've been speaking to on the phone, are you from 'Help Africa'?"

"That's correct. Merjam Babuba."

"Samuel Johansson."

They shook hands, but the old millionnaire wasn't content with just a handshake, he leaned forward and kissed Merjam on her hand. Merjam became a bit abashed, she didn't expect this.

"Thanks for that, and thanks for the gifts you gave us", Merjam said politely, "they will surely help many needy."

"Oh, that's nothing. Those were just gathering dust in the cigar-room anyway."

"We at 'Help Africa' would like to give you a little gift as a way of thanking you."

Merjam gave him the painting.

"Oh, look at that, thank you." Samuel looked at the painting casually.

"Excuse me", Merjam asked discretely, "but I have to ask you, are you from America?"

"I was born in Minnesota, my parents emigrated from

Värmland (a province in western Sweden) in 1915."

"Oh, how interesting! So you like going for long walks?"

"Absolutely! Long walks in the Swedish countryside. It helps me stay young and healthy. But my feet are ruined though."

"Oh, what happened? Have you been walking with pointy shoes?"

Samuel laughed out loud, a chuckling laughter that told you he had swallowed a whisky or two over the years.

"No, no, no."

"Excuse me for being so curious, but what happened?"

Samuel had charm and charisma. He resembled a mixture of the French comedian Louis de Funès and Benny Hill from the waist up. When he talked he looked as if he were standing on a stage somewhere, with wild gestures, capturing the attention of everyone around him. From his waist down he walked with the speed of a snail, because of the illness he desperately wanted to hide.

"You know, Merjam, it's really no problem, I like curious women. You see, this happened a long time ago, back in the States. My uncle had a ranch not far away from the house I was living in at the time. I used to help my uncle at the ranch whenever I wasn't busy doing business. He had lots of cows at the ranch, and when this happened they where out grazing, and I was watching them when suddenly the biggest bull of the whole ranch came rushing towards me! I didn't have time to think, the bull kicked me on my right foot, I just threw myself to the left, got up and jumped at him. I managed to get him in a firm and good headlock, and threw him over with a thump. He was heavy as hell, but it worked. Just as I was about to tie him up with my lasso he kicked me on my left foot. Man, did it hurt! I was able to tie him up, and limped away to my uncle's house. Turns out my feet were crushed, both feet are just like mashed potatoes. I was driven to the hospital for surgery. At the hospital, you know the doctors and nurses, they couldn't believe it. 'You can't walk one yard with those feet', they said. But I could!"

"Unbelievable, you're Minnesota-Tarzan!" Merjam said. "What happened to the bull?"

"He lay there moaning, oh my, oh my, I remember it like it was yesterday."

Samuel fired away his whisky-laughter again. The very same moment, Linnéa came driving up the road. She stopped at the other side of the street, stepped out of the car and said, "Hello, everyone".

She went up to Samuel and the chauffeur.

"Thanks for your contribution, we're really glad you could help us", Linnéa said.

"Bah, you know I have so much furniture, just glad to get rid of some", Samuel bragged.

"It's good you help the needy, this money will do much good you know", said Linnéa.

"Oh, that's certain", Samuel said, and turned to Merjam. "By the way, we're going to have a little party here on Walpurgis Night. If you're free and feel like it, you're more than welcome to come. It would be an honour."

"Thanks for the invitation", Merjam answered, "but Linéa and I have plans, we're going to celebrate Walpurgis with some co-workers from 'Help Africa'."

"Ah, that's a shame", he exclaimed. "Don't hesitate to call me if you need help in the future, I'm happy to contribute. Or, maybe I could have your phone number, Merjam?"

"Sure, here you are."

Merjam gave Samuel her visiting card.

"Oh, lovely! Now, if you excuse me, I have to take a bath in my Jacuzzi. Nice meeting you!"

"You too, Samuel. Take care of your feet! Thanks

again!"

Merjam and Linnéa got into the car, and drove towards Mörby shopping centre in Danderyd. Samuel threw an air-kiss at the car as they left. Merjam and Linnéa met Elisabeth in Mörby shopping centre. The three continued working the rest of the afternoon.

Fly while you can – tomorrow it might be too late!

It was seven o'clock in the evening on Walpurgis Night. Merjam and Fatima were at Bibbi's place for Walpurgis dinner, and Ali was meeting his new girlfriend Bente. Mustafa was alone in the flat in Skärholmen watching al-Jazeera. At the moment, he had only 20 crowns. After getting his paycheck from "Keep Stockholm Clean" he had paid the rent and food for Merjam and he had paid back an old debt to Ali. The rest of the money he had blown away on a three day long party at the clubs around Stureplan.

He went to the stable to fetch the donkey Besbussa. He dressed the donkey Besbussa in green and white. A Hammarby-scarf (Hammarby, also known as "Bajen", is a football team from Södermalm, Stockholm, plays in green and white) around the neck, and a Hammarby flag makes for a nice costume on the donkey's back, sides and belly. On one side of the flag he had made Ali write the words "Fly while you can - tomorrow it might be too late". Mustafa tied the flag on Besbussa's back, so that the words were clearly visible on the donkey's side. He took Besbussa with him and walked down to Skärholmens gård. On his way down he saw a shiny black Saab 9-5. The driver honked the horn at him, the Saab pulled over and the window on the driver's side rolled down. Mustafa could now see the driver was Lasse, the owner of Bux-Biou.

"Hey, Mustafa! Taking your dog out for a walk this late?" Lasse joked and smiled. "Boy, they get big these days! What do you feed it?"

"Strictly confidential. We've put him on a diet, it's classified material, but I'll tell you, he'll be the size of an elephant in a year!"

Lasse laughed and squinted at the donkey.

"What, you're taking it to a Bajen game?" Lasse wondered. "They let creatures like that in at Söderstadion (Hammarby's home arena)?"

"'Course they do, don't you know the donkey is the official Hammarby mascot?" Mustafa replied.

Lasse shook his head.

"You don't know much about Hammarby, Mustafa. But she's dressed in great colours, that's good to see."

"Thanks. By the way, what are you doing here, Lasse?" Mustafa asked. "I didn't think you were allowed to pass the Liljeholmen Bridge (the bridge that separates Södermalm and Stockholm's inner city from the southwest suburbs)!"

"Haha, no I had to get a visa for it, a lot of paper work, you know."

"I thought Lasse was lying in the pool at Bux-Biou on Walpurgis, lapping drinks like some cat."

"You need variety, you just can't sit and lap at the same place all the time, you end up a domesticated cat! No, we're going to Mälarhöjden (a leafy suburb in south-western Stockholm), one of those cocktail parties, the beautiful people you know´."

"So what are you doing there?"

Lasse laughed.

Suddenly, the car's back doors opened and two young, nice looking girls stepped out. Mustafa recognised them. It was Tia and Sandra, bartenders from Bux-Biou. They walked up to Mustafa and Besbussa.

"Oh, such a cute donkey, never seen anything like it!" Tia said and stroked Besbussa's wither. "What's it called?"

"Besbussa", Mustafa replied.

"What does that mean?"

"Hug and kiss. 'Boussa' means kiss in Arabic, the 'bes' part we just put in to make it sound good."

"Man, what a good name. Right, Lasse? Sounds like drink, doesn't it?"

"Not bad, rolls well on your tongue."

Lasse laughed.

Tia discovered the Hammarby flag on Besbussa's back and read the message.

"What do you mean by this, Mustafa, 'Fly while you can'?"

"That everyone should take advantage, take a plane and travel, enjoy life, soon only millionaires can afford to do it."

"Are you advertising for Air France, SAS, Lufthansa or something?" Tia wondered.

"No, this is no commercial, it's reality. The demand for oil is sky high, and soon the oil is gone. History! The prices will rise even more and ordinary people won't be able to fly", Mustafa said.

"Have you become a prophet? How can the oil be gone?" Tia asked.

"Everything ends, sooner or later."

"Oh?"

"Yes! Because we have new superpowers like China and India and other countries, they're getting rich now, people can afford a car, they want to live like people in the Western world."

Tia gave Mustafa a doubtful look.

"Mustafa, I've seen you with your coloured moustaches and I've been thinking, 'This must be a crazy artist'. And now it's verified! Written in stone!"

"No, I'm not crazy, I just want to be a sign, warning people of things to come."

"So you mean that we will start walking with

donkeys?"

"Absolutely! The roads will disappear, asphalt is made of oil! There are thousands of examples of what might happen." Lasse looked at Mustafa in mistrust.

"Mustafa, you ARE a crazy artist. You walk around with a Bajen-dressed donkey, talking about the end of car roads, damn, have you been drinking? I can't stand this crazy Tunisian anymore, get in the car, girls!"

"Speak for yourself, I could stand here patting this beautiful donkey all night long", Tia said and turned to Besbussa.

"Well, aren't you the cutest donkey, Besbussa, aren't you?" Sandra said.

Tia and Sandra were totally enchanted by Besbussa.

Lasse patted Besbussa on the back.

"Haven't seen much of you at Bux-Biou lately."

"You haven't? You are either looking too deeply into your beer glass or you are staring so much at the girls that you miss the action, Lasse." Lasse laughed and shook his head.

"Mustafa, how long have you been in Sweden?"

"Yeah, more than three years now."

"Hmm", Lasse mumbled and looked at Tia and Sandra.

"Come on girls, we have to go now, otherwise the prominent host will treat us like the Södermalm scum we are when we get there. Come on, get in the car! Mustafa, come in for a drink next week, OK?"

"Sure Lasse, sure." Tia and Sandra let go of Besbussa and jumped into the Saab. Lasse turned on the engine, then turned it off again.

"Hey, Mustafa, by the way, I've got some free tickets for the Bajen game on Monday. Come along and leave the oil talk at home, OK?"

"Sorry, Lasse, can't go. Got big plans, you know."

"What big plans? Are you going to hug a tree?"

Mustafa grinned.

"No, but Robert Johansson is singing at the Concert Hall on Monday."

"So now you're going to the opera as well? You mean this Robert guy is so wonderful he takes priority over Bajen?"

"Priority over Bajen? Hardly! But his wife is fantastic! Monday evening is my only chance to see her on this tour. I have to do it while he's at the concert hall singing."

Lasse laughed and handed over a game ticket to Mustafa.

"Here, give it to Ali, at least he's got some passion for Hammarby left."

"Nice of you, Lasse, Ali will be happy for this one. Hold on, I'm going to give you a present in return." Mustafa took the Hammarby flag off Besbussa's back and gave it to Lasse.

"From a crazy Tunisian to a crazy Hammarby fan."

"Oh man, a Hammarby flag with a political message on it! I'll bring this one to the game, for sure!"

Smiling, Lasse unfolded the flag and gave it to Tia. She looked at the donkey and then at Mustafa.

"Where does the donkey live, at some farm or what?"

"She lives in a stable. A couple of hours each day she is with us at home."

"What! You're insane!"

Mustafa was, like his brother Ali, against Merjam bringing Besbussa from Tunisia. But Merjam was the boss.

"No, I'm not insane. In fact, I'm very wise. Donkeys are part of the future, get used to it."

"I understand Lasse now, you really are one crazy artist, Mustafa", Sandra said.

"Everybody said this to me, 'Mustafa, you're crazy, you're a madman'. But soon, the truth will catch up with them, and I will stand there with dear old Besbussa next to me, and say 'I hate to say I told you so'."

Tia interrupted: "Mustafa, I don't understand that you can keep a donkey in the flat for two hours."

"Why not?"

"I've been to the market in Morocco", Tia replied, "and there the donkeys bray all the time, I think it's because there are lots of people around."

"But Besbussa doesn't do that."

"Is she ill?"

"No, she brays only when a virgin passes by."

"Shame on you!" Tia said and waved her index finger in the air.

Lasse started the car.

"OK, here we go. Happy Walpurgis Night, you crazy artist!"

"Bye, Besbussa!" shouted Tia and Sandra.

The Saab flew away at high speed. Mustafa followed the fancy car with his eyes until it was gone in the distance. He felt that sting of jealousy in his stomach and envied Lasse and the girls who were going to a party tonight. He stroked Besbussa over the back.

"It's just going to be you and me on Walpurgis night, Besbussa", he said. "Just you and me."

A sober Walpurgis night

Mustafa and Besbussa reached Skärholmens gård, and Mustafa found a stone to sit on. He watched the Lake Mälaren water flow and wondered how to make ends meet for the months to come. This was the worst Walpurgis Night since coming to Sweden. After a while a Walpurgis Night celebrating gang came down to Skärholmens gård and sat down a few meters away from Mustafa and Besbussa, putting out blankets on the ground, bringing out fruits and salads. They lighted a grill and threw hamburgers and sausages and salmon on them. Mustafa looked enviously in their direction. Besbussa started drawing the barbecue people's attention. They pointed and gestured towards her and Mustafa. Soon enough, one of the barbecuers headede over to them.

"Hi, how are you?" asked the barbecuer.
"Guess it's all right ", Mustafa replied grumpily.
"Cute donkey, is it yours?"
"Guess it is."
"That's amazing, having your own donkey?"
"Guess I have."
"What's its name then?"
"Besbussa."

The barbecuer stroked Besbussa's back.
"Hi, Besbussa, aren't you nice?" he said and turned to Mustafa. "My name's Peter, what's yours?"
"Mustafa."

They shook hands.
"Mustafa, shouldn't you and Besbussa come over and sit down with us? We've so much food and drink it's enough for you too."

Mustafa's face lit up.
"We can do that!"

They walked over to the other barbecuers. Peter introduced Mustafa to everyone. Besbussa immediately became a success among the barbecuers. Mustafa sat down and looked around. There was food everywhere, but he couldn't see any drinks. Where was the beer, the wine, the can of moonshine?

"OK, let's eat", said Peter. "Get the beverage out, Kristian!"

The guy known as Kristian brought out a rucksack and opened it. To Mustafa's despair, soda bottle after soda bottle came out of the rucksack, Coca Cola, Fanta, Sprite… Mustafa thought that it might just be mixer that the guy was bringing out of the rucksack and that the booze might come any minute.

"You sure have a lot of mixer, how much booze are you guys going to drink?" Mustafa joked.

Loud laughter.

"We're not going to drink any booze at all, we like soda better."

Mustafa felt confused, he had never seen anything like this before during his time in Sweden, particularly not on Walpurgis Night. He wondered if he finally had run into Swedish Muslims, and for a second he let the question roll on his tongue, but he stopped himself from asking and tried a different method...

"How do you guys know each other, are you childhood friends, or...?" Mustafa asked.

"No, we're in an association, the Skärholmen temperance society", Peter replied. "Maybe that explains a few things. I mean, the soda and all." Mustafa giggled nervously. Peter looked at Besbussa and saw the words on the legwarmers.

"What's that text on Besbussa's legs?" Peter tried to read the text on the donkey's legwarmers. "WHAT'S THE AL-TER-NA-TIVE... what do you mean by that?"

"What's the alternative to the car when we run out of oil? Is it going to be bicycles? Horse and wagon? I think donkey's going to be the new lifestyle."

"Hmm, interesting. I usually try not to think about the oil situation, that we're running out of it."

"Mustafa!" Kristian interrupted, "Do you want hot dogs or salmon?"

"Salmon!" Mustafa replied. "You have to eat a lot of salmon now, while it's cheap. Soon it will be a luxury, only for the rich!"

"So we're running out of salmon as well?" Kristian wondered.

"No, but when we're out of oil, what's the fuel for the fishing boats going to be? Will the fishermen have to stand on land fishing with casting rods, or what?"

"Are you one of those prophets of doom, Mustafa?" Peter asked.

"No, no, no" Mustafa bragged. "I study at the al-Jazeera University, best university in the world!"

"The TV channel al-Jazeera?"

"Exactly! I saw a show recently, it was about what's going to happen when we're out of oil. I've dressed Besbussa with different messages that call for attention, that make people wonder, 'What does he mean'? And then I tell them, just as I am doing now."

Peter studied Mustafa with an interested look.

"It's good you do that! But maybe we shall get a better world when the oil's gone? No stress, just listen to the birds, people might get time to actually see each other, maybe we will become more harmonious."

"Or maybe it will come as a shock for people?" Kristian asked.

"Shock, yeah, you know what?" Mustafa said. "I have a mate, he had a nightmare about the judgement day, he screamed and cried in his sleep, and when he woke up he discovered that the house on the other side of the road was on fire. He thought he'd died and gone to hell! You know, he became unconscious for a week!"

Everyone laughed.

"Pretty funny, huh? But there's a serious point with this story: we can't just sleep and then wake up one day and become shocked by what we might see! We have to be prepared."

"That's very true", Peter said. "What a nice illustration. You're a real poet, Mustafa!"

"I try my best."

"Here's to life without oil!" Peter burst out. "For a better life! For a better world! Cheers!"

"Cheers!" shouted the rest of the bunch. Mustafa found the whole scene a bit odd, but he tried to seem interested in front of Peter and the rest of the gang.

"How interesting with your temperance society. So where are you located, here in Skärholmen, or?

"Yeah", Peter said, "we have a place on Skärholmsgatan 10. You're more than welcome to come by any day."

"Thank you, Peter, I appreciate that." They started eating and drinking and talked about everything between heaven and earth. Later they lit a campfire. One of the abstainers was a keen guitarist and had brought a guitar. He played it and everyone sang classic campfire tunes. At eleven o'clock, Mustafa and Besbussa decamped and started walking home. At the end of the day it was a pleasant night. Mustafa felt that he was really welcomed among the abstainers, he felt like he was part of something good there for a while, and while walking home, he thought that this wasn't such a bad Walpurgis Night after all.

Mustafa and the temperance society

Next week Mustafa started visiting the temperance society. He had come up with an idea for how to finance his comedy. He felt that he was quickly becoming good friends with Peter and the other abstainers. At the same time he missed Stureplan and the good life at the clubs, the beautiful people with the fancy designer clothes, all the cute girls and the intoxicating drinks. He had developed the taste for the good life and he didn't want to give it up, even though he couldn't afford it. During his third visit to the temperance society, when he sat in the temperance society's meeting place with Peter, drinking tea, he got an idea.

"Hey Peter", Mustafa began, "I've been thinking of something. What's the main purpose of this temperance society?"

"To keep young people off alcoholic drinks, to show

them that there are other ways of living this life", Peter replied.

"OK, cool. So which methods do you use to show that to the kids then?"

"We try to promote the temperance society, to show the world that we exist, but like with so many things, it costs money. We get some benefits from the government, but it's not much."

"I know another way for you to get hold of some cash."

"How?"

"The mosque! You have no idea how much Muslims appreciate Swedes who stay off the booze. You and I can go there, I go inside and pray, and you stay outside with a sign that says something like 'Support the Skärholmen temperance society, make your donation here'. I promise you, man, the cash is going to flow in!"

Peter looked at Mustafa with a grave look on his face for a few seconds. Then he opened his mouth.

"You know what, Mustafa? That sounds like a good idea! Let's do it!"

"Is next Friday OK with you?" Mustafa asked.

The next Friday, Peter and Mustafa met outside the mosque in Skärholmen. Peter had brought a big sign with the words "Support the temperance society in Skärholmen, make your donation here". They decide to stand just outside the mosque's entrance. Mustafa took his bandana off and put 100 crowns in coins and banknotes in it and gave it to Peter. Then he went into the mosque to pray for the first time since he came to Sweden. He came out again an hour later. By then Peter had collected almost 3000 crowns.

"You're a fantastic entrepreneur, Mustafa!" Peter exclaimed on his way back to the temperance society. "You could do a lot for our temperance society with all that resourcefulness of yours. What do you think, would you like to become a member?"

"Do I want to join the abstainers? Absolutely!" Peter smiled at Mustafa.

"OK, we'll get you in then!"

Beef Wellington à la Qatar

A few days later, Mustafa and Peter met up at a café in Skärholmen shopping centre.

"Hi, Peter!"

"Hi, Mustafa!"

"Is cake and a cappuccino OK with you?" Mustafa offered.

"Oh, thank you Mustafa! It's not often you meet someone who's treating you these days."

"Oh, it's nothing."

They sat down at a table.

"Hey Mustafa, you think we can go to the mosque and collect some money on Friday?"

"You can't do it every week, you know there are other organisations standing there", Mustafa lied.

"Oh, really?"

Inspired by the successful fundraising at the mosque, Mustafa decided to pursue an idea he had got a few days earlier, he started to make his "Beef Wellington à la Qatar."

"But I have good news for you!"

"And what's that?"

"I met two students from Qatar who were here in Stockholm on vacation, I told them a bit about our work. They told me that a safe thing to do if I wanted to make our finances grow was to invest in Qatar funds."

"OK, and…" Peter asked curiously.

"Funds in Qatar! We will open a fund and spend 20 000 on advertising. Many mosques will contribute. Qatar is a generous country, within a month we'll have tripled the money!"

Peter looked thoughtfully at Mustafa.

A week later, Mustafa had got 70 000 crowns from the temperance society to invest in a Qatar fund and 20 000 for advertising.

Days passed by, they became weeks and months. It was now mid-July and Peter and the rest of the abstainers hadn't seen Mustafa since the end of May.

It was Saturday and Merjam was on her way home to Stockholm from Dalarna (a province in northern Sweden) together with Bibbi. The two had visited Bibbi's grandmother in Borlänge.

At home in Skärholmen, Ali was lying on the sofa playing video games and Fatima sat in front of her computer working on the "Fabizaists" homepage. The "Fabizaists" was an organisation that worked for peace and it consisted of Fatima (a Muslim), Bibbi (a Protestant) and Zaza (a Jew), three childhood friends who had spent their holidays on the island of Djerba in Tunisia. They had a mutual dream of peace and understanding between people of the different world religions, to make other people follow their example, to try to cross borders and to communicate with one another. Fatima tried to work really hard with the home page, in order to forget about what had been going on in the flat, or rather outside it. Peter from the temperance society had tried to get into the flat for an hour, shouting menacing things about Mustafa and what was going to happen to him if he didn't open the door. But Mustafa wasn't at home. After about an hour it seemed as if Peter had finally given up. Fatima went out to the kitchen to have a cup of tea. Suddenly she heard the voice again: "Mustafa, Mustafa, open the door! You have to give us our money back!" Peter threatened.

Peter stood outside the Babuba family's flat shouting

through the letterbox.

No one replied. Ali and Fatima were scared. Ali started running around the flat out of control, Fatima dropped her cup of tea on the kitchen floor; she was at a loss what to do. Peter raised his voice to scare Mustafa.

"You have no chance of getting away with this! I'll bring a mattress, and I'll stay here until you come out", Peter went on, repeating his threat, over and over again.

"You have no chance, Mustafa! You have no chance, Mustafa!"

At last he seemed to give up, there was silence outside the flat. Ali and Fatima recovered their composure. They stood still, shaking. After a while, Ali walked out to the vestibule and the entrance door. He stood there for a while, looking through the keyhole. At last he turned to Fatima.

"I think he's gone", he said at last. "Why hasn't Mustafa paid these people their money?"

"Yeah, why hasn't he?" Fatima said. "We can't have it like this. People standing outside our door, shouting obscene things.

The phone rang. Ali tried to toughen up and act as a leader. He hit the wall with his fist.

"Enough's enough!" he shouted. "Answer, Fatima!"

Fatima got herself together, sat down in the armchair and picked up the phone.

"It's Fatima."

"Hi, it's Daniel from the temperance society. Can I speak to Mustafa?"

"Eh… he's dead."

Daniel was surprised by the reply.

"Oh really? When?"

"For… four days ago."

"Oh… Is he dead? Was he shot in the head?"

"Erm… we don't know, and that's the problem. When he was alive, the Swedish tax authorities didn't know what he lived on, and now the doctors don't know what he died of."

The doorbell rang. Fatima quickly hung up so that no one would hear them. She and Ali panicked again.

"What are we going to do?" she whispered to Ali.

They ended up under the dining-room table. The donkey walked towards the vestibule. Peter let out a squawk.

"Mustafa, you HAVE to give the money back! You have NO chance of getting away with this!" It became silent again. After a long while Fatima walked to the vestibule and looked through the keyhole.

"Seems as if he's gone for now. But he'll be back. I'm going to call mum now, I'm going to tell her the truth. We can't hide this from her any longer."

Fatima called Merjam's cell phone, but there was no answer. Maybe the batteries were dead? She called "Help Africa", maybe Merjam and Bibbi had dropped by there before coming home? One ring. Two. Elisabeth picked up the phone on the other line.

"Help Africa, Elisabeth!"

"Hi, it's Fatima! Are mum or Bibbi there?" Fatima asked anxiously.

"No, but they're on their way here. They said they'll be here within an hour."

"When you see mum, please tell her to call me!"

"OK Fatima, no problem!"

Fatima hung up.

"OK, let's go! I have to see Claudia."

"Yeah, let's leave. Quick!"

Bibbi and Merjam back from Dalarna

When Bibbi and Merjam reached the centre of Stockholm, they went straight to Mariatorget, a square on Södermalm, where "Help Africa's" headquarters were located. They were going to leave some clothes they had collected in Dalarna, so they parked Bibbi's car and went to the beautiful old house and down to the cellar. They knocked on the door but no one opened. They opened the door and walked in, passed through the office and coffee room but there was no one there. Then they went through a corridor that led to the laundry room and found Elisabeth and two other "Help Africa" workers washing and ironing clothes.

"Hi, everyone!" Bibbi and Merjam said.

"Welcome back!" Elisabeth greeted them. "Merjam, Fatima called us, she wanted you to call her, it was something important."

"OK", Merjam said. She was a bit worried. "Let me just give you the clothes from Dalarna, then I'll go home immediately."

A couple of hours later, Peter was back, right outside the Babuba family's door.

"Mustafa! Mustafa! I know you're there! Open the door!" he shouted through the letterbox.

He raised his voice even more.

"Open the door! What wrong with you, Mustafa?"

Peter didn't notice the person standing behind him. It was Merjam who had come home.

"I've asked that question a million times myself."

Peter turned around, surprised.

"You're the mother?"

Merjam imitated Peter's Skåne accent (Skåne is a province in the southernmost part of Sweden, where the accent is a bit similar to Danish).

"Yes I am. Can't you respect the people living here for one minute? Do you have to stand here squealing like a stuck pig? You think he'll open if you shout loud enough?"

"Listen, your son had ripped quite a lot of money off us", Peter yelled.

Merjam looked him straight in the eye.

"There is such a thing as a police here in Stockholm. Why don't you turn to them? You don't have to stand here terrorizing us and our neighbours. They haven't ripped you off too, have they?"

Peter calmed down a bit.

"You have to understand us…"

Merjam opened the entrance door.

"Please, come in! We have to get this straight. How much money does my son owe you?" Merjam asked.

"90 000 crowns."

That sum of money made even Merjam shocked.

"90 000! Oh my, that's bad."

Both Merjam and Peter were so upset that they couldn't bring themselves to sit down.

"And you gave him this large amount?"

"Yeah."

"But why?"

"To invest in a Qatar fund."

Merjam shook her head. She felt that something wasn't right. She wanted to know the truth so she played along.

"What kind of a fund, the Usama bin Laden-fund or what?"

"No, your son had opened a fund in Qatar, it's called 'Dialogue'. Mustafa had advertised in several Qatar newspapers, appealing for financial contributions to our temperance society."

"How did he manage to do that? Mustafa's an illiterate, he always holds the newspaper upside down when he tries to 'read' it."

Peter was surprised.

"What? He's an illiterate? He told me he's an expert on Muslim funds."

Merjam burst out in laughter.

"Expert? Listen, Mustafa is an expert at a lot of things, wine, booze and women for example. But Muslim funds? I don't think so."

"Wine and booze? He told us he's an abstainer!"

"He's so much an abstainer that he can hurt and ruin the entire night for a South American girl, just because she said no to wine and booze.".

"What do you mean? What happened?"

"About a year ago, he invited my daughter's best friend Claudia, a real Brazilian treasure by the way, to a dinner at a restaurant. After an hour Mustafa got out of his chair. Claudia was upset and asked if he was going to leave already. 'Yeah, I don't like girls who use bad words', he replied. Claudia defended herself saying that she hadn't used any bad words. Mustafa became upset. 'You haven't?' he said. 'You've said no to wine at least ten times tonight'! Then he paid and left her in the restaurant."

"I'll be damned", said Peter and looked puzzled.

"What about this then", he said. "Every time Mustafa came into the temperance society headquarter, he mumbled and fiddled with a strand of pearls. He said he's afraid of God."

"Not only is he afraid", Merjam said, "but he didn't even dare to go outside in the evenings without a Scandinavian blonde by his side!"

Merjam opened a bureau in the vestibule and took out a rosary.

"Is this what you mean by 'a necklace'?"

Peter nodded. Merjam sighed.

"Everything's just comedy and theatre", she explained. "When he mumbles and plays with a rosary, then he's about to come up with a sophisticated bluff, you can be sure of that. Report him to the police if you want to."

"No, I don't dare do it", Peter said nervously. Merjam walked into the living room and picked up the receiver just to scare Peter.

"There's something fishy about this, I'd better call

the police."

Peter walked up to Merjam and put his hand over the telephone.

"Please don't do it! Hang up, please!" he asked.

"OK, talk to me then! Who are you?"

Peter sat down in the sofa.

"My name is Peter, and I'm in charge of a temperance society here in Skärholmen. We have a little basement studio that we use as a meeting place, and now we've collected 90 000 crowns to invest in restoring the place and advertising to recruit some new members. You know, we want to attract young people to the temperance society, and we want to offer them fun and meaningful activities that don't include alcohol or drugs. Your son convinced me to open a fund in Qatar, putting in 70 000. The rest of our money, 20 000, was going to be used for advertising in the local newspapers and the mosques down in Qatar. Mustafa said that through advertising you could reach the serious mosque visitors and thus triple the invested money within a month. He told me that people in the Arab world are very positive towards things like temperance societies, and that everyone is more than willing to participate. Mustafa gave us the impression of being an honest and serious person. But now we haven't seen him in nine weeks, and no one knows what has happened to the money."

Merjam burst out in her characteristic sound "RRRA, RRRA, RRRA…", she went on for a while and then calmed down.

"Have you any receipt from Mustafa?" she asked.

"No, nothing."

Merjam sat down in the sofa. She understood that there was something suspicious going on.

"What a mess!"

"Please, Merjam, you must know where Mustafa is, tell me!"

Merjam looked down on the floor and shook her head.

"Honestly, I don't know, I've been on vacation in Dalarna for two weeks. I'm going to call my daughter and see if she knows."

"That sounds good. Please do that. I want to know where he is."

Merjam called Fatima's cell phone.

"Hi Fatima!"

"Hi mum, I called you earlier."

"I know, Elisabeth told me. What is it that you wanted?"

"Big troubles with Mustafa."

"Yeah, so I heard."

"What? You know? Who told you?"

"Doesn't matter. Important thing is, where is he?"

"Don't know, he hasn't been home for two weeks."

"Two weeks? But where can he be?"

"Don't know, he said he was going to Stureplan to study 'the meaning of life'."

A big sigh from Merjam.

"OK, listen Fatima, I'll take care of this, just take it easy. I'll call you later, OK?"

"OK."

Merjam hung up and looked at Peter.

"Guess you heard, he's been gone for two weeks, we don't know exactly where he is, but a wild guess is he's somewhere around Stureplan, studying 'the meaning of life'."

"What does that mean?"

"To Mustafa it must mean binge drinking and picking up girls.".

"But he's a member of our temperance society!"

"Listen here, my son is more sophisticated than a politician. He may be very convincing, but he doesn't always speak the truth, so to speak. I guess you've noticed that."

"OK, so he's at Stureplan partying then. I really didn't think this of him, he was always really economical, always looking for discounts in the stores when we went shopping for the temperance society. Really thrifty!"

Merjam looked sceptical:.

"But that's really true, he really IS thrifty! He's so thrifty he even sleeps with Swedish girls just to not wear out his own sheets here at home."

Mustafa at Stureplan

Mustafa had begun his night out with a drink at Spy Bar, one of Stureplan's hot spots. He hadn't seen any familiar faces, so he took his delivery bike, "Mustafa's Volvo", and biked down to Kungsträdgården and the most classic of all classic hot spots in Stockholm's night life, Café Opera. Mustafa had put on tons of perfume, from several different brands, and you could even smell him from a long way away. He wore a Gucci-jacket over his Armani shirt, and the Sinbad pants on his legs. He dropped elegantly in at Café Opera and looked around. Men and women danced. A long, blonde waitress, Diana, smiled at Mustafa.

"Hi, monsieur Nyponros!"
"Hi, gorgeous!"
"You smell good!"
"Well of course, mademoiselle!"
"You're early tonight?"
"Yeah, I'm early, and there's a reason for it."
"What reason, if I may ask?"

Mustafa put on a big smile on his face.

"Did I really spend two thousand crowns on wine and beer last night?"

"Something like that, yeah. You ran from the bar to the toilet and back, over and over again."

"Oh, mon dieu, good to hear that, I thought I'd lost

the money!"

Diana couldn't help but laugh. Mustafa looked at her, then around the venue. He discovered a familiar face, Oscar, a real estate agent, and his sister Victoria, a glamour model, sitting at a table together with a girl he hadn't seen before. Oscar and Victoria were part of the in-crowd at Stureplan, always beautiful, always well-dressed.

"Can I have a bottle of champagne?" Mustafa asked. "I'm sitting over there, with the crew, you know." Mustafa smiled when he said "crew", Diana smiled back. He pointed towards Oscar's table.

"Sure!" Diana replied.

Diana tried to clear the table but dropped a few glasses on the floor.

"Oh, I'll help you", Mustafa said.

"No, you don't need to, I'll manage."

Mustafa turned his head and attention to the bar. There he discovered Mona and Sara, two girls who ran a beauty salon at Stureplan where Mustafa was a regular. They were standing by the bar talking intensively to: a girl dressed in tight white trousers under which Mustafa could spot a beautiful, pear-shaped bottom.

"Hey, Diana! Bring a bottle of white wine over to those two girls over there too. You see those with the pink dresses, right there, yes."

After making sure that Diana had seen the right girls to give white wine to, Mustafa headed over to Oscar and Victoria's table.

"Hey, you old geezer", said Mustafa to Oscar, "it wasn't yesterday I saw you here. Or wait a minute… it WAS yesterday! At the bar!" Everyone around the table laughed at Mustafa's joke.

"You have coloured your moustaches again?" Oscar asked.

"Dear Oscar, one thing you must know. My moustaches are my accessories. You can't have a Gucci jacket, an Armani shirt and French moustaches. You have to have Italian moustaches, otherwise the Italian fashion kings will go mad!"

Mustafa turned to Victoria and kissed her hand.

"Mustafa, do you even know what 'gamla galosch' in Swedish means?" Victoria asked.

"No, but in Mustafa's own dictionary it means 'good looking guy in expensive designer clothes'."

Loud laughter at the table again. Victoria shook her well-formed body a little. She wore a low-cut dress that almost showed more than it hid.

"And what do you call a girl like me then?" she asked.

"A girl like you I call 'Mademoiselle Gauguccina', 'Gau' like in Gaultier, 'gucci' for Gucci and 'a' for Armani. You are well aware what you are wearing."

Victoria giggled. Mustafa turned to the other, still unknown, girl.

"Hi, I'm Mustafa."

"I'm Sabina", she replied.

They shook hands. Sabina turned out to be a tall and beautiful blonde, nineteen years old. Mustafa took a free chair and sat down at the table. Diana came with a tray with four glasses and a bottle of champagne and put them on the table.

"Here you go!"

"But we haven't ordered any champagne", said Victoria.

"Mademoiselle Gaguccina, this one is from me to you", said Mustafa.

"Oh, what a gentleman!" said Victoria.

"Oh, it's nothing", said Mustafa and turned to the waitress.

"How are you doing today, Diana? Seems like a busy night, huh?"

"Oh, it's just my head. It hurts like hell."

Mustafa opened his jacket and showed his white shirt. It had a foot printed on it and the footprint had a number of zone points in different colours on it.

"How lucky for you then, that I'm an expert at zone therapy! I can fix your problems."

"That's sweet of you Mustafa, but I really don't have time for that."

"That's ridiculous! This is an order: take off your right shoe and lift your foot."

Diana put her right foot on Mustafa's thigh. Mustafa pushed with his thumb on Diana's middle toe and explained.

"This is number three, it goes straight to the head. Now I'm going to push it really hard."

Diana screamed in pain.

"Ouch, ouch, ouch! It hurts!"

"It'll soon be over", Mustafa assured her.

Diana kept on screaming.

"Ouch, ouch, ouch!"

She's calmed down a bit.

"Oh, now it's starting to get a bit better. My dad blames me for always walking around in pointy, high heel pumps."

"Please Diana, what would Stockholm be without girls in high heel shoes that make their bodies look attractive."

"Yeah, but my father tells me that a reasonable girl wears comfortable shoes that don't make her head or back hurt."

"Aha, tell your father from Daddy Mustafa that a reasonable girl is a girl who took birth control pills before going into a Stockholm underground train during rush hour."

Everyone started laughing. Mustafa continued to massage Diana's right foot.

"What do those figures on your shirt mean?" Diana

asked, to change the topic.

"You treat different illnesses by pushing these different spots on the bottom of your feet" Mustafa explained. "After a while, the illness and the pain go away."

"Yeah, it's a little bit better now. But it still hurts here."

Diana pointed at her forehead. Mustafa acted puzzled.

"Hmm, strange. Could it be that you are wearing underwear made of cotton today?"

"Yeah", said Diana, "I am! How on earth did you know that?"

Mustafa was a guy with extraordinary powers.

"There is a connection between cotton underwear and headache. You know, your whole blood circulation is disrupted, and you get a headache." All the girls stared at Mustafa with their mouths wide open.

"You really mean that, Mustafa?"

"One hundred per cent!"

"Thanks Mustafa, you're simply amazing!" Diana said. She put her shoe back on.

"So you mean that cotton knickers cause headaches?"

"Absolutely!" Mustafa said and twisted his mustaches. "Many girls wear string tangas."

She went back to work. Mustafa raised his champagne glass.

"To all the "gamla galoschers" and Gaguccinas on and around Stureplan!" he shouted and turned to Victoria.

"Do you want zone therapy to revive your spirits tonight?"

"Well, it's difficult, you know, my boyfriend is very warm and kind, but he's also very jealous."

"Your boyfriend? Where is he, I've never seen him here with you!"

"He's in Kuwait."

"Well then it's no problem, is it? He's far away."

"That's what you believe, you don't know how Kuwaiti men are when it comes to their women." She lifted her foot. "You see this gold necklace on my foot? He's installed a burglar alarm in it!"

Everyone started laughing.

"I'll be damned", Mustafa said.

"And within five minutes the police will be standing here calling my boyfriend", Victoria said. "And they will receive a big check, you know how much money the oil people have!"

"That explains why the police never arrive in time for break-ins in flats and cabins, they're too busy taking care of girls dating rich oil men."

"That's right!"

Mustafa turned to Sabina.

And how about you, mademoiselle, would you like some zone therapy?"

"If you put something in the collect" said Sabina and held out her purse.

"How much?"

"Two thousand crowns."

"That´s too much – a hundred"

A guy came up to the table and asked Sabina for a dance.

"May I?"

"Sure", said Sabina and turned to Mustafa.

"I'm not impossible, try raisning your bid, put another zero to the amount, I'll be back in a minute, OK?"

"Aha", Mustafa replied, "the girls from Stureplan, the girls from Stureplan…"

Mona, Sara and Eva at the bar

At the bar Diana served white wine to Mona, Sara

and the girl in white pants. Hanging out with Mona and Sara had been the key to Mustafa's success at mixing with the Stureplan in-crowd. Through Mona and Sara he had managed to get to know many of the hippest in Stockholm's nightlife. But he knew that sexually he didn't stand a chance with Mona and Sara, since they were both lesbians. But he treated them with wine anyway.

"Here you go, taste it", Diana said when she poured the wine into the girls' glasses.

"Hey, this is my favourite wine!" Mona said. "Did Mr Happy Hour pay for this?"

"Of course Mustafa paid for this", Diana said.

"He's so sweet", Sara said.

"So he's here tonight?" Mona said. "Where is he then?"

"Over there, with Oscar and Victoria", Diana said.

The girls toasted Mustafa and Mona headed for his table. She said hello to Oscar and Victoria. Mustafa was nowhere to be found.

"Where's Mustafa?" Mona asked.

"He went to the toilet, he'll be here soon", Oscar replied.

After a little while Mustafa showed up at the table.

"Hi Mustafa, thanks for the wine!" Mona said.

"Oh, no problem."

Mona took off her outer skirt that looked like a beach towel, rolled it up and threw it round Mustafa like a lasso, caught him and pulled him to the dance floor, towards Sara and the "white pants-girl".

"Hi, Mustafa, thanks for the wine! This is Eva, she's an old school buddy of mine from Dalarna, she's here visiting me in Stockholm", Sandra said.

Mustafa and Eva shook hands.

"Hi! You've got such amazing eyes!" Mustafa exclaimed spontaneously. "One could drown in them!"

Eva was flattered and at the same time embarrassed by Mustafa's compliments. From the bars at home in Dalarna she was not used to this kind of go-get-'em attitude.

"Oh, thank you", she said.

"Oh, I get so frustrated with you, Mustafa", Sara said. "What a strange tie are you wearing. Why don't you wear that tie I gave you last week with an Armani advertisement on it? Don't you like it or what?"

"Of course I like it! I'm wearing it, right now! Here, on the other side!"

Mustafa turned around, took of his jacket and showed the tie hanging down on his back. The girls laughed.

"But Mustafa, why aren't you wearing it like a regular tie, in the front?" Sara asked.

"I wear it on my back because I know you love to dance the Lambada!"

"You're insane, Mustafa!"

As if it had been planned, the DJ started playing the Lambada dance song. Sara pulled Mustafa to her using his Armani tie and grabbed hold of him from behind. Mustafa took hold of Eva's hips so that he had her beautiful pear-shaped bottom in front of him. Eva grabbed hold of Mona from behind. This dance train reached all destinations on the dance floor.

"Stockholm, je t'aime, Stockholm, je t'aime!" Mustafa cried out, over and over again. When the song was almost finished he received a call on his cell phone.

"Where are you?" Ali asked with an angry voice.

"What? What did you say? I can't hear you! Speak up!" Mustafa said.

"What is happening?" Ali yelled.

"Hold on, Ali."

Mustafa turned to the girls.

"Excuse me, ladies."

He left the dance floor for the less noisy bar, in order

to hear what Ali was saying.

"OK brother, where are you?"

"Where are you hiding?"!

"At Café Opera, studying the meaning of life according to Swedish social codes", Mustafa replied.

"And what is that supposed to mean?"

"If you had seen this curve that was in front of me on the dance floor tonight, then you'd understand me talking about the meaning of life."

"Stop playing the fool and go home! Mum is worried about you."

"OK, OK, Ali, I'll come tomorrow."

Mustafa shook his head as he hung up and ran back to the dance floor.

The dancing continued.

Two hours later, Mona, Sara and Eva were getting tired and considered going home.

"Thank you for a pleasant evening, Mustafa!" they said in chorus.

"Well thank you", replied Mustafa, "it's always a pleasure being out on the town with you people."

He turned to Eva.

"Can I see you tomorrow?" he asked.

Eva didn't answer him straight away. It looked like she was considering the whole thing.

"It's kind of difficult…"

"But I would love to take you to the new hot-spot here in Stockholm, 'Bux-Biou'. It's summer all year round there!"

"What's that?"

"A really exotic place, they have a big swimming pool and a big bar by the swimming pool."

"That would have been nice, Mustafa, but I'm getting married tomorrow, at four o'clock!"

"What?"

Mustafa was instantly devastated, it was as if someone had hit him in the head. Here he had been struggling and fighting all night, giving her free drinks and all. He changed his tactics.

"But can't you get away afterwards, around six, so I can show you 'Bux-Biou'?"

"I was just kidding, I'm not getting married, but I'm going back home to Dalarna tomorrow. I'm just here for the weekend."

"Oh, you freaked me out there for a while, my heart's not strong enough for such jokes! When are you going home tomorrow then?"

"Four o' clock."

"That's great, then we can go there tomorrow! If we meet at twelve I can take you to lunch at the floating pier at Norr Mälarstrand on Kungsholmen, or at 'Bux-Biou'. It's not far from the Central Station."

"I heard that it's going to rain tomorrow."

Mustafa had also seen the weather forecast, but he really wanted to take Eva to "Bux-Biou."

"We can meet outside the Central Station, then we'll see what the weather's like. If it's good we go to Norr Mälarstrand, if it's bad we go to 'Bux-Biou', OK?"

Mustafa looked straight into Eva's eyes while waiting for an answer.

"You know what?" she replied. "I have to think about it. I'll call you tomorrow when I know. Can I have your number?"

Mustafa had realized that this was a tough girl to play ball with. He gave her his number.

"Please Eva, come with me! I just want to get to know you a bit, maybe hold your hand, look into those beautiful eyes of yours, and then you take the train home, OK?"

"Is that it?" Eva asked.

"Yeah, that's it!" Mustafa replied.

"OK, I'll be standing outside the main entrance at the Central Station at twelve o'clock tomorrow!"

They hugged and the girls left, heading for Mona's and Eva's flat, where Eva was staying for the weekend. On their way to the underground, the girls talked about their night.

"Mustafa's a real gentleman" said Eva and smiled at her friends.

"Yeah, he's a good guy", said Mona, "and generous with the wine and the champagne as well."

"But why do you call him Mr Happy Hour?"

"Because he's a load of fun to hang out with", said Sara. "And so generous with the drinks without expecting anything in return. He just treats, without any hidden agenda."

"Ah, that's lovely! I really appreciate guys like Mustafa, guys who respects girls! This is the first time that a guy gave me wine and drinks and actually wanted to see me the day after. Every time I go out, guys come up to me and say 'shall we go to your place or to my place'?"

"But it isn't like that with Mustafa", said Mona. "And that's a relief!"

The truth was, Mustafa couldn't decide whether Eva turned him on or not. He could never decide about a girl until he had seen her in her underpants or in a bikini. He thought Eva was really cute, but he also wanted to take a look at her bottom. According to Mustafa, curvy girls rule the world. He could not be turned on by a girl unless he could see her bare bottom, not even if he swallowed a pound of Viagra. Because of this, he usually dated girls at "Bux-Biou", where there was a swimming pool and everyone had to be dressed for bathing.

To Eva, he appeared to be a gentleman because he didn't try to make her sleep with him on the first night, but in fact, he didn't even know if she would turn him on. Thus the date at "Bux-Biou."

Mustafa at Pedro's house

Mustafa couldn't sleep at home after all that had happened. He thought it was better sleep over at Pedro's place in Farsta instead. He took the underground from the Central Station and discovered Pedro on the train, half-drunk.

"So you're here?" Mustafa said.

"Yes", Pedro slurred. "What's your real name, Mustafa?"

"What do you mean?"

"I was at a party and a girl said she knew 'Mustafa Happy Hour'. Ali calls you 'Le Saharien imagineux'. At Stockholm University they call you 'Monsieur Nyponros'. How can people give you such beautiful names? I want names like that too!"

"I'll give you some advice."

"What advice is that?"

"If you bluff five times about the same thing, people will believe you the sixth time! There's proof for that", Mustafa said.

"Why five times?" Pedro asked.

"Ask ex-president Bush, he knows! But I think it's because Muslims pray five times a day."

"I don't understand. Why should I ask Bush?"

"Because Bush said, 'Saddam has weapons of mass destruction', 'Saddam has weapons of mass destruction', 'Saddam has weapons of mass destruction', 'Saddam has weapons of mass destruction', 'Saddam has weapons of mass destruction' five times. The sixth time the American people said 'Amen, Amen!' It's called the Bush effect!"

"Ah, I see", Pedro said, "bluffing five times…"

"Oui, Monsieur", Mustafa interrupted. "People will believe you the sixth time! It's a formula!"

Eva on Mustafa's bicycle

The next day it rained. Mustafa took his delivery bike and headed for Farsta shopping centre, where he bought a bouquet of flowers and a box of chocolates. Then he headed for central Stockholm. Just before twelve o'clock he parked his delivery bike outside Stockholm Central Station. At twelve o'clock, Eva arrived, dressed in tight jeans, high heeled shoes and a short leather jacket.

"Hey you!" Mustafa said.

"Hi", Eva said.

Mustafa gave her the flowers and the chocolate, a gesture that surprised Eva.

"Oh thank you, Mustafa, I didn't expect this!"

"Flowers and chocolate for a sweet girl", said Mustafa and smiled, "that's a must, an old rule you have to follow!"

"What a sweet thing to say", Eva said smiling.

"It looks as if the weather gods force us to go in Bux-Biou's direction, doesn't it?"

Eva giggled.

"Guess it does. Is it far?"

"It's some distance away, but we'll be there in no time, I mean, we have Mustafa's Volvo!"

Eva smiled a curious smile.

"OK then, what's that then? Where have you parked?"

"Follow me, I'll show you."

Mustafa took Eva's hand and walked over to the delivery bike.

"Nice, huh? I'll drive you!"

"Oh, how cute", said Eva. She studied the vehicle with an amused smile. "But I don't know if I dare to sit in the front!"

"Dear mademoiselle, you're safe with me behind the handlebars, I promise you that. Just sit down here and I'll give you Stockholm Sightseeing with Mustafa's Volvo!"

"OK, but you must promise me to drive safely."

"Of course, mademoiselle, you're dating a gentleman!"

Eva sat down on the delivery bike, and Mustafa headed for Slussen and "Bux-Biou." Eva began to laugh as soon as Mustafa had gained some speed with the bike.

At café-bar Bux-Biou

When they reached "Bux-Biou" they walked into the lobby, where they saw a big sign saying that all guests must change into bathing clothes before they can entered the place.

"If you want to buy something from the bar you have to wear beachwear" Mustafa informed Eva with a proud smile.

"Yeah, I can see that. But I don't have any beachwear with me!"

Mustafa opened his jacket and picked out a number of string bikinis and mini bikinis in various colours and sizes. He had bought them from a surplus stock.

"No need to worry! I brought mini bikinis that fit with your skin colour."

"Oh, I don't know if I dare to wear such a garment."

"Try them, Eva! You if anyone shouldn't be afraid of wearing these."

Eva thought about it for a moment.

"OK, if that's what it takes to try the drinks here, I might as well put on one of those bikinis!"

They decided to meet by the pool and went to the locker rooms to change clothes. A couple of minutes later Mustafa came out to the pool and bar area. He looked for Eva, but didn't spot her anywhere.

He hid behind one of the artificial trees, pretending to

study the tree, while keeping score of who was coming out of the locker rooms. Suddenly he could feel how someone grabbed hold of his left ear and pulled it.

"You should be ashamed of yourself! Standing here behind the tree and spying like some dirty old man."

"Lasse!" Mustafa shouted out. They laughed and shook hands.

"You should be ashamed of yourself, not only are you standing here sneak peeking, you steal my favourite girls right in front of me as well!" Lasse said.

"You mean that red haired, freckled, English girl from last week?"

"Yeah, Mustafa, you know well how much I like red haired freckled English football birds. You can't go on like this, stick to your Queen Latifah ladies, freckled ladies is my territory!"

"If there's any sort of consolation, it went straight to hell. I was at her place, she was going on about United for a few hours…"

"Mmm, that's my British girl."

"And then she just told me to leave. God damn bad luck."

"It's not about luck and bad luck. You just don't know how to handle these brit-girls. Take advice from an anglophile."

"What advice?"

"This is how you do it if you have a red head from Great Britain on the hook. You put on some Tom Jones music, preferably 'Delilah'. Then you give her some English ale, like Newcastle. Dimmed red lights is a must. Then you give her a little gift, a red nightgown with United's badge on it. Ask her to put it on. Then you open the window!"

"Open the window? Why should I do that?"

"Because you have to shout 'United'! Then I come and help you out with the rest!"

Mustafa made a grimace.

"United? I thought you were a hardcore Hammarby fan!"

"I am! But I have my English heart as well, and United have a little special chamber of their own in there."

Suddenly Eva appeared. She walked to the bar and finally Mustafa got the chance to see her bottom in a tight bikini. He certainly wasn't disappointed. She had a nice pear-shaped bottom that made Mustafa drool like a dog. His tongue immediately fell down dangling like a tie down his chin.

"OK, where is she?" Lasse asked.

"Over there in the yellow bikini."

"OK, no brit-bird this time, well done, Mustafa."

"Dalkulla! (Girl from Dalarna) Best type! Good to see you Lasse, but if you'll excuse me, I have a little project to work on."

Mustafa almost flew over to the bar where Eva stood waiting for him.

"Hi! Oh, you look so good in yellow! Fits you perfectly!"

"You think?" Eva asked in an anxious tone. "I feel so fat around my bottom."

Mustafa dragged out his favourite line, presented it with an Italian accent since he had his Italian moustaches.

"No, no ,no, all girls say that, 'my bottom's too fat', but it's wrong! You have a beautiful, buxom behind, very female. It's mmm... Marabou chocolate! (Marabou is one of the largest chocolate factories in Sweden.) It's so sexy, that if I had a camel tail I would be waving it by now!"

Eva laughed, then blushed, and held her hands over her mouth. A couple of other barflies stood nearby waiting to order, and they happened to hear Mustafa's line. They burst out in loud laughter.

"You really mean that?" said Eva. "Mustafa, I'm embarrased. Is it a Tunisian expression, that one?"

Mustafa made up something to reinforce his favourite expression.

"No, actually it's a Saudi expression. Usama bin Laden says that when he's happy with his wife."

Eva didn't know what to say, she just smiled. Never before had her behind had so many compliments from a guy. She changed the subject.

"It's really cool in here! Very well done, an authentic vibe! It's like being at the Mediterranean."

She looked around. Everywhere she saw buxom and sturdy women and men.

"What's was the name of this place, I didn't catch it?"

"'Bux-Biou'. It means 'Buxom is Beautiful'!"

"What a cool name!"

"Yeah! These cheerful girls like their curves and refuse to go around starved!"

Eva laughed. "It's wonderful to be here!"

"What do you want to drink, my darling?"

"Which drink is the best they have here?"

"Oh, there's so many of them. I prefer Mojito, you want one too?"

"Sounds good."

Mustafa turned to Tia who was wearing a yellow apron with black letters that said "It's cool to be buxom".

"Two Mojitos!"

"No Mustafa, no Mojitos for you today", said Tia.

"What? Have I gotten a liquor ban or what?"

"No. Take it easy, Mustafa, I didn't mean to scare you. No, I just wanted to make you try Bux-Biou's hottest drink at the moment: Besbussa!"

"What? You named a drink after Besbussa?"

"You bet we did! I couldn't let go of the name, it's just so beautiful!"

"Who's Besbussa?" asked Eva.

"Erm, thing is… we have a donkey named

Besbussa." Mustafa explained.

"Cool!"

The drinks came in.

"Here you go!" said Tia.

"Thanks, how much?" asked Mustafa.

"Nothing, these two are on the house!"

Mustafa and Eva studied the drinks.

"What's in it?" Mustafa asked.

"Do you think we just share that information for nothing?" asked Tia. "It's a secret, we have a potential goldmine here and we are not going to give 'Besbussa' away! That's why we have these sports-drink bottles to pour the content from."

"But it's not sports drink in these 'Besbussa' drinks, I suppose", said Eva.

"Depends on what sport you're into", said Tia.

Mustafa burst into loud laughter, while Eva blushed.

"Water wrestling is my favourite sport", said Mustafa and smiled. "I only compete in the mixed class! Anyway, Tia, your secret's safe with me, I'm only a happy and thirsty Saharian."

Tia smiled and took the next order.

"Cheers, and welcome to Stockholm", said Mustafa smiling, looking at Eva with love in his eyes.

"Thanks, and cheers!" said Eva.

They took a sip from their drinks.

"Mmm, how good!" they said in unison.

"Thanks Tia" Mustafa shouted.

Tia nodded and smiled. She was busy serving other guests at the bar. Mustafa looked at Eva.

"OK, so what are you doing in life, if I may ask?"

I'm an agriculturalist", Eva replied, "I take care of my family farm. I love it, I'm out-of-doors a lot, which is what I like, and I'm crazy about animals."

"Interesting, and your hobby must be chess, then."

Eva was surprised.

"As a matter of fact, yes! HOW on earth did you know that? Are you a psychic or what?"

"No, but whenever I ask you something you really take your time before you answer, so I thought that this girl must have chess in her blood!"

Eva couldn't help but laugh, it was the first time she had dated an immigrant and she was thinking she had never had so much fun on a date before.

"And how about you, what are you doing in life?"

Usually when Mustafa got this question from girls he dated, he lied and exaggerated to impress them, but he felt genuinely interested in Eva and didn't want to lie to her.

"I work as a cleaner and I have zone therapy as a hobby. But my big dream is to become a comedian!"

"Interesting! And your family's here in Sweden?"

"Sure, my mum, her name is Merjam, and two siblings, my sister Fatima and my brother Ali."

Suddenly Mustafa discovered Ali and Pedro a few tables behind Eva.

"By the way, he's very good at imitating birds, Ali."

"Really? That's funny!"

"Yep! In fact, my brother is behind you, watching us with his hawk-eyes."

Eva turned around, and saw two guys waving at her and Mustafa. It was Ali and Pedro

"How about a swim?" Mustafa asked.

"Sure!" Eva replied.

They said hello to Ali and Pedro, shook hands, did some small talking and then jumped into the pool. Mustafa swam under water and lifted Eva up, so that she flew up in the air, then swam away again. She couldn't find him. He hid from her, swimming under water, back and forth.

"How have you learned to swim so fast?" she asked him.

"I worked as a sailor once upon a time."

A slight exaggeration from Mustafa. He had never

been a sailor, but he had lived near the ocean, on the island of Djerba in Tunisia.

"Oh! Then you must have had a girl in every harbour."

Mustafa bragged. "Absolutely, some girls swam out to meet the boat before we even reached the shore! They just couldn't wait for me!"

Eva laughed heartily.

"Seriously, wouldn't you like to move here, to Stockholm, Stockholm je t'aime?"

"Why do you wonder?"

"Because I like you. You're easy to talk to, relaxed, you know. You laugh a lot and you seem a nice and happy person. I want you to be here!"

"Oh thanks, that's sweet, Mustafa. But it's like this: first of all, I have the farm. I inherited it from my parents, I can't just leave it. I love taking care of the farm and the animals, I love the nature around the farm and I love Dalarna. The whole region's so beautiful"

"Mmm, I see. It isn't easy to compete with a farm and everything that goes with it."

Eva laughed.

"Mustafa, please don't misunderstand me, I really like you. You don't think you could move to Dalarna instead?"

"Hmm, that would be tough. I'm a city man and I love Stockholm, it must be the most beautiful city in Europe. I fit in here, like a fish in water. I wonder if I would fit in the countryside."

Eva became silent, she didn't know what to say. Mustafa took the initiative.

"I fit in like a fish in this water as well! Now I'm going to teach you how to swim under water like a fish!"

They had a good time until Eva had to get ready. They changed, left 'Bux-Biou' and took the delivery bike back to the Central Station.

"I really had a good time, Mustafa."

"What do you think I had? Such an ugly fish like me, swimming with such a beautiful mermaid, never thought that'd happen!"

"Mustafa, you must promise to call me soon!"

"I promise."

Eva jumped onto the train to Falun (a small town in Dalarna). Mustafa waved her goodbye and he kept waving as the train left the platform and disappeared in the distance. Then he walked into the main station building. Downstairs he had hired a locker. He opened and emptied it. It was the entire collection of party clothes that he had been stashing away. He had finally decided to end his nomadic life and go home to Skärholmen. He tied the bags with the party clothes onto his delivery bike and started pedalling home.

The Qatar money

At home in Skärholmen Fatima gave Mustafa the evil eye when he appeared in the vestibule.

"Hello, everyone!" he shouted.

No answer.

He walked into his and Ali's room and started to stuff his wardrobe full with newly bought brand-name clothes. At last Fatima couldn't hold it in anymore.

"Where have you been?" she burst out.

"I've been here and there", Mustafa replied proudly, "among other places I was at Café Opera, and guess who I saw? Princess Madeleine! She was so nice and ordinary, she waited for her turn in the bar like everyone else."

"Really? So you've spoken to Princess Madeleine?" Fatima wondered.

"No, but we looked at each other, and I noticed how she studied my Italian moustaches, 'Made in Italy'."

He fixed his moustaches with a nonchalant know-all

attitude.

"Drop your bluff-talk and give that temperance society their money back."

"I don't have any money. Why is everybody blaming Mustafa? What money are you talking about?"

"Well, the society's money, stupid, what have you done with their 90 000?"

"They know I opened a fund in Qatar, put in 70 000 and invested 20 000 in advertising. That money will at least triple."

"You think I'm stupid, Mustafa?"

"No, you're not stupid, but the money's on its way!"

"Stop it, how did you afford all these fancy clothes all of a sudden?"

"What's that badge on your jacket?" Ali interrupted.

"Gucci", said Mustafa proudly.

"And what did it cost?"

"Eight thousand crowns."

"You're insane, Mustafa! A cleaner who pays eight thousand for a jacket!"

"Brother Ali, you have to integrate."

"What do you mean, integrate?"

"Integration means 'Mustafa's recipe'!"

"And what is Mustafa's recipe?"

"Yep! Now listen closely, brother, and write it down on your pyjamas so that you can read it the first thing in the morning!"

Ali sighed.

"Integration", said Mustafa, "is buying a new identity! If you don't stand out, you're nothing at Stureplan, they don't let you in anywhere, you HAVE to stand out in the crowd. That's what integration is. Buying the bouncer at Café Opera, at every sort of place. To walk past all the Swedes in the queue, to order first at the bar, to offer a Swede a free drink, to buy a new friend, THAT'S integration! Bribing the hairdressers, buy their friendship and their friends, that's integration."

"God damn it, Mustafa, you have missed the point totally, integration is not about that", Ali said.

"No, Ali, YOU have missed the point! This is the truth about integration. I'm Sweden's most integrated foreigner! I tell you this: the night before last night I was sitting in a bar and staring at two good-looking girls. I guess I was a little obvious and after a while one of them came up to me and said: 'Hey you, either stop staring at us or come over to us with another guy with designer clothes!"

"Chicks like that have no brains - how old were they?" Fatima asked.

"About ten plus sales tax!" Mustafa said.

Ali shook his head. "Your stories about designer clothes and integration are boring enough, but when you try to spice them up with dirty jokes, I just fall asleep!"

Fatima applauded Ali's point.

"Listen", Ali continued. "In truth is integration is about paying your way, working hard, paying taxes, being kind to your fellow employees and not telephoning to say you're ill just because you're lazy. And most important: going to sleep at ten at the latest, so that you're fresh and sharp in the morning. Swedish employers really appreciate that. And, like mum said, it means living within your means."

"No, brother Ali, integration is about going out and having a beer with the Swedes and getting to know them. The Scandinavians appreciate that."

"No chance in hell, I'm an abstainer!"

"No, no, Ali, you're a fanatic. And that's what's wrong with you, you don't want to integrate in Sweden."

Fatima broke in: "You're sick, Mustafa. Sick, sick, sick!"

"No, Fatima, I'm not sick. In fact, I feel perfect. I've been appointed Mr Happy Hour at Stureplan, and that's the finest award an immigrant can get here in Sweden. You should be proud of me!"

"So you're not ashamed, Mr Happy Hour, for taking money from people who have great confidence in you?"

"But I haven't taken anything; why is everyone always accusing me? The money's on its way!"

"I don't believe you!" Fatima shouted. "You think integration is about going out at Stureplan. If you do want to go out, there are loads of other places in Stockholm that you can go to, and you don't have to wear designer clothes to get in. You don't have to go to Stureplan to be happy and enjoy yourself. Stockholm's big, you've got Södermalm, Kungsholmen, Farsta, Täby, Bromma; there are pubs and restaurants everywhere."

"Really?" said Mustafa sarcastically.

"Let me finish, Mustafa", Fatima asked. "You know Bibbi was born in Östermalm (a smart district) and works as a cop, she knows a lot about what's going on over there. Drugs, suicide, bluff, theatre, flummery, curing your problems with pills, ruined marriages…there's so much tragedy!"

"But there's a lot of comedy as well!"

"Mustafa, you don't understand", said Ali. "Listen to this then: people have been calling our telephone, ringing the doorbell, shouting through the letterbox, threatening us, over and over. We can't live like this! It has to end!"

"Those abstaining fools should calm down. The money from Qatar is on its way!"

"Just like the eight thousand crowns that you owe me? Stop lying, Mustafa!"

Bente comes to visit

The doorbell rang. All three froze and became silent. Fatima walked up to the door and looked through the peephole. It was Bente, a girl who worked with Fatima at the Kindergarten and also happened to be Ali's new friend.

"It's Bente", Fatima whispered and opened the door.

"Hi Bente!"

"Hi Fatima!"

Ali came into the vestibule.

"Who are you? Have I seen you before? joked Bente. "You're cute though, I can give you a kiss!"

Ali smiled and walked up to Bente. She kissed him on the cheek.

Mustafa stepped out from the shadows.

"And you must be Mustafa?"

Mustafa smiled.

"You see? I keep getting more and more famous. Soon the whole country will recognise me!"

Fatima sighed. Mustafa and Bente shook hands.

"Shall we go now?" Ali asked.

"Yeah, might as well, the movie starts in half an hour", said Bente.

"OK, let's go."

Ali gave Mustafa an angry look and walked out. Soon Fatima left too, to meet Bibbi. Mustafa was left alone in the flat and went to take a shower.

When he had finished showering, Mustafa got dressed. He opened the bathroom cabinet and picked out an exclusive perfume from Lagerfeld. Just as he was about to give himself a perfume shower he heard another ring on the doorbell. He winced and tried to figure out what to do. The doorbell rang again. He pulled himself together and started walking towards the door with determined steps. He was not even aware that he still held the perfume bottle in his hand. He looked out the peephole and saw a cute girl. He unlocked and opened the door.

"Hi!" he said.

"Hi! Is Fatima around?" asked the girl.

"No."

"Mm, OK… it took you a long time to open the door."

"Sorry about that. I was in the bathroom to pour some water into my perfume bottle."

"Water in the perfume bottle, why?"

"Well, you know, the girls were really chasing me yesterday, it got a bit out of hand, I just have to dilute the perfume."

"Not bad. What's the name of the perfume?"

"It's called 'Heart of mine. Come closer'."

"Amazing! I also wear a 'come closer' perfume, but for women! Its smell is a little more discrete, you know about it?"

"No."

The girl wanted Mustafa out of the flat so she took a step back.

"There's too much perfume in your flat, come here, come closer!"

Mustafa took a step forward.

Peter was standing behind the entrance door. The girl whom who he had engaged to make the Babubas open the door was his cousin, a really cute girl that hopefully could get Mustafa out of the flat. And Peter's plan worked perfectly. When Mustafa stepped over the threshold Peter came out of the shadow and attacked Mustafa. And suddenly, from another direction, came Kristian who also joined in.

"Now you've got no chance of escaping!" Peter shouted in a mad voice.

"Idiot, thief, swindler, bluffer, you said you were an abstainer!" Kristian filled in.

"Of course I'm an abstainer", said Mustafa, "but I had a spring depression, hung out with the wrong crowd and started drinking again!"

Kristian pushed Mustafa into the flat, twisted his arm the way angry policemen do. He forced him into the living room and threw him onto the couch.

"I don't believe you", Peter hissed, "why haven't you answered the phone or returned our messages?"

"Ouch, ouch, stop it!" Mustafa screamed.

"I'm not going to stop until you give me the money back!" Peter said.

"You can hit me as much as you like, I don't have any money now. But tomorrow night at eight, you'll have at least 270 000 for that little organisation of yours."

Cable from Doha

"You're bluffing again, why would I get 270 000 tomorrow night?" Peter asked.

"Hold on, hold on, I'll show you." Kristian let Mustafa go. He rose from the couch and took out the telegram from his pocket.

"Read this telegram that just arrived."

Peter read the telegram aloud.

> Doha, the 28th of May 2003
> From: Imam Lotfi
>
> "The 15th of August 2003 at 4:00 pm, my colleague's son Nabil will arrive at Arlanda Airport, travelling with flight SAS FA 343 from Geneva, Switzerland. He will stay in Stockholm for one week, together with some friends."

"You see? I said you were going to get your money within a month, OK, so we get it a little late, it took us about two months instead", Mustafa said with a smile.

Peter threw the telegram in Mustafa's direction, angry as hell. Kristian walked over to Mustafa again, put him in a headlock, and lifted him towards the armchair, where Peter stood. He grabbed hold of Mustafa's ear and pushed him down onto the couch. Peter grabbed hold of Mustafa's other ear and pulled. They really were hurting Mustafa.

"So I see, some guys are coming to Stockholm from the Middle East to hook up with some Swedish blondes", Peter hissed. "So how does that change our situation? Where's our money?"

"Ouch, ouch, please, let go of me!" Mustafa cried, "try and understand me!"

He kept screaming.

"Ouch, ouch, ouch, I'll explain. Ten imams from several differents mosques have collected money for our project. Nabil is the son of the big Imam Jibril, he's on his way here with the money."

"It's all just a big scam", said Kristian and pulled Mustafa's ear even harder.

"Ouch, ouch, don't pull so hard!"

"Yes I will pull hard, because not only have you swindled us but also you look like the Spaniard that my girlfriend ran off with!"

"You don't have to pull so hard just because of that!"

"What I do to your ear is none of your business!"

"You think we will fall for this?", said Peter angrily. "So the mosques are willing to give us money? Yeah, right!"

"They do, they're generous! If you let go of my ears, I'll tell you the truth about the mosques in Qatar."

Peter and Kristian let go of Mustafa, who shook his head a few times, adjusted his clothes and started serving his famous "Beef Wellington".

Beef Wellington à la David Letterman spiced with the Emir of Qatar and his prime minister

"You know where the TV company al-Jazeera comes from?"

"No idea", said Peter, "a wild guess is it's from somewhere in the Middle East."

"Ouch, very close! It's actually from Qatar. In 1996 two very important things happened in Qatar. First: a new TV company was founded, with a TV channel that was meant to be controversial, a TV channel that lets everyone speak their mind. That TV channel was al-Jazeera. The other big thing was the realisation of an idea with a rather famous source: none other than… David Letterman!"

"And what was the idea?" Peter asked.

"The 'Letterman concept' was based on research showing that people who are generous are happier, live longer, and have better sex lives."

"OK", said Peter, "that part about al-Jazeera, I'll have that, but the 'Letterman concept'?"

"Listen, just listen. The authorities in Qatar stole the 'Letterman concept' just like that, all of it, and you know why? Because it fitted Islam like a hand in a glove!"

"Really?"

"Yeah. You'll understand if you don't interrupt all the time. An important pillar in Islam is the 'zakat', almsgiving. The zakat means that people should give a part of what they earn to the needy. If you do that, you end up in paradise. So, the authorities in Qatar fixed two things in one, with the 'Letterman concept' they could both extend people's lives, better their sex lives and also prepare a place for them in paradise!"

"Really?"

"Yeah Peter, really! So, the Qatar authorities legislated the birth-control pill. A law that's unique in the whole world."

"And what's so unique about that law then? They have to put the pills in their nostrils or what?"

"Very funny, Peter! No, the Qatar authorities wanted every family to react if any female family members showed the slightest tendency towards greediness. As soon as there was any sign of greediness, the woman had to take birth control pills!"

"And why?"

"Because the Qatar authorities want to prevent greedy and egoistic women from reproducing. So you see my friend, your money's coming, for sure!"

"How can I be sure of that?"

"Because it's statistically proved! Peter, let me ask you one thing. How many inhabitants does Qatar have?"

"Three million, four perhaps?"

"Good answer, Peter, if it had been ten years ago. Today it's only 850 000. Work it out Peter. It's gone down, hasn't it?"

"That sounds weird, how can the population go down that much in ten years? There hasn't been any war there, has there?"

"No, it's just the 'David Letterman concept, live longer and have a better sex life'! What more can you ask for?"

"I really don't get it."

"The birth control law is very effective, only generous women are allowed to have babies!"

"Incredible!"

"I'll tell you", Mustafa said, "that the emir of Qatar, Hamad bin Khalifa Al Thani, and his Prime Minister, Hamad bin Jassim bin Jaber Al Thani, were so happy over this concept that they have given a gift of one million dollars to the city of New York because they have such a fine guy as Letterman who can come up with positive ideas like that."

"I didn't know that."

"Call the city of New York if you don't believe me. It's a fact that wherever there is a flooding or an earthquake the emir of Qatar and his Prime Minister is there donating money."

"Really?"

"Sure. And not only that, they love to solve problems and to mediate – between Lebanese, between Palestinians, between northern Sudan and Darfur. It's their greatest hobby. And it's thanks to Letterman."

The home phone rang. Peter took the receiver and held it against Mustafa's ear.

"Hi, I'm calling from the local post office", said a female voice. "I'm looking for a Mustafa Babuba."

"That is I."

"You've got five boxes with CDs at our stores", the female voice said.

"What kind of CDs, where do they come from?"

"It looks like it's the Koran on CD, it's from Doha, Qatar."

Peter and Kristian tried hard to hear what the voice on the phone was saying.

"Is this going to cost me anything?"

The telephone voice chuckled.

"Yes, it will cost you 1652 crowns."

"I can't pay that much, I can give you half the price for them, not more."

"I'm afraid you can't bargain with the Swedish Postal Service.

"Of course you can! When I buy a CD in the store or go to the movies, I never pay more than half the price."

"Is that so? Never heard of that before. How do you do that?"

"I'm deaf on one ear!"

The telephone voice laughed out loud.

"OK", Mustafa continued, "I'll come and pick them up some day this week. Thanks and goodbye."

Peter hung up and turned to Mustafa, who looked at him with a triumphant smile on his face.

"There you go! As I said, the birth control law in Qatar is highly effective, I haven't even ordered CDs, and now I get five boxes of them! And money is on its way…"

"But what do we need CDs for?"

"We'll give them to the mosque of course! Do you realise how much money we'll get this time?"

The atmosphere in the room lightened up a bit.

Peter picked up the telegram from the living room table and read it again, silently this time.

"So you mean we're getting our money back tomorrow night?"

"Yep. 270 000, just like I said. Maybe even more.".

Peter shook his head.

"Mustafa, can I trust you?"

Mustafa smiled and looked squarely into Peter's eyes.

"Of course you can, Peter!"

Peter became quiet and he inspected Mustafa, from his head down to his feet, and up again.

"OK, this is your last chance. Have your cell phone on, I'll be calling you tomorrow. And don't even think about running away. If you do, I promise you it won't be pretty next time."

"I'll be waiting by the phone as if I were waiting for my loved one!"

"You'd better. See you."

Peter and Kristian left.

Merjam comes home

A little bit later, Mustafa walked down to the flower shop in Skärholmen shopping centre and bought flowers for his mum. Then he walked back home again. After a while, Merjam came home.

"Hi, mum."

"Hi."

"Look, mum, I'm sorry about the mess I stirred up."

"I'm not going to forgive you until you tell me the

truth about the temperance society and the Qatar fund, the truth and not some 'Beef Wellington' that you've taken out of thin air."

Mustafa took out the telegram from his pocket and showed it to Merjam.

"You see, mum, Imam Jibril's son is on his way here with the money. I talked to several people from different mosques down in Qatar. They've collected money."

"But how and why would they do that, just send some money to this temperance society, just like that?"

"Mum, the truth is a religious concept. You know, Allah builds a house in heaven for those who build a mosque here on earth."

Merjam nodded. She was coming to grips with how things fit together by now.

"Did you say you were going to build a mosque?"

"No, but renovate one", Mustafa replied and went on: "I told them among other things that we have a temperance society here in Skärholmen, that we are against alcohol, and that we needed financial support in order to help people with drinking problems. It didn't take long before they replied. The people of the mosques thought that this was a brilliant initiative, and they told me that they had already started to collect cash."

Merjam shook her head.

"What I just can't seem to understand is how you became friends with the people of the temperance society in the first place."

"What's wrong with being friends with abstainers? Ali is an abstainer."

Merjam shook her head.

"Are you collecting money for them for friendship?"

"Good question, mum! You remember when I was a kid and worked in the ceramics workshop in Tunisia. Friends of the workshop's owner came by all the time, chit chatting and having a cup of tea, and I remember this old man citing Charles de Gaulle. 'There is no friendship without self-interest'. That quote had stuck in my head, so I set up this goal, that the temperance society would get triple the amount they put in within a month, 90 000 times three, 270 000. Then I could pay my debt to Fatima and invest the rest in my comedy show!"

"I see... So how much you think they will send?"

"At least a million, the Arabs of the Persian Gulf are very generous!"

"So you're going to use these Arabs' generosity to launch your comedy show, huh?"

"No mum, it's just a loan, I'm not going to use anybody. As soon as I get my comedy show rolling, I'll give my first paycheck to poor people, or give it to 'Help Africa'."

"Who wrote your letters to Qatar; was it Ali?"

"No, it was an Iraqi mate who lives here in Sweden."

Mustafa had sent ten letters to ten mosques in Qatar. The letters contained a photo of the temperance society in Skärholmen, taken by Mustafa, and a message written by Mustafa's Iraqi friend Hamadi: "You who want to build yourself a house in Paradise, help us restore our house here on earth".

"Wouldn't it have been better", Merjam said, "to have gone to school and learned how to read and write instead of ripping kind people off?"

"Mum, I have told you a million times, I hated school."

Merjam shook her head, not just once but over and over again.

"How come you can afford to buy such fancy clothes, when you have sent all the money to Qatar?"

"Wait", said Mustafa and ran off to his room. He got his piggy bank and came back.

"Look here, mum, only two crowns left! I had sixty in there and I gave it to Hamadi, he's a wicked gambler, we won 40 000 on a horse race! We shared it fifty-fifty, I went shopping for 20 000. He's my lucky star, that Iraqi!"

Merjam sighed heavily.

"I'm sick and tired of you, and all these naïve people from oil countries tossing their money over hoaxers like you. I can't stand this anymore."

Merjam went to the stable and took Besbussa for a walk. Mustafa waited a while, then he also left. He took the underground into central Stockholm, to Kungsträdgården and Café Opera. He really hoped Diana was working today.

Back to Café Opera

There was no life at Café Opera, it was early and people weren't yet in the party mood . Mustafa sat down at the bar, made eye contact with one of the waitresses.

"Can I have a cup of coffee, please?"

"Here you are."

"When is Diana coming in?" he asked.

"Any time now", said the waitress, "her shift starts in fifteen minutes."

Mustafa stayed at the bar, and soon enough, Diana was on her way in.

"Hi, Diana!"

"Oh man, now you're even here before I am! Why don't you put up a tent next to the bar?"

Mustafa smiled, but the smile faded quickly. He was there for a reason

"Hey, Diana, I need your help."

"Anytime, baby. What can I help you with?"

"Do you know anyone who leases limousines?"

"OK, Mustafa, what have you got going this time? Arranging a concert with Michael Jackson? Is this the last little puzzle piece in the arrangement?"

"Even better! Mr Hollywood is coming!"

"Who's Mr Hollywood?"

"Mr Hollywood is a person who has money to invest in films and TV shows. You know Diana, these days you don't need to go to Hollywood to make movies. Hollywood is everywhere, as long as you have the money. You see, someone's going to visit me tomorrow, kind of a Mr Hollywood actually, from Qatar. He and his friends are going to hit the bars here in Stockholm. I want to give them a royal welcome."

"Hmm, interesting. And you have some movie project in the pipeline?"

"No, but a TV show! I have a script ready, it's recorded on an mp3, every line. I would love to do a trial run. If only I could talk SVT (Swedish national television) into it!"

"That's sounds great, Mustafa! Do you have a name for the show?"

"Stockholm, je t'aime!"

"What's it about?"

"That's classified material, but I can reveal one thing: Café Opera is VERY present in the show!"

"Oh, that's so exciting! Can I get a part?"

"Absolutely, I've already thought about that, I see a star in you! And if you can help me with the limo thing your chances will increase dramatically!"

"Well in that case I'll fix the limo immediately!"

"Good. One more question. You work here among all these celebrities and media people. Do you know any photographer, any editor?"

"Oh, there's plenty of those here! They have their union meetings here in the bar!"

"Awesome! Thanks Diana, you're an angel! This is very important information you're giving me."

"You know, when you work here, you can't avoid picking up a lot of useful information. So when does this Mr Hollywood and his posse land on Swedish soil?"

"At 3:45 PM, so if the limo is parked and ready at Arlanda (Stockholm's international airport) by four o'clock it would be good."

"OK!"

Diana was just about to dial a telephone number when Mustafa stopped her.

"Hey Diana, there's one more thing. Can you be with them in the limo, from Arlanda and in to the city centre? Welcome the boys? You know, they've never been here before, I want to give them a warm welcoming."

"So I have to go with a limo to Arlanda and back here?"

"That's correct. If you bring a few friends, it's even better."

"That sounds pretty good, actually, sipping champagne in the backseat like some Jay-Z."

Diana burst into laughter.

"So you're in?" Mustafa wondered.

"I'm in, but I have to be here at seven at the latest."

"Absolutely, no problem. Damn it, I'm so glad, thanks Diana, so great of you to do this!"

Mustafa leaned over across the bar and kissed Diana's hand. He said goodbye and left, walked straight out into the sunlight. Kungsträdgården was blossoming and summer had arrived. Mustafa looked up to the clear blue sky and thought to himself…

"Tomorrow night a star will light up that sky, and that's me. Finally a new life is on the way. Oh, soon I'll just walk into the office at 'Keep Stockholm Clean', throw the wastepaper basket in the boss's face and tell him 'I'll send you a postcard from Cannes'."

Nabil and his friends arrive in Sweden

The next day, SAS flight FA 343 from Geneva with destination Stockholm left the ground. Among the passengers in the plane: Nabil, son of the Imam Jibril, and Nabil's three friends from Japan, Thailand and Indonesia. They were about to travel together in Scandinavia for a month. Stockholm was the first stop, after that they were going to Norway, Finland, Denmark and Iceland. The captain went through his usual speech in English with a Swedish accent before landing.

"This is captain Gustafsson speaking. In about ten minutes we will be landing in Stockholm. The time is 3:35 PM local time. It's about 27 degrees Celsius, it's Friday and it's a very special night here in Sweden, Stockholm is vibrating."

The boys looked through the plane window and cheered.
"Wow, there's Stockholm, look, look!"

Mustafa, Diana and three of Diana's cutest girl friends sat in a limousine on its way to Arlanda International to welcome the boys.

In the arrival hall, Mustafa, Diana and her friends were waiting eagerly. Mustafa held up a sign with Nabil's name on it.

People started streaming into the arrival hall. Suddenly a tall and chubby boy, who probably weighed about 100 kilos, appeared in the hall with three young Asian-looking boys right behind him. Mustafa realised it must be Nabil and his entourage. He greeted the boys and escorted them to the limo. An elegantly dressed chauffeur helped the boys with their bags.

The plan was that the three Asian friends were going stay at Radisson Hotel right by the Central Station, while Nabil was going stay with Mustafa and the Babuba family in Skärholmen. The limo stopped at Vasagatan and dropped the company off. When they came out and met the sweet summer weather it all clicked for the three Asian boys: they fell in love with Stockholm! A steady stream of cute girls in their summer clothes passed one by one, while boys sang: "Stockholm Je t'aime, Je t'aime, Je t'aime!"

Nabil and Mustafa watched them, laughing. Nabil turned to Mustafa.

"Man, the girls you have here! Everywhere! Never seen anything like it", he said.

"I know, Stockholm is both exotic and erotic", Mustafa said.

"Is it like this in all the Scandinavian countries? We're going on to Finland, Norway, Denmark and Iceland."

"Absolutely!"

Nabil looked around.

"Damn, these chicks! And those mini-mini-skirts!"

"Oh yes, the summers here in Sweden will kill you slowly, the doctors actually recommend men with heart problems to stay indoors!"

"How do you manage?"

"It's pure hell, next summer I'm going to Qatar to escape this suffering."

The crew walked across the street over to Radisson hotel, where Nabil's three amigos were to stay during their visit in Stockholm. Mustafa looked at Diana. He saw that she was in a hurry and looked at her watch.

"Thanks for all your help Diana, you're free to go now."

"Thank YOU! It was nothing, just fun, I felt like Beyoncé in there. But now it's back to reality, work calls."

Mustafa raised his voice.

"Listen everyone. I've got some plans for tonight. How about champagne at Café Opera tonight? Ten o'clock, how does that sound?"

Everyone cheered, Nabil's three friends louder than the others.

Mustafa gave Diana a wink.

"Keep the champagne chilled, darling."

They said goodbye. Mustafa and Nabil took a cab to Skärholmen. Already they felt like friends and chatted without any awkward silences.

"Nice boys you brought with you", said Mustafa, "how do you know them?"

"You know, the world is small these days. I know people from all over the world, I meet them on the Internet."

"Interesting."

"They're really into Arabic culture, and I'm into their culture. I talked to them on a net community for months, and a while ago we decided to go on a trip together."

"So you met in Doha first or?"

"No, I have only just met them, in Geneva, we hung out there a couple of days, to get to know each other, live so to speak."

"Hmm, interesting."

Nabil in Skärholmen

When thet arrived, Mustafa introduced his family to Nabil.

"This is my mum Merjam, my brother Ali and my sister Fatima", he said.

"Welcome", Merjam said and did her cry of joy, "RRRA, RRRA, RRRA..."

"Thanks", said Nabil.

"Where are your friends?" Merjam asked.

"They're staying at a hotel", Nabil said.

"That's a shame, they're going to miss a tasty experience, we've cooked some Tunisian food."

"Unfortunately I'm going to miss that too", Ali interrupted. "I'm going home to my beautiful girlfriend. But it was nice meeting you, Nabil."

"You two will see each other tomorrow, right?" Merjam said.

"Sure", said Nabil.

Ali put on his shoes and left. Merjam and Fatima had laid the table in the living room.

Mustafa and Nabil sat down at the table and started eating. Merjam was in the kitchen and Fatima served the food, which Nabil shamelessly stuffed himself full with.

"Mmm, tastes good!" he managed to get out of his mouth before stuffing in more. "Magnifico! Prima! Excellent! This food melts in your mouth. I've got a great appetite."

Mustafa tried to make friends with Nabil. He did his best to eat at the same furious pase as his visitor. It became a veritable contest.

"Me too!" he said.

"You can't speak with your mouth full of food, Mustafa", said Fatima.

"Of course I can, it's just a matter of practice!"

Fatima sighed.

"You've really developed an exceptional appetite lately," she remarked.

"Ssch", hissed Mustafa. He didn't want anything to disturb his growing friendship with Nabil.

"Is there any more meat?" Nabil asked with his mouth stuffed with food.

"I'll get some more", said Fatima.

She turned to Mustafa who was dipping pieces of bread in the stew with his right hand while eating sauce with his left, using the knife.

"Mustafa, don't put the knife in your mouth", Fatima urged him.

"I have to." He tried to eat some sauce with the fork. "Look, dear sister, the fork leaks!"

Fatima shook her head and walked into the kitchen where Merjam was cooking.

"Mum, this Nabil guy eats like a hippo, and now Mustafa tries to do the same. Is there any more meat?"

"No, we're out of meat now."

Fatima tried to get Mustafa into the kitchen.

"Mustafa, come quickly", she said. Then she walked out to the living room and took his plate away from the table.

Mum, stressed and angry, pulled Mustafa's chin when he got inside the kitchen.

"You have to go shopping, we need meat and vegetables immediately. This guy's a dinosaur! Hasn't he had any food for weeks?"

"Don't know, mum", Mustafa replied. "I'm as surprised as you are."

Fatima came in to the kitchen with Mustafa's plate and moved the meat he had left on the plate to another one.

"Hey, what are you doing?" Mustafa exclaimed. "I'm not finished!"

Merjam pulled her son's ear.

"Silent! You should be ashamed, bringing a food swallowing machine to our house when you know we're short of cash. And what's more, you try to be like him!"

Fatima walked out to living room to serve Nabil the rest of the meat.

"Here you go, monsieur Nabil!"

"Thanks. The best thing in life is good food", Nabil said. "Excuse me, is there any more bread?"

"Sure!"

Fatima picked up bread in the kitchen and came back.

"Thanks, is there any more of this dish? By the way, what is it called?"

"Tajin, and I'm afraid we've got no more left."

Fatima picked up the plate and held it in her hand. There was a tiny piece of tomato sauce left on it. Nabil took a piece of bread and wiped the tomato sauce off the plate. Fatima couldn't believe her eyes.

"Wait, wait", said Nabil diplomatically, "it's a sin to

throw food away, my teacher in Qatar said the Swedish people are famous for their awareness when it comes to the environment. I heard that the Swedes are really mad at all the countries that pollute the air with all these chemicals."

"Oh, really?"

"Yes, washing-up detergent. It's a chemical product", Nabil replied with his mouth stuffed

He took a piece of bread and wiped off a last microscopic piece of tomato sauce that was left on the plate.

"Look at the plate you're holding in your hand, now you don't need any washing-up detergent, just a little water!" Nabil said. "We must save nature, as Al Gore says."

"You really need water?" said Fatima with an ironic tone, "I mean, this is clean as a mirror, I can do my make-up in front of this one!"

Fatima kept walking between the kitchen and the living room, serving Nabil the food that was left. After a while, he finally seemed to give up.

"Oh, thank you so much, this was what I call a proper dinner!"

"Here you go, a little tea over on the sofa, perhaps?"

"Thanks, thanks a lot."

Mustafa and Merjam went to the supermarket. They were almost out of food in the household again, after Nabil's little food show.

Fatima sat down on the sofa next to Nabil, who was quiet as a wall. He seemed to be completely numb after the marathon dinner. Fatima tried to flirt with him to find out how much money he brought in his big travelling bags.

"I'm cold", she said in a feminine voice.

"Really?" said Nabil.

"Yeah, I'm so cold."

Nabil got up, got his barnous (a warm coat) and put it over Fatima.

"There you go", he said.

Suddenly Fatima threw the coat on the floor. Nabil stared at her.

"If you don't stop staring at me like that I'll call my mum", she said.

"OK, and where's your mum?"

"She went shopping with Mustafa?"

"Shopping?"

Fatima looked at her watch.

"They're back in twenty minutes", she said.

"But Fatima, I haven't done anything to you."

"True, but if you planned to do something, you'd better speed up!"

Nabil leered shyly at Fatima.

Mustafa and Merjam came home. Merjam put the fruits that she had bought in a bowl on the table.

"Here you are!"

"Thanks!" Nabil said.

"So, Nabil, how does it feel to be here in Stockholm?" Mustafa asked.

"Perfect!"

Mustafa didn't have the patience to wait and try and be nice, he wanted to know how much money Nabil had brought.

"Hey, I want to know, how much money have the mosques in Qatar sent for our temperance society?"

"What? What temperance society?" Nabil replied. "Don't know what you're talking about. My father told me to put the money into his account in Switzerland, that's all I know."

RRRA, RRRA, RRRA!" Merjam shouted viciously. "This is the second mishap in three days for the Babuba family! So, Nabil, you've taken donated money from the mosques and put it into your father's Swiss account, is that right?"

"I didn't know who's money it was, I just deposited it."

Mustafa fell backwards and when he was on his back on the floor he started kicking about like a little child having a tantrum.

"My life is over, can this be true?"

"Well", said Nabil, "I can tell you, my father's so tight he didn't lend me money to sleep in hotels or eat in restaurants. He told me before I left that the week in Sweden would be my savings week. So he blocked my credit card in Sweden, it works in the other Scandinavian countries but not here."

"My life's over, my life's over", Mustafa repeated, still lying on his back on the floor.

"Have you spoken to my father on the phone?" Nabil wondered.

"No, but I spoke to Imam Lotfi. He said the money was on its way."

"Imam Lotfi hasn't given me one single dollar to give to you."

"Don't be stupid, Nabil. Imam Lotfi gave the money to your father."

Mustafa's cell phone rang. It was Peter.

"Hi there, old friend! Are you ready with the money?"

"My stomach hurts, I'm in the toilet", Mustafa lied, "I'll call you back"

"But…"

Mustafa ended the conversation and continued to twist and turn around in agony, lying on the floor. Another call came, now it was Diana.

"Hi, Mustafa, my boss told me that you have to come up with four thousand for the limo. He wants to speak with you."

"Excuse me, Diana, my stomach's on fire or something, hurts like hell, it must be the dates I ate for lunch, I'll call you back, OK?"

He turned the phone off again. Soon the phone was ringing again, over and over.

"How can your dad do this to me? How much have you stuffed into his account?"

"Can't tell you."

"But what kind of behaviour is that, put money into some freaking Swiss account and arrive here without a penny!"

"I promise you, Mustafa, I don't know anything about this story."

"It's just wrong to do that. Wrong, wrong, wrong!"

Merjam now realised where this was going, and she didn't like it one bit. She had no desire to cook six dinners for this guy over the whole week and immediately decided to alter her course. She walked into the kitchen and prepared a very special drink, consisting of pineapple juice and barbitone. The she came back into the living room with the glass of juice and a Tunisian pastry. On the couch she saw a yawning Nabil.

"Here you go, Monsieur."

"Thank you, thank you, I really appreciate Tunisian generosity."

"Are you sure your dad wasn't supposed to give Mustafa any money? What's your dad's name, by the way, and where does he live?"

"His name is Jibril ben Tahar, and our address is Rose street 35, Doha."

Nabil emptied the glass in one go. He went on talking with Merjam for about 45 minutes and then fell into a deep sleep on the couch. Merjam sat down and wrote a telegram: "Your son is ill, it's a matter of life and death, you must come to Stockholm immediately, Merjam Babuba." She said to Mustafa: "Go to the telegram bureau and send this to Nabil's dad. He must come here, it's really important!"

Mustafa was still paralysed by Nabil's wet blanket. He was wondering how to explain this to the abstainers and as yet had no idea what to do.

"Sorry, mum", he said.

Merjam was angry and she didn't answer him. Instead she walked to her room and launched into a telephone conference with Elisabeth and Bibbi. She told them the whole story.

Nabils second day in Stockholm

The next day Nabil woke up from his long sleep at around noon. He was dazed and tired. Fatima was the first to discover him awake, lying in Ali's bed with shaggy hair and tired eyes.

"Good morning, Nabil. How are you?" she asked.

"A little tired", was the short reply from Nabil.

Fatima made up a story.

"You just passed out yesterday, we were so worried about you, we called for a doctor, but he said you were OK."

"I don't remember a thing! Just the food being fantastic, so good I must have fallen asleep."

Fatima's heart took a little jump, he didn't seem to remember how he fell asleep yesterday! She managed to calm down.

"I was thinking about taking Besbussa out for a walk to Skärholmens gård. It's really nice down there, right by the water. And there's a nice little café there as well, I'll buy you breakfast, what do you say?"

"Yeah, that sounds perfect! But tell me, Fatima, where's your mum? I would like to thank her for the delicious food yesterday!"

"Mum and Ali are out shopping, but she told me she was going to make you a fine dinner later today."

Nabil rubbed his hands. He looked hungry already.
"Mmm, I can already taste it!"
"Get dressed so we can go. You want breakfast, don't you?"
Nabil threw on his clothes, Fatima got Besbussa ready and they went out in the summer heat.

A quarter of an hour later, Merjam and Ali came home. Mustafa had told Merjam that Nabil's father, Imam Jibril, was coming to Stockholm and was scheduled to land at Arlanda at seven in the evening. Merjam started making dinner. Ali, who had a degree as a pastry chef, started with the dessert, a wonderful Schwarzwald cake for Nabil, spiced with a crumbled sleeping pill, a pill with enough power to put the young boy to sleep again for a few hours.

At four o'clock Fatima and Nabil came back to the flat, and Nabil was very hungry. Fatima knew that the little café would be closed today, and deliberately took Nabil for a long walk along the shore of Lake Mälaren just to feed his hunger.

Nabil stuck his head inside the kitchen door and he could immediately feel the wonderful smell of food teasing his nostrils.
"Hi, Merjam. Hi, Ali!"
"Hi, Nabil!" The cook and the pastry chef said in unison.
"Mmm, it smells delicious in here! I have to take the opportunity to say thank you for the lovely dinner yesterday, fantastic!"
"Thank you, Nabil, glad to hear you liked it. But I have to say I was a little worried about you yesterday, you ate so much that you passed out", Merjam said.
Nabil laughed nervously.
"In fact I was so worried that I contacted your father.

We sent a telegram to Qatar, telling him that you passed out, and now he's coming to Stockholm!"

"Oh my, is it true?"

"Yes, he'll be at Arlanda at seven o'clock tonight. Mustafa is meeting him. So I thought we might eat at nine, all of us."

Nabil froze. He didn't want to bother Merjam with his incredible hunger, but the hunger was now stronger than his will to act politely. He couldn't help himself but tell her...

"Oh, that is late!"

"Too late for you to eat at nine?"

"No, I can wait, sure."

"Are you sure, Nabil? Because I can fix an early dinner for you and Fatima, I mean you've been out running today and all."

"No that's... or... I guess..."

"I can see that you are hungry, Nabil. But you know, I'm preparing for a big dinner tonight, so if you want to have some now, it's OK, we have enough for tonight. And you, Fatima, do you want some as well?"

"No thank you, mum, I'll eat tonight. I'll be in my room working with the web page."

"OK. Nabil, please sit down at the dinner table, I'll be out with some food any second."

After a short while, Merjam came out to the living room with a big portion of food, but Nabil was just happy to see the mountain of food on the plate.

He stuffed the food into his mouth with something that was close to obsession. The plate was clean in such a short time that if the publishers from Guinness Book of Records had been present, they would have put him in the book without hesitation.

"Did you enjoy the food, Nabil?" Merjam asked.

"Mmmm", was all Nabil came up with.

"Are you full?"

"Mmmmm, or, I mean, I can go for a little bit more."

Merjam went to the kitchen and came back with yet another mega load of food.

Incredibly enough, Nabil swallowed it even faster than the first portion.

Afterwards he looked like a drunk realising that the bar is closed and it's time to go home. Merjam came out to the living room again.

"Was it good?"

Nabil nodded.

"Good, and guess what? We've saved the best for last!"

Nabil lit up again.

Ali came out with the dessert, Ali's little Schwarzwald cake spiced up with just the right dose of crumbled sleeping pill. It looked seductively delicious.

"Fantastic!" shouted the food monster.

"Yeah, isn't it?" Merjam said. "Feel free to take some!"

Merjam handed over the cake.

"Here you are! Feel at home!"

He grabbed the spoon and lifted several chunks.

"Mmm... magic! This is the best so far! Merjam, you've done it again!"

"Actually", Merjam said, "it's Ali who made this, he's a trained pastry chef, he makes the best cakes in the world!"

"Fantastic, Ali! Best cake I've ever eaten! You have to taste your own masterpiece!"

"Thanks a lot, Nabil, but fact is, I can't even if I wanted to. I'm lactose intolerant", Ali bluffed. "I would get all red in the face if I ate that cake. Maybe that's why I can bake such good cakes!"

"Lactose intolerant? Poor thing! How about you then, Merjam?"

Merjam had got her alibi ready.

"Oh, I don't eat cake anymore. Order from my doctor, have to think about my health you know."

Merjam clapped her big, round stomach. Nabil didn't seem to doubt her.

"Well, well, more left for me then", he chuckled merrily and continued to eat the cake at Olympic sprinter speed. He swallowed what was left of the cake and patted his big stomach. Twenty minutes later he passed out again, this time in Ali's bed.

Imam Jibril in Stockholm

Nabil's father Jibril, a short man in his sixties, was Imam at a mosque in Qatar. At seven o'clock he arriverd at Arlanda where Mustafa was waiting for him in the arrival hall holding up a sign with his name on it. The two took a cab to the Babubas in Skärholmen.

"RRRA, RRRA…" Merjam did her sound.

"Welcome, welcome, my name is Merjam."

"Imam Jibril."

"Sorry for bothering you, but your son is fine. He's sleeping in here."

"What happened then?"

"Nabil came here yesterday. We offered him dinner, and he ate as if he had never eaten before. Suddenly he passed out, just lost consciousness. We were worried, in state of shock. We called the doctor and sent you a telegram. The doctor didn't arrive until after two hours, he examined him but told us everything was fine. Nabil apparently had too much to eat, that's all", Merjam lied.

"Hmmm, that's not good."

"Mmm, no, but today he woke up at twelve. Then he was fine", Merjam said.

"No, not really", Fatima said. "He was a little tired when we were out taking a walk. Maybe it's the change of environment?"

"Yes, you're wise. You can get tired from travelling", Jibril said.

"Mmm, yeah", Merjam said, "you could be right, but this afternoon we had dinner, and he just ate and ate and ate, then he went to bed."

"We'd better wake him up", Jabril said.

They walked into Ali's and Mustafa's bed room where Nabil was lying, sleeping soundly.

"Nabil! Nabil! Wake up! Your father's here!" Merjam said.

Nabil opened his eyes slowly, wrinkled his forehead and squinted, unused to the light.

"Dad?" he said in a surprised tone.

"Yes, Nabil. It is no dream, I am here. What happened to you?"

Nabil waited a long time before he answered, he didn't seem to be completely awake yet.

"What happened, Nabil?"

"I just eat and sleep" he said slowly, "dad, the food is so good here, I eat so much good food, and then I get tired and fall asleep."

"They told me you slept fifteen hours yesterday. Are you sure everything is all right?"

"Yes, I promise you, I'm OK, dad! But I'm tired, so tired."

Jibril stroked his son's hair.

"Go back to sleep, my son. I am here now, we'll talk when you wake up again, OK?"

Nabil didn't answer, he had already drifted off to sleeping land. Merjam and the Imam went into the living room.

"You have much love for your son, you came to Stockholm so quickly", Merjam said.

"I love all my children. It's fortunate that I had a visa for Europe. I was planning to go to London... But it is really strange, that he sleeps like that. Apart from that he seems to be all right."

"Yeah, really strange. Has the Imam seen anything like this before?"

"Well, he likes to eat, no question about that, and he used to have a siesta in the daytime. But that's just for a few hours."

"Guess I have to stop cooking such good food all the time."

Jibril smiled and shook his head.

"Perhaps. He seems to appreciate it a lot."

"Yes, I'm afraid we're out of food, but maybe I can take you to a restaurant instead?"

"Yes you may, that would be very nice."

"Is there anything you want to see in Stockholm?"

"You can be my guide."

"We can go to a restaurant called 'Stockholm je t'aime' and enjoy the famous Swedish smorgasbord."

"What's that?"

"It's a buffet with all kinds of delicacies. 'Jamais, jamais vu' (never, never seen before), as the French say,"

"Sounds like a good idea!"

Beef Wellington à la Bob Geldorf and U2-Bono

When Merjam realized where the mosque's money had gone, she decided to serve the Imam a "Beef Wellington à la Bob Geldof and U2-Bono", to take from the rich and give to the poor. She took the Imam to the restaurant "Stockholm Je t'aime"

The restaurant was run by a women's association called "We are all sisters." A big chunk of the profit from the restaurant went to Africa. "Stockholm Je t'aime" had an elegant interior design, with beautiful paintings of European capital cities: Prague, Paris, Rome, London… There was a romantic atmosphere to the place. A violinist played "Strangers in the night" and attractive men and women dressed in sandwich paper were lying on tables covered with food; herring, meatballs, raw spiced salmon, gratins, sausages, cold cuts, goose, salads and much more... Only their heads, necks and feet were visible. Merjam had asked Elisabeth to be the head waitress for the evening.

"Welcome, bienvenue", Elisabeth greeted Merjam and the Imam. The other waitresses, two very nice-looking blondes, came up with a small plastic wash basin, a watering can, soap and towels.

May we bother you for a moment?" they said.

Merjam and Jibril held out their hands. One of the waitresses poured water and the other one cleaned their hands.

"Such good service", said Jibril delighted. "Is it a dream or is this real? Thank you, thank you!"

"It's reality", replied Merjam.

"Excuse me, Merjam", Jibril wondered, "but why are some men here picking food from other men and not from the women?"

"They're homo."

"Ah... OK. I've never seen anything like!" said Jibril.

"Let's go and pick some food. From the women, of course!"

"Such beautiful women, such luxury! It looks really good, I don't know where to start", Jibril said.

Merjam put food on her plate, while Jibril stared at the women, who smiled seductively at him.

"Start with salmon, Béarnaise sauce, salad and tomatoes."

Jibril started walking around, picking food here and there, from different lying women.

"Exciting, it's like Arabian nights", he said.

Merjam thanked and nodded.

Jibril bowed.

"Thank you, thank you, thank you", he said.

"Not like that!" Merjam shouted. "The blondes of Stockholm like men to kiss their feet."

"Can you do that?"

"Well, a gentleman has to start somewhere, and the feet are clean, right?" Merjam replied.

Jibril stepped up to the lying woman and bowed again, looking at her. She had blonde hair, big blue eyes… a real looker. Jibril stood up again.

"Excuse me, what's your name?" he asked.

"I'm Siri."

"Oh, what a beautiful name!"

Jibril bowed again and kissed Siri's feet, once, twice, he didn't seem to stop.

"That's enough", Merjam said.

They went to their table and started eating. They continued to discuss, eagerly gesturing.

A beautiful sign made of black velvet hung on the wall behind the girls. There was a text written in gold letters in several different languages.

"What does that sign say?" asked Jibril. "I can't see it, I forgot my glasses."

"I can't read it either", Merjam said and turned to the violinist Linnéa Blixt, who was playing a couple of meters behind their table.

"Mademoiselle Linnéa, what does that sign say?"

"Monsieur, monsieur", Linnéa read aloud, "Don't divorce your wife just because she can't cook! Eat at our place and keep her as a hobby! Welcome to Stockholm! Bienvenue à Stockholm!"

"Allah, I lost my head", Jibril mumbled, "my heart beats…, it's a feeling I can't describe!"

Linnéa went back to playing the violin, she walked over at Merjam and Jibril's table while playing. Merjam stretched her leg out in front of her. Linnéa pretended to play on Merjam's leg and pulled the bow over her foot. Jibril stretched out his leg and Linnéa did the same trick on him.

"That was the first sign that you've landed in Stockholm", Linnéa said to Jibril. "The second sign is that your socks have a hole!"

"That can't be, these socks are new. How can you be so sure of that?"

Jibril took his shoes off and saw the holes in his socks.

"Unbelievable! How is that possible?" he burst out, puzzled. "Is it the blondes or is it my high blood pressure?"

"Dear friend", Merjam said, "tu es à Stockholm (you´re in Stockholm), Stockholm, Stockholm."

The Imam laughed out loud.

"Come, let's have some more food."

They walked over to the food tables and took food from the reclining women.

"The person who came up with this smörgåsbord idea was really clever", said Jibril.

That quote became the starting signal for Merjam. She decided to release her "Beef Wellington à la Bob Geldof and U2-Bono."

"You know the woman who welcomed us when we got here?"

"Yes?"

"Her name is Elisabeth Nordström. We call her 'Madame Volunteer'. She's a psychologist, and she works with several different projects. Among other things, she's the inventor of the Swedish smörgåsbord. And she started this restaurant. Brilliant concept, isn't it?"

"Oh yeah, it's amazing!"

They finished picking food and went back to their table.

"So Madame Volunteer started all this, but she's not the one financing it. I can tell you who does, but you have to promise that it stays between you and me."

"Well, of course!"

Merjam leant over the table.

"It's rich Arabs who are financing this little Swedish smörgåsbord project", she said in a low voice.

"Rich Arabs!" Jibril spat out in surprise. "Is it really true?"

"Please, Imam Jibril, think about it. What can they do? Allah forbids Muslims to charge interest. Poor Arabs! And Americans and Europeans of course take advantage of the situation and put interest in billions right into their pockets."

"That I know."

"And not only that! Every time I watch al-Jazeera or BBC and they show the stock markets from the Persian Gulf I feel so sad. I see all these well dressed Arabs with rosaries in their hands counting how much they lost."

"I've lost a whole lot on the stock market myself, so I know what you're talking about."

"So, what are we going to do? Well, some smart Arabs invested in 'Stockholm je t'aime' and now they get payment in kind instead of interest, and voilà! Everyone's happy and content."

"How do they do that then?"

"It's very simple. These Arab businessmen visit Stockholm, where they have invested money. They eat for free and in addition they have young, beautiful lady companions, taking care of them, guiding them. And this doesn't cost them anything."

"So, if I understand correctly, you mean that these girls follow the rich Arabs back to their hotel rooms?"

"Absolutely! The Arabs collect interest in kind! And that's not forbidden as far as I know."

"How did all this start?"

"There was this chap from Kuwait who had inherited a lot of money from his dad. He went to Stockholm and jumped at the idea. He told his uncle that he shouldn't let the interest slip away to the Americans and the Europeans. 'I want to live an exciting life and meet beautiful Scandinavians and enjoy the interest', he said. 'And, dear uncle, you shouldn't keep me from Scandinavian women'. The uncle said, 'I don't want to prevent you. On the contrary, I'm going to join you when you're going to Stockholm'. And after that, the word spread."

The Imam laughed, his eyes glowing.

"What do you do with the interest yourself?" Merjam asked him.

"I follow the rules of Islam, I leave the interest to the bank, as a Christmas present", Jibril replied.

Merjam of course wanted to see money collected in mosques in Qatar going to "Help Africa" instead.

"Well, you can stop doing that now", she said to Jibril. "Put your presents here instead and enjoy life!"

"I have to say, it sounds very interesting. I'm glad you brought me here, Merjam. And I'm glad you told me about this little… what shall we call it…"

"'Blonde interest rate', according to the Babuba dictionary!"

"What a wonderful name! Thanks, Merjam!"

"Oh, that was nothing. It's a pleasure having you here, Jibril."

They become silent for a while, enjoying the food.

"This was very good", said Jibril.

"It was even better with sauce", Merjam said.

Jibril rubbed his moustaches while throwing dirty looks at Siri.

"You're right, I'll go and get some pepper sauce."

He walked over to the sauce-lady and tasted some of the sauces with a spoon.

"Mmm, this is super! Do you work here every day?"

he asked Siri.

"No", she said in a sexy voice. "I only work here two nights a week, I work at Huddinge Hospital normally. I'm a nurse."

"If you're a nurse, I wish I were ill and could go to the hospital so that you could take care of me!"

"I couldn't do that."

"I'm willing to pay you twenty thousand crowns a day."

"But I can't do it."

"I'll give you forty thousand a day!"

"I just can't."

"Are you a racist? You don't like foreign patients?"

The Imam started to get desperate.

"No, we like all our patients, but you see, I work at the maternity ward!"

"Oh, sorry… how stupid of me."

Jibril took pepper sauce from between her breasts, which were covered with black and green olives.

"Well, how can I meet this nurse?"

"This weekend I am working as an escort. Here, there's a brochure under the pillow."

Jibril lifted the pillow, took a brochure and smiled.

"Is this from tomorrow on?" he asked.

"Yes. Write down your cell phone number on this napkin, I'll contact you tomorrow."

Jibril wrote down his number and walked back to his table, happy and content.

"This sauce is a real winner!" he shouted. "Can I get the recipe?"

Merjam turned to Madame Volunteer.

"Excuse me, Elisabeth, may we have your recipe for the pepper sauce, or is it confidential?"

Madame Volunteer looked at Merjam, confounded.

"It's the standard recipe, look it up in any cook book!"

The Imam shook his head.

"That's impossible! I've eaten pepper sauce many times in my life, but never had it been this good! It's superb, splendid, it must be something special, something unique!"

"It's every woman that is unique! You know, a woman has a lot of power. If you put the pepper sauce between a woman's breasts and let it lie there for 15-20 minutes, the taste improves colossally!"

"Aha!" Jibril cried out. "Now I understand. Brilliant!"

The Imam continued to eat with great appetite. Suddenly he took a break from eating, looked at Merjam. He rubbed his moustaches...

"Merjam, life is short. I want to invest in this project. How does one become a member?"

"Oh... wait..."

Merjam turned to Elisabeth.

"Excuse me, Elisabeth, monsieur Jibril here wants to become a member. How will he be able to enjoy the interest?"

"Monsieur Jibril will get his interest within one week! How long is he staying in Sweden?"

Merjam looked at the Imam.

"Stockholm is so beautiful, I'm planning to stay for three weeks", the Imam said.

"You know that it takes time to approve your membership, but we can find a solution. Are you coming back to Sweden soon?"

"Hmm." The Imam looked doubtful. "I don't know whether I'll be back in Stockholm in the near future", he said. "Most of the upcoming year is already booked up for me, I'm going to travel a lot in different countries in the Muslim world."

Elisabeth, who knew the story, leaned forward and

the Imam's glance got caught in her décolletage.

"Where are you from?"

"Qatar."

"Oh, Qatar! al-Jazeera!"

The Imam smiled proudly.

"We'll make sure the company sends one blonde down to Qatar every month to meet monsieur Imam."

"That can't be", said Jibril, "I have a wife and kids. You know, I'm known to people, I work as an Imam. I'm afraid I'd be exposed."

"I think we can overcome that problem. This is how we do it. Every month the company sends a young woman and a young man down to your home country. The company makes reservations at the best hotel in Doha. The only thing you need to do is to leave two copies of the Koran in the reception. When the young couple arrives at the hotel they each get room keys and a copy of the Koran."

Jibril had trouble understanding all the information.

"Why does a man have to be with her?" he asked.

"Please", Merjam explained, "this man is just a cover-up, so that everything seems to be in order. You know, some of the guys working here are homosexual."

"OK, now I get it", said Jibril and smiled. "But one thing is still uncertain. What are they going to do with the Koran?"

Merjam was well on her way to bake her "Beef Wellington" now.

"Dear Imam Jibril! That is also just a cover up! You get two things for the price of one here, you get beautiful Swedish blondes, and back home in Qatar people think that Scandinavians are coming to convert to Islam. You're going to appear as a good missionary for Islam in Scandinavia."

The Imam rubbed his moustaches and looked at Merjam thoughtfully.

"When do we sign the contracts?"
Elisabeth looked at Merjam.
"Shall we say tomorrow at twelve?" she asked.
"Sounds excellent", said the Imam.
"Where are you staying?"
"Erm…"
"Sheraton Hotel, near Kungsholmen", Merjam said.
"Oh, good choice", said Elisabeth, "Kungsholmen is a gem! Then I would like to offer you a dinner at one of the boat restaurants along Norr Mälarstrand."
"Sounds excellent", said the Imam.
Elisabeth bowed, kissed the Imam's cheek, put a chaplet of flowers around his neck and left.

Jibril and Linnea

Behind Merjam and Jibril, a beautiful woman was standing, playing the violin. It was Linnéa Blixt, another actor in Merjam's theatre. The Imam really enjoyed her violin-playing. He turned around and applauded after she finished.
"Amazing! She plays wonderfully!"
"She's a music teacher normally", Merjam said, "and in her spare time she works for a non-profit organisation, raising money for the needy in Africa."
"Interesting", said Jibril.
Merjam turned to Linnéa.
"Who's this week's escort girl?"
"It's Siri! But I'm free a couple of hours tomorrow as well."
She looked Jibril straight in the eyes and went on.
"We could go and have a cup of coffee tomorrow if monsieur has time for that?"
"Time and money I have plenty of!"
"If monsieur would be kind enough to put his hand in my back pocket, and pick up my visiting card?"

"Well, of course!"

Jibril felt turned on but he managed to avoid groping Linnéa's bottom, and just picked up the visiting card.

"See you the day after tomorrow, then?"

"Of course! I'll call you to make an appointment."

"Sounds excellent."

"So your new life begins the day after tomorrow?"

"Yeah", said the Imam with an Arabic smile, "but don't wake me up too early!"

Linnéa continued to play and the Imam turned to Merjam.

"What does 'escort girl' mean?" he asked.

"An escort girl is a girl with charm and charisma, but most important, a girl with experience. She knows how to treat a man like a king."

"But how do you know she has experience?"

"Well, here in Stockholm, the escort girls proudly carry around their grades!"

"Grades?"

"Yeah, when you apply for a job in Qatar you have to show your theological grades, right?"

"Sure, but how does an escort girl show her grades?"

"Look at Linnéa, what a beautiful and original necklace she wears, made out of her old wedding rings, count them!"

The Imam stared at Linnéa's necklace that Merjam had given to her and counted the rings.

"Nineteen."

"Well, you can see that this girl had been married nineteen times, girls like that are much sought after by some men!"

"OK. I have to check if I have any holes in my other sock, Stockholm had made me so confused!"

"Why?"

"It's so hard to understand why men prefer women who have had a lot of guys."

"What's it like in Qatar?"

"Girls should be virgins."

"You see, this is what you call a collision of cultures. Here, some men appreciate experienced women…"

They were interrupted by the waitress.

"Excuse me, can I take your plates?"

"Of course", Merjam said and caught sight of the waitress's bracelet which had beads in different colours.

"Where did you buy this beautiful bracelet?"

"You buy beads in 100 gram bags and make the bracelet yourself. The beads show the number of boyfriends you have had."

"Interesting. Is this the new fashion?"

"Yes, some guys appreciate an experienced girl. And it is also a way to remember how many boyfriends I have had."

"We better go home now, Merjam, I can't take any more", the Imam said and held his hand on his head.

"Why? The night is long in Stockholm."

"Yes, but I have to go to a clinic, I need sedation to sleep tonight. My head is spinning!"

"No, you don't need to go to any clinic, there are women here who can sedate both you and 'Monsieur anaesthetist'.

The Imam at the Sheraton

The day after Mustafa took his delivery bike and rode to Sheraton Hotel. He walked over to the reception.

"Hi, I would like to speak to Imam Jibril, what's his room number?"

"Do you hear that man speaking loud in his cell phone?" said the receptionist. "That's him, over there in the café, do you know him?"

"Sure!"

"Can you tell him to change to an Ericsson

telephone? Then he can speak lower and still be heard on the other side of the globe!"

"Or, even better, a Nokia", the other receptionist interrupted with a Finnish accent, "then he can even whisper and it will be heard on the other side of the globe!"

"Hey, miss Finland", said the first receptionist, "no bragging here, watch out!"

"I wonder if it helps", Mustafa interrupted, "some people, regardless of phone brand, like to talk loud on their phones and entertain people on the bus, on the underground, everywhere! I'll tell you a story: A man got on a bus in Tunisia, he was a bit tipsy. The man found a seat next to an angry person who was talking loudly in a mobile phone. 'Hello, hello', he went on, 'we're on our way to hell'! The tipsy guy thought that he sat next to a suicide bomber and got totally crazy, shouting to the driver, 'Stop, stop, please drop me off, I'm on the wrong bus'!"

The receptionists laughed and Mustafa walked over to the bar. He sat down and heard the Imam talking admiringly about "Stockholm Je t'aime's" excellent service. He was speaking to Linnéa, Mustafa could only see his back. The Imam became silent and listened…

"Sure," he said in the receiver, "no problem, I'm going to become a member of 'Stockholm Je t'aime', I am meeting Merjam and Elisabeth at twelve to sign contracts… I guarantee, it's no problem."

Suddenly, Mustafa's cell phone was ringing and he saw that it was Merjam. He walked out in the lobby to answer.

"Hello."

"Where are you, Mustafa?" Merjam asked angrily.

"I'm in town, mum!"

"I told you to stay at home and take care of Nabil! We can't leave him alone! You have to come home at once!"

"But mum…"

"You have to come home NOW!"
"OK, I'm coming."

Mustafa took his delivery bike and began the ride home. He cursed in Arabic, French and Swedish...

When he reached the Liljeholmen bridge all he wanted to do was throw the bike in the water and jump after it.

After an hour he was back in Skärholmen.

Merjam and Elisabeth were sitting in the lobby at Sheraton Hotel, waiting for the Imam.

He was supposed to meet them at twelve o'clock, but he had taken a walk. Close to half past twelve he sauntered in. Merjam looked at her watch. When she looked up she saw the Imam walking towards her and Elisabeth.

"Hi, what happened?" both women asked.

"Sorry I'm late! I got lost in this beautiful city, but a couple of kind Swedes helped me find the way here."

"Good", said Elisabeth, "I was a bit worried. You're almost half an hour late."

"You don't need to worry about me", said the Imam. "I feel great here in Stockholm! I have to say that the Swedes have surprised me."

"You mean that?" said Elisabeth. "In what way?"

"Well, you know, on the plane here I happened to be seated next to an English businessman, and we started talking about Sweden and the Swedes. He told me 'The Swedes are silent and shy'. And now I come here, and it turns out it's not like that at all, everybody is so kind and happy here!"

"You came to Sweden at exactly the right moment" Elisabeth explained. "You know, it depends how the Swedes are feeling. The winter here is long and cold, and the Swedes are more inward looking then. But now, in the summer time, Swedes are social and outgoing."

"And most important", Merjam said, "the flirting energy among the girls is on a record high, like the Eiffel Tower!"

"Yeah, I noticed that! And I must say, I've never seen so many nice-looking blondes wearing dark blue police uniforms as here in Stockholm! The best-looking one I've seen so far was as beautiful as the moon shining over Arlanda airport!"

Merjam wondered if it was Bibbi the Imam was talking about. After all, it was she who had stamped his passport when he arrived at the airport.

"Aha, aha!"

"Glad you appreciate the Swedish women", Elisabeth said and looked at her watch. "We've booked a table for half past twelve, we have to go at once!"

"Oh, OK, better hurry then. I'm just going up to get some things from my room, OK?"

"Sure", said Elisabeth and Merjam in unison.

The Imam got his room key in the reception and walked up to his hotel room. He brought out a briefcase from the wardrobe. In the briefcase he had 900 000 crowns in cash which he had withdrawn from the Nordea bank earlier this morning. It was money that had been collected from various mosques in Qatar, and which had been deposited in a bank in Geneva by the his son Nabil a couple of days earlier. The Imam took his briefcase and walked down to the lobby. The trio took the walk over to Norr Mälarstrand, and the floating boat restaurant "Strandbryggan". They got a table and sat down. The Imam looked around. From where he was seated he had the city hall to the left, and he looked happily at the proud building.

"That one I've seen in the tourist brochure", he said. "What is it for?"

"It's the city hall", Merjam said. "The Nobel Prize dinner is held there."

"Oh… interesting!"

A waiter brought the food, beef steak with pommes chateau and green pepper sauce. They all enjoyed the delicious food.

"What do you think about the food?" Merjam asked.

"Mmm… it's perfect! Everything is perfect here! It's like a dream, sitting on a floating pier, with this food, and this view. This body of water… what's it called?"

"It's Riddarfjärden", said Elisabeth.

The Imam turned his head and looked right.

"So many people out walking alongside the water", he said. "Where is everyone going?"

"The whole shoreline is called Norr Mälarstrand, but that particular part, over there at the water's edge, a good friend of mine calls it 'Kungsholmen's Little Champs Elysées'!"

"So there's a Champs Elysées here as well?"

"Yep! It's hard not to fall in love with Stockholm, isn't it?"

"Definitely! It's so green and beautiful here. Back home in Qatar everything's yellow from the sun and the heat."

"Yeah, Sweden is a dream country in the summer time!"

They enjoyed the main course and a dessert. After that, it was time for business. Elisabeth brought out the contract for membership in "Stockholm Je t'aime" and handed it over to the Imam.

"How much are you planning to invest in 'Stockholm Je t'aime?" she asked.

The Imam looked at Elisabeth and tried to look as trustworthy as possible.

"900 000 kronor. It's most of my savings. I expect a good return."

"Considering the success we've had lately, I think you can count on that. And you can also count on royal treatment whenever you visit us, of course."

"And the interest?"

"It will be paid monthly."

The Imam smiled excitedly.

"Thanks. Just one thing… I hope that I can meet escort girls during my stay in Stockholm."

Elisabeth and Merjam were shocked.

"No problem", Elisabeth said. "We'll arrange that. OK, then, if nothing in the contract looks odd or inappropriate, I suggest you sign it!"

The Imam signed the contract. They made a toast for "Stockholm Je t'aime's" new sponsor and member of honour, Imam Jibril.

"I know I haven't got the right to butt in your business strategies", Jibril started, "but I just have to say that I think you should open restaurants like this one all across Europe! That would help a lot of Arabian businessmen in Europe to get around the 'interest problem'."

"Oh, we have plans, don't you worry, Jibril", Elisabeth reassured him. "This is only the beginning, our ambitions are high. By the way, I have to say 'Hi' from Siri, the escort girl… your first interest payment…"

"Thanks. I'm seeing her today."

Imam Jibril looked out on Riddarfjärden.

"How are the winters here in Stockholm?"

"Oh", Elisabeth burst out, "it's a long cold winter here."

"How do you manage? You must wear a lot of clothes of course."

"That doesn't help the slightest", said Merjam.

"No?"

"But there are a lucky few who receive portable bedwarmers."

Jibril looked at Merjam, confused.

"Bedwarmers?"

"Sure, every winter, in December/January, we launch a contest all across Sweden, 'Portable bedwarmer of the year'."

"What's that?"

"It's men and women that can radiate warmth, you don't need gloves or long underclothes. Their body warmth is infectious."

"Ah! A friend who works at the Saudi embassy told me that Swedes eat ice cream outside even when it's minus 15 degrees. But now I see how it all fits together!"

"Yeah, by the way, Siri was voted portable bedwarmer of the year in 2003."

"That I can understand, you can sense her warmth from far away! By the way. when can I get my first interest payment on home court, so to speak?" the Imam wondered.

"Well, it might take a little while, we have to arrange with transport, accommodation and things like that. But it shouldn't take longer than a couple of weeks, I can promise you that", Elisabeth said.

"Mmm, sounds perfect. What time and place?"

"We usually stick to one hotel in Doha, the Millennium Hotel. Is that OK with you?"

"Sounds good! One of the best hotels in Qatar! So I can expect a first payment of interest at the Millennium hotel in a few weeks?"

"You can be sure of it, Jibril."

The Imam looked at his watch.

"Oh, it's late! I have to leave at once! I'm seeing Siri. Just one question: Is Linnéa part of the interest payment?"

"I'm afraid not. Are you seeing her too?"

"Yes, tomorrow. Bye for now."

When the Imam had left Merjam turned to Elisdabeth and made thumbs up. "I have to go, Bibbi's coming for dinner. We're going to discuss the next step in the plan."

"How are we going to arrange escort girls for three weeks?" Elisabeth wondered.

"My daughter is a police woman", Merjam said.

Beef Wellington à la Swedish Prostitution Law

The next day...

Along Kungsgatan were a couple of horse-drawn carriages with number plates, in Roman numerals, on them. There were also a bunch of cycle taxis there. Jibril had forgotten his glasses back home in Qatar and had trouble reading, so he walked over to one of the cycle taxis and took Linnéa's visiting card from his pocket. He handed it over to the taxi-driver. "Linnéa Blixt, cab V" it said on the card.

"Excuse me, where's this one?" the Imam asked.

"It's the third cab from the right", replied the cycle-taxi driver, a young, cute girl. "But it's better to go with these, then you will support 'Help Africa' at the same time."

"Some other time", said Jibril and pointed at the visiting card. "I have to meet this girl."

"OK, promise to go with us next time", the girl said and pointed to the cab on the other side of the street.

"Sure, absolutely."

He crossed the street and spotted Linnéa sitting in the front of a horse cab, next to a girl holding the reins. He waved with the visiting card.

"Hello!"

"Hello! Guess we're a little late", Linnéa said.

"Sorry", said the Imam, "but it's not easy to find your way here in Stockholm. So, you sit in the horse cab during daytime and play the violin at night?"

Linnéa smiled a captivating smile.

"No, not really. I work as an S-volunteer."

"An S-volunteer? What does that mean?"

"Sex volunteer – our organisation "Stockholm je t'aime" earns money from sexual favours for men."

Jibril couldn't believe his ears. In a second he changed from horny to frigid.

"You call that S-volunteering? It's prostitution!"

"Sure", said Linnéa happily. "Prostitution is a fantastic business. You use what you have, you sell it and afterwards you still have it."

"Dear child, you're so beautiful and have such great talent for music. You cuold have any man you wanted – the great love."

"Love, l'amour, Liebe – as far as feelings are concerned, that's bad business for a woman."

Jibril was confused but he had to ask:

"Why?"

"Men are so egoistical", giggled Linnéa, "and women get so little back from what they invest in a relationship."

Jibril looked at her, affected by her words.

"Don't you feel ashamed? You work as a teacher, you should be a role model for your students!"

Linnéa was politically aware and familiar with social problems

"Ashamed? Don't you think it's a shame that millions of people die from starvation or lack of medicine and water, while politicians buy weapons for billions?"

"But you don't need to sell your body because of that!"

"Why not? Isn't it a shame that people have become so selfish? They just want everything for themselves. They cannot give even one per cent of their salary to help starving children."

"Allah helps them."

Linnéa was well familiar with Catholicism, Islam and Judaism.

"How can Allah help when some Muslims don't want to give even the two-and-a-half percent that he demands?

And not all Catholics and Jews are willing to pay a tithe either! How are we going to make the world a better place? Well, it doesn't get worse if I make a contribution my way."

Jibril shook his head.

"Selling one's body to help the third world children. I've never heard of anything so drastic in my entire life."

"A cold world calls for drastic solutions."

"What does your father say about you selling your body on the streets?"

"Ah, my dad… he doesn't have time for me. All he thinks about is Saddam and the hidden weapons."

Linnéa had seen Hans Blix, head of the United Nations' weapons inspection in Iraq, on al-Jazeera at Babuba's in Skärholmen.

"You know who my father is, right? Read on the visiting card!"

Jibril picked up the card again.

"Sorry, I've forgotten my glasses", he said.

"Take mine", said Linnéa, "they're strong."

Jibril put the glasses on and looked at the card. After a little while he discovered it.

"Hans Blix? The UN weapons inspector? Are you…, are you…"

Linnéa wanted to impress him.

"His daughter, yes!"

Jibril didn't see the subtle but important difference between Linnéa's surname, the common Swedish surname "Blixt", and the famous UN secretary's name, the much less common and more aristocratic "Blix."

Jibril was shocked. He was a big fan of Hans Blix, this prominent and righteous Swede. He gave the glasses back to Linnéa, took off his Arabic slippers, pulled up his shirt and ran off on Kungsgatan, screaming.

"It can't be true! Doctor Hans Blix, the man of justice, 'allô, allô, Stockholm!' I'm losing my mind. I'll go home at once, no, no, I'm going home!"

Linnéa ran after Jibril. For a moment, the car traffic stagnated. Everyone looked out of their car windows. The pedestrians turned around, looking at each other. Was it a thief or someone running away from a restaurant without paying? Had Usama Bin Laden finally been caught? Where were the police? Jibril kept running with Linnéa behind him.

"Stop, stop, what's the matter with you?" she screamed.

"This can't be true! This is a dream!" Jibril shouted back. "When Hans Blix speaks in the UN, the world stops for a moment, and here in Stockholm, his daughter sells her body for the sake of the children of the third world!"

Jibril had little knowledge about Sweden, he didn't know the names of the Swedish king or the Prime minister, or how many people live there. To him, Sweden was Volvo, Saab, Ericsson and Hans Blix.

"I'll call al-Jazeera, I'll call al-Jazeera!" he shouted.

Before his eyes he could see Hans Blix, whom he had seen on al-Jazeera back home in Qatar. Linnéa ran after him, screaming loud in the traffic chaos on Kungsgatan. She ran faster than he did and got closer and closer all the time. Next to her came the horse cab with her friend holding the reins.

"Stop, stop!" she huffed.

"Why?" said the Imam.

Linnéa was surprised by his reaction.

"I want to buy you a drink!"

"No thank you, I'm a Muslim, an abstainer!"

"OK, sorry then. But I want to buy you lunch!"

"No thanks, I've already eaten!"

Linnéa managed to catch up with the Imam, and she grabbed his jelaba. Jibril gave up, stopped and turned around.

"I want to hug and kiss you", she said.

"I caught a cold, got tons of germs", said the Imam.

Linnéa leaned forward towards the Imam. He backed off instinctively.

"A kiss from Hans Blix's daughter can kill all of those germs", she said.

"I don't understand! Your father is so powerful the whole world stops when he speaks."

"I am too, in my own way", Linnéa Blixt countered in a warm and sexy voice. "Do you know what 'blixt' means in Swedish?"

Jibril shook his head.

"It means lightning! And that's a suitable name, because when you lie on my stomach, you feel as if you were flying to the moon like a flash of lightning!" Linnéa put her forefinger to Jibril's mouth. "But if you are going to fly like a flash of lightning, you must listen to me…"

She turned her back on Jibril.

"Pull down the zipper and kiss my back."

The Imam immediately became aroused by this invitation from Linnéa. He tucked away her long blonde hair, pulled down the zipper on the back of her dress and kissed her beautiful, sunburned back.

"Allah, Hans Blix's daughter, Hans Blix's daughter!"

Linnéa played along…

"How does Hans Blix's daughter taste? Good?"

"Oh yeah!"

"OK, that's it, let's go up to the horse cab."

"How much is it?"

Linnéa lit up.

"1500 for Swedes, 2500 for tourists."

"The Swedes are honest, they you how it really is. But I have to ask you, why do the Swedes pay less?"

"At the end of the day, the Swedes pay the same amount, I do a little blackmailing on the side."

Jibril laughed and counted his money. 1000, 1500, 2000, 2500. He gave her the money.

"Remember, it's for a good cause." They went into the cab and sat down opposite each other.

"Give me your right hand", Linnéa said.

Jibril gave her his right hand and Linnéa started kissing it, over and over.

"When I make love to a man, it's important that he gets a hundred per cent pleasure. And love's secrets are to be found in the man's hand!"

The Imam smiled a silly smile.

"In the man's hand are the lines with the replies to all of love's secrets!"

"I have never heard of this before! Sweden is a lover's paradise!"

Linnéa studied his hand and stroked her hand over his.

"You have a soft hand, that tells me you have an enormous sexual energy within. You just have to wake it up!"

"That's very true, I love sex. But I lost my lust!"

"You're not alone. Let me see in your hand which position is the best for us. The love line reveals it all."

She pulled her thumb across the palm of the Imam's hand.

"Stomach against stomach! That didn't work. Let's see here... the crossed legs position! No, that didn't work either..."

The Imam started to get impatient. His eyes wandered towards Linnéa's cleavage. She had a chain around her neck, with two jewels in it. The jewels were shaped as cars, one of them in gold, Volvo, and one in silver, Saab. Linnéa noticed that the Imam looked at her cleavage and looked up at him.

"You seem to be more interested in cars than in what position to make love."

"I do?"

"Tell me, Jibril, which one of the cars fascinates you

the most?"

"None of them! I just want to drive drive through that beautiful highway!"

Linnéa giggled.

"Yeah, you have to find the right highway, 'cause here in Sweden not all of them lead to Stockholm!"

The Imam smiled. Linnéa started to study his hand again. She moved her thumb across his palm and found a new line.

"Cross-bar position? No, that won't work either. The crab position? No…"

"What's the crab position?"

"It would take all day to explain that, Jibril."

Linnéa continued.

"Love's fusion…"

The Imam became more and more impatient, he wanted to make love to Linnéa. He was very fond of her big breasts à la Pamela Anderson.

"Speaking of fusion… how can you have such large breasts and still have such a flat stomach?"

Linnéa smiled.

"This you must learn, Jibril, things don't grow well in the shade!"

Jibril laughed.

"You're as intelligent as your father."

Linnéa didn't pay any attention. She continued to check Jibril's hand.

"Ah, here it is! The joiner! Suits us perfectly! Let's try it with the clothes on first."

"What? Do you make love with your clothes on here in Sweden?"

"No, but I have my principles, I want to satisfy my man one hundred per cent and the most important thing is, don't hurry."

They sat down on the floor inside the horse cab. Linnéa put her right thigh over Jibril's left. She instructed him to put his right thigh over her left thigh. They grabbed hold of each other and started to move in rubbing moves by leaning forwards and backwards.

"Please, Linnéa, this is too difficult! You need to be a Chinese acrobat to master this position!"

"But there's help!"

Linnéa managed to get herself out of the difficult position. She tapped on the wall of the coach. The cabbie understood and immediately tugged the reins. Suddenly the horse started to tramp on the spot causing the carriage to rock. Linnéa pushed herself against Jibril and after a while she started to moan, at first very quietly and then after a while a little louder, then even louder. Jibril became very aroused hearing Linnéa's moaning, and he liked the fact that despite them both being fully dressed, this little game had obviously made her all fired up.

At the same time, people on the street started noticing the horse cab.

The horse was a mare, and she started to neigh, a very peculiar sound, coming from deep down her throat. It sounded as if she were aroused too. She neighed more and more and soon the whole cab was rocking. People started gathering around the cab and soon there was a large crowd of curious bystanders there.

At the police station

A cop plain clothes policewoman made her way through the crowd and knocked on the cab door. It was Bibbi's colleague Ronnie, who had filmed and photographed Linnéa and the Imam during the whole process.

"It's the police. You have to come with us to the station."

Jibril was surprised and offended at the same time .
"Why?" he asked.

"I'll explain it to you when we're at the police station", Ronnie replied.

Jibril reluctantly followed Ronnie. They went by car to a building nearby. Jibril didn't understand where he was, but it looked like an ordinary residential building. The came up to a door with a newly applied sign of the Swedish police logo.

They walked into a small office and there sat Bibbi. "Can I see your passport?" she asked Jibril.

"It's at the hotel."

"What's the name of the hotel?"

"Sheraton Hotel."

"Have a seat." Bibbi sat down in front of a computer and started writing a police report.

"What's your name?"

"Jibril ben Salem."

"Where do you come from?"

"Qatar."

"When were you born?"

"24th of March, 1940."

"Where were you born?"

"Doha, Qatar. But please, I haven't done anything, what is this all about?"

"You've committed a crime that can give up to six months in prison or fines." Ronnie replied calmly.

Jibril started pondering whether this wasn't the Swedish "Candid Camera".

"Excuse me, but was that a joke?"

Bibbi got out of her chair.

"I'm afraid this is serious, Jibril. There's a law here in Sweden saying it's not illegal for a woman to sell her body, but it's a criminal offence to buy sexual favours."

Jibril became perplexed.

"Excuse me, but I did not have sexual relations with that woman."

Bibbi shook her head.

"All men say that", she said.

"You were in the horse cab for fifteen minutes and thirty one seconds", Ronnie said.

"I promise, I promise, I promise, I haven't touched her!"

"So you paid 2500 crowns for nothing? Tell that to the judge on Monday", said Bibbi. "Lying doesn't pay off very well here in Sweden, it just makes things worse."

The Imam looked completely devastated.

"Please, please, police, try and understand me."

"Please, please, Jibril ben Salem, try and understand ME! You've caused chaos on Kungsgatan, Stockholm's Broadway! It was anarchy out there, it was as if we changed to left-hand traffic or something!"

"In what way have I caused chaos?"

"Your passionate lovemaking with the prostitute inside the cab made not just her, but the horse pulling the cab squeal from sexual pleasure! It was extremely noisy out there, the horse was moaning at 200 decibels! It has never happened before in Stockholm! And who can do such a thing?"

Bibbi looked at the Imam.

"Only Qataris can do that!"

The Imam was standing still staring at them. He shook his head.

"And who can make a horse so shaky it almost falls down to the ground in a big pile, right there on Kungsgatan, Stockholm's Broadway!" Ronny said.

"Only Qataris can accomplish that", Bibbi said. "Is it the wonderful smell of oil that gives you your sexual energy?"

"Can I say something?"

"Yeah?"

"I HAVEN'T MADE LOVE TO HER!"

"What did you do then? Did you tell her about the

TV channel al-Jazeera?" Bibbi asked. "You were inside the cab for fifteen minutes and thirty one seconds!"

At the same time, Fatima was at a café on Kungsgatan. She called Jibril on his cell phone.
"Hi there, Jibril, how are you?"
"Bad, I feel very bad. You have to come here and help me!"
"Where are you?"
"Wait, Fatima, there's someone here who can explain."
Ronnie took over the phone and explained to Fatima where they were.
"Yeah. Linnégatan 30B, yeah. OK, see you!" Bibbi printed out the police report. Jibril looked at her, worried. Then suddenly Fatima came running into the police station.
"What has happened?" she asked, playing along with the script.
"I don't get it, they accuse me of making love to a woman... But I haven't touched her!"
Fatima turned to Ronnie.
"Imam Jibril here is a tourist. He came here yesterday. He doesn't know about the Swedish law on prostitution. Why doesn't it say anything about that in the tourist brochures?"
"You're right, there's no information to the tourists about these things."
Bibbi smiled in collusion with Fatima, and shook her head.
"What will happen now?" Fatima asked.
"There are two options" Bibbi replied. "Either the Imam stays here and defends himself in court. Or he pays a fine..."
By now Jibril was frightened. He suspected a mighty scandal was on the way. He interrupted Bibbi and dreamed up an excuse.

"No, no, I can't do that, I'm going to London, I'm going to speak about Islam at a conference there. I want to get out of here, now! How much must I pay in fines?"

"The judge will decide on Monday, then you'll know", Bibbi said.

"But I can't stay here all weekend, I have to go now!"

"Can't you give him an idea about how much the fine would be for this type of crime?" asked Fatima.

Bibbi brought out the Swedish code book outlining laws and regulations and studied it thoroughly. She turned to Jibril and exaggerated... "20 000 kronor if you make love in a cab. 15 000 if you make love against a tree or a wall."

"And if I stand on one leg and kiss a girl on her back, what would the fine be then?"

Bibbi giggled.

"Do the Arabs stand on one leg while kissing?"

"No, the Arabs kiss just like you. But it was such an honour for me kissing Hans Blix's daughter.

Bibbi's giggle turned into laughter.

"OK, you've been nice to us, and you have a sense of humour, I'll give you that. You know what? Let's forget about this."

The Imam went from sad to happy in a millisecond and looked hopefully at Bibbi.

"But on one condition", she said.

"Anything!"

"That you leave the country right now. Where were you going, London?"

"Absolutely! I'm going right now!"

"OK."

Bibbi tore the police report to pieces.

"Now go to the Sheraton and gather your belongings, I'll come and pick you up in two hours. I'll take you to Arlanda."

"Oh, thank you!"

Jibril and Fatima left. Bibbi took up a plastic bag full of food.

"Oh, it smells good!" Ronnie said.

"Merjam has made it for us."

"Exciting!".

They left through the main entrance of the small office and locked the door. Ronnie took down the police logo and they left.

Fatima and Jibril took a taxi to the Sheraton.

"Fatima, I've been so mad at the laws in some of the Arab countries, you know some of them are really stupid. But this breaks all records! This is SUPER-IDIOTIC!"

"I understand what you mean, Jibril, but every country has its own laws."

"What's the name of this law?"

"The law on prostitution", Fatima replied.

"It's a Taliban law! Unbelievable! A man has to go to jail just because he needs to make love!"

Fatima didn't reply, she just laughed

Fatima at the Sheraton, Mustafa at the City Hall

They reached the Sheraton. Jibril got his room key and went up to his room to get his stuff.

Fatima called the Babuba residence in Skärholmen. No answer. She tried Mustafa's cell phone.

"Hi!" she said. "Is Nabil with you?"

"Hi, Fatima! Yeah, he's here."

"Where are you two?"

"At archangel Gabriel's porch! Right up on the top of Stockholm city hall's tower!"

Mustafa and Nabil were just about to walk up the stairs of the city hall tower. Mustafa really wanted Nabil to see Stockholm from above, and they had a great view from the top of the city hall tower. But it was hard work for the not so fit Nabil to climb up the stairs up to the top. While Mustafa was almost up on the top of the tower, Nabil still hadn't completed his task. He had walked almost 200 steps, but there were another 164 left. Mustafa heard Nabil screaming at him from down the dark spiral staircase.

"Wait a moment, Fatima."

Nabil screamed from down the staircase again.

"I can't do any more, which Jibril are we going to meet? Jibril up in the sky?"

"No, Nabil, Jibril up here! Go on and you will meet him soon!"

The archangel Gabriel is called Jibril in Arabic. Mustafa used to call the summit of the city hall tower "Gabriel's porch" because it was so high in the sky, 106 meters. Mustafa returned to the phone.

"Yes, Fatima?"

"You have to get down now! Nabil's father is going to Arlanda in two hours! We're at the Sheraton now."

"I'll be damned. OK, we'll be there soon!"

They hung up, Nabil had worked his way up a bit in the staircase, Mustafa could hear him panting now.

"Oh, man, if I can't climb up to Jibril's porch, I'll never come down again!"

"Keep at it, Nabil!"

At last, a weary Nabil stumbled up the last stair and fell down to the floor of the small look-out platform.

"Get up, Nabil, Jibril is waiting for you!"

"You're pulling my leg, Mustafa. For the last time, tell me, which Jibril? Jibril in heaven or Jibril on earth?"

"Jibril on earth. Your dear father."

"No way! I'm dead tired."

Nabil gasped for air. After a few minutes he was revived enough to be able to stand up again. He jacked up his heavy body, and suddenly, he had all the beauty of summer-time Stockholm in front of him.

"Oh, it's gorgeous."

"Isn't it?"

"Stockholm… Stockholm Je t'aíme", he panted.

Mustafa pointed to the southwest, to Södermalm and the cliffs of Skinnarviksberget.

"Over there we have one of Stockholm's main attractions - the drunks on Skinnarviksberget! There they sit, all intoxicated. Lucky bastards."

Nabil didn't listen to Mustafa. All of his senses except his vision were switched off when Stockholm's panorama materialised in front of him.

He stood there for a while watching it, then he turned to Mustafa.

"I've never heard of the city hall or Jibril's porch before."

"You know, Nabil, the Swedes are bad advertisers, they don't like to brag."

"I see. But this, this they should brag about!"

"Stockholm or the chicks?"

Nabil laughed a shy, embarrassed laugh.

"But hey, Nabil, you know what? I spoke to Fatima while you were trying to climb the stairs here, and she told me that your father is leaving Sweden. In two hours. But they're at his hotel, and it's just a few blocks away from here.

"But then we have to walk down!"

"Yep."

Nabil looked doubtful, he wanted to see his dad but he didn't dare to think about how to get down the hellish spiral staircase.

Mustafa smiled a dodgy smile.

"Come on, Nabil, I'll carry you!"

Nabil nodded to the staircase, and they started walking down again.

At the Sheraton, Fatima and Jibril were sitting in the lobby waiting when Mustafa and Nabil stumbled in.

"Hi, dad!"

"My son."

They hugged. Jibril made up to Nabil.

"Good to see that you're OK!"

"Yeah, I'm all right now. The Babuba's serve such good food that I fall asleep, but today I've been awake all day! We've just been up in the city hall tower, it was amazing!"

"That's good, my son, I'm glad that you're having such a great time."

"But dad, why are you leaving so soon?"

"It's a conference in London, I have to go there."

"That's a shame."

Fatima sat on a chair behind Nabil's back. She shook her head when she heard Jibril's fairytale. She decided to tell a tale of her own.

"We're going to Gotland (an island in the Baltic Sea) tomorrow. We are going to be there for two weeks. What are you going to do about your son? Where will he stay?"

"OK, but that's great, then he can take my room here at the Sheraton, I haven't checked out yet.

"Excuse me." Mustafa broke into the conversation. "Imam Jibril, can I speak with you in private for a moment?"

"Sure."

The two walked away a bit further into the hotel lobby.

"Dear Imam, I was wondering something. Have the mosques in Qatar collected any money to give our temperance society?"

"Oh yeah, good of you to remind me. They have collected 35 000 Swedish crowns so far", he bluffed.

"Is that it?"

"Yeah, but we're counting on Ramadan, then we're going to get a lot of money. But it's still another five months until then."

Mustafa felt as if he had been knocked out by Mike Tyson. He had no idea how to pay Peter or Fatima back, or pay for the limo.

"That's odd, they told us in a telegram that money was on its way."

"It sure is! The 35 000 that is." Jibril handed over the money in cash to Mustafa. "This is the best I can do."

Mustafa thanked him politely and then walked back to the others. The Imam discussed with the receptionists and managed to find a solution so that his son could take over the room. He turned to Nabil.

"Nabil, did you bring your passport? You have to show them your passport."

"Sure."

Nabil stepped up to the reception. Mustafa and Fatima were now within safe gossiping distance from Nabil and Jibril.

"I wonder if they have a breakfast buffet here", Fatima whispered to Mustafa. She could barely hold her laughter back.

"Gosh, they are going to have to work hard in the kitchen", she continued. "They have no idea of what's waiting for them." Mustafa nodded.

"But it's good", he said. "You know, new job opportunities at Sheraton, they're going to need at least two new chefs here."

Fatima giggled. The Imam turned to the youngsters.

"Oh my, are we having fun over here! Is everything always this amusing in Sweden?"

"Yep", said Fatima.

"Now it's settled with the hotel room."

"That's good", Fatima said.

"Then we have to go and get your stuff, Nabil", Mustafa said.

"OK, but I have to take the time to thank you, kids, thank you for taking care of Nabil here in Stockholm. You have to say hello to your mother too, say thanks to her for serving such good food and showing me the city."

"We will", Mustafa assured him. "Let's go. Or, sorry, erm, give me a hug first!"

The Imam smiled.

"You seem to be a happy chap, Mustafa. Good luck with your project, I promise to stay in touch. I'm going to try and help you guys as much as I can."

"Sounds brilliant, Jibril."

They hugged goodbye and the kids continued to the Central station. Jibril ended up alone in the lobby. He sat down in an armchair and pondered over his short visit to Stockholm. What a crazy place! Restaurant "Stockholm Je t'aime" with food straight from women's bodies just dressed in panties, Hans Blix's prostitute daughter in the horse cab on Kungsgatan, the arrest …

With Bibbi to Arlanda

He didn't reach any further in his train of thought. Suddenly Bibbi was standing right in front of him.

"Hello, Jibril!"

He looked up towards the adorable creature, and realised just how beautiful Bibbi really was now that she didn't pose any threat to his freedom.

"Hello!"

"Shall we go at once?"

Jibril nodded and took his travelling bag. They walked out on the street and Bibbi unlocked her beautiful Saab cabriolet.

"Beautiful car for a beautiful woman", Jibril tried.

Bibbi pretended to be flattered.

"Oh, thank you, Jibril, that's sweet of you."

She opened the car door for the Imam, walked around the car to the driver's seat, started the car and drove away. She pushed a button on the dashboard and the car's roof dropped backwards with a mechanical sound.

"We have to enjoy the Swedish summer, don't we?"

Jibril nodded. He looked at Bibbi from his passenger seat and watched her long blonde hair waving in the wind like a flag. He though that he was a happy man, despite all that happened. Bibbi turned left and drove onto Sveavägen.

"If I'm not mistaken, you stamped my passport at Arlanda when I arrived here", said Jibril.

"Maybe", said Bibbi and played ignorant, "I stamp hundreds of passports every day."

"Well, I don't forget a face like that, you must be the most beautiful police officer I've ever seen", the Imam said and added, with an Arabic saying: "You are as beautiful as the moon that shines over Arlanda International airport."

"Thank you!"

Bibbi smiled. She was used to these kinds of compliments. She had heard them since she was ten years old and visited Tunisia for the first time.

Jibril stood up in the passenger seat, happily unaware of the fact that the money that he had invested in "Restaurant Stockholm je t'aíme" was going straight to the Red Cross. And he was happily unaware of the fact that he wouldn't get any visit from any beautiful blondes back home in Qatar. Now he stood up in the cabriolet, waving to people walking along Sveavägen like some Jacques Chirac on a motorcade through the Champs Elysées.

"Stockholm, je t'aime, je t'aime! La rose pour un jour et Stockholm pour toujours!" (The rose for a day and Stockholm forever)

They drove out of central Stockholm and out on the highway to Arlanda. Bibbi pulled down the roof over the car, it was getting windy out on the highway.

Back in Skärholmen

Afternoon became evening and Merjam took Besbussa for

a walk through Skärholmen. She had a lot on her mind and her thoughts became clearer when she walked with the grey donkey. The thing with Mustafa and the temperance society. She couldn't get it straight. Something was fishy with this Peter fellow, why hadn't he reported Mustafa to the police, if Mustafa had run off with the temperance society's money? 90 000 is many months' salary on "Keep Stockholm Clean". She decided to contact this fellow Peter again. After a two-hour walk she came home to the flat. Fatima was sitting in her room at the computer. Merjam knocked on the door.

"Fatima?"

"Yes mum?"

"You know Peter, from the temperance society. Do you know if he had any cell phone number?"

"No, but I might be able to fnd out. Mustafa told me that he had a funny surname, Strö-something... Strövare?"

"Good, can't be many people with that name. I can look it up in the phone book."

"That won't be necessary, mum!"

A couple of mouse clicks, and Fatima had Peter's number on eniro.se (the Swedish phone book on the Internet).

"Here it is! There's only one Peter Strövare, that must be him."

"Please write it down, Fatima."

"Are you going to call him, mum?"

"Yes, but don't worry, Fatima, he won't threaten our family any more."

"I trust you, mum."

Fatima wrote the number down on a piece of paper and gave it to Merjam, who walked out to the living room and lifted the receiver. She hesitated for a second, and then dialled the number. A couple of signals passed. Then she heard a scraping sound.

"Peter Strövare, who am I speaking to?"

"Hello, Peter Strövare, this is Merjam Babuba. I just wanted to tell you something."

"Yeah?"

"I expect visitors tomorrow. At one o'clock."

"OK."

"A couple of friends are coming over."

"OK. So?"

"It's a few journalist friends from Aftonbladet and Expressen. They are coming to my flat for a cup of coffee."

It became silent for a while.

"Hello? Still there, Peter? You're so silent. I just wanted to tell you that you are invited as well."

Peter didn't answer.

"Listen, Peter. I'm going to tell the truth to the journalists. My son had no ninety thousand for you, but it's wrong to terrorise us day after day. And I know you've been ripping off your fellow members in that wonderful temperance society of yours", Merjam said ironically.

"You can't do that. I'm going to sort this mess out, but please don't tell the press, OK? We can fix this."

"They know enough already and tomorrow I'll tell them the rest. Bye, Peter, good luck with the temperance society."

Merjam hung up and stared down at the floor with cold eyes.

"I'll strangle them, both of them", Merjam shouted.

"Who?" Fatima asked.

"Mustafa and Peter!"

"You have to forgive them, mum. Everybody can make a mistake. It doesn't matter if you're a politician, an Imam, a Swedish priest, rabbi, a worker in the local temperance society or Mr. Happy Hour."

"I wonder if Mr. Happy Hour had some sort of brain damage or if his development has stagnated. What are we going to do about this boy, Fatima?"

Fatima walked up to Merjam and gave her a hug.

"Give him our love, mum, that is what he needs. Love and warmth."

"I've given him love and warmth but it's like spitting in the sand, it doesn't help one bit! And we must teach this Peter chap a lesson, that's the least we can do."

"Why, mum? What are you going to do?"

"I'm going to find out what really happened here, why he gave all the money to Mustafa, without the temperance society's permission."

"Good luck, mum."

Expressen and Aftonbladet

An hour later Mustafa was standing inside a flower-shop on Regeringsgatan, not far from Café Opera. His cell phone rang. When he saw the name on the phone's display he hesitated for a moment. Should he answer? At last he pushed the green button on the phone.

"Hi, Peter."

"Do you have the dough?" Peter wondered.

"I received some money, yes."

"Some money? How much money do you have then?"

"Hey, Peter, I'm busy right now, can I see…"

"Listen, Mustafa. Your mother is completely mental! She called me and said she would nail me. And you. Apparently she's being visited by some 'journalists' from Expressen and Aftonbladet tomorrow at one o'clock. She's going to reveal everything to the media!"

Mustafa winced.

"Godammit!"

"You have to come up with the whole sum, the 90 000 kronor you got from me. Deposit them in the temperance society's account, then the media will have nothing on either of us."

"OK, Peter, here's what we'll do. We'll meet

tomorrow at twelve thirty outside the metro station in Skärholmen. I'll fix this, trust me."

"Of course I trust you, Mustafa, because you're so trustworthy, aren't you?" said Peter sarcastically.

"Of course. But you are going to have to trust me - what choice do you have?"

"OK, twelve thirty tomorrow. I really hope you're there with the money then."

"No problem!" Mustafa lied.

Mustafa ended the conversation, giving the red button a hard push. He snapped up a bouquet of expensive-looking flowers and walked up to the counter. He threw down two hundred crowns and left without waiting for change. He had never been economical, Mustafa.

When he came out of the flower shop the evening sun was glistening over Kungsträdgården, but the weather was the last thing on Mustafa's mind. Problem-clouds were hanging over him that not even the most beautiful evening sun could penetrate. He walked through Kungsträdgården, found an empty park bench and sat down. He dialled his home number with a deep sigh.

"Merjam Babuba!"

"Hi mum, it's me, Mustafa."

"Hi."

"I heard you've invited journalists from Aftonbladet and Expressen over tomorrow. Why?"

"Not only that, Janne Josefsson from 'Uppdrag Granskning' on SVT (a Swedish TV show where journalists scrutinise the potentates) is coming as well!"

Mustafa had never heard about Janne Josefsson.

"Josefsson who?"

"Josefsson who protects the ordinary people from all the evil crocodiles who lie in wait everywhere!"

"What are you bladdering about, mum? Josefsson, crocodiles... Why do you want to hurt your own son?"

"I just don't want a son who rips people off. Good bye, Mustafa."

She hung up the phone. Mustafa stared at the display with empty eyes. What was going on? Could his own mother really do this? And what did she mean with crocodiles? Had she finally lost her mind? His thoughts flew around. Maybe she had gone nuts, and, if so, why shouldn't she be able to do something like this to him? He thought for a while, then he called Fatima on her cell phone.

"Hi, Fatima, what are you up to?"

"Hi, Mustafa, I'm at Kafferepet, waiting for Claudia and Bibbi. What are you up to?"

"Nothing special. But hey, Fatima, I'm coming over to you soon, I'm close by. Are you going to be there for a while?"

"Yeah, I'll wait."

"OK, see you soon!"

Mustafa ran over to Kafferepet. It takes about ten minutes to walk from Kungsträdgården via Hamngatan and Sergels torg over to the fine old café, but Mustafa was there in four minutes. He spotted Fatima sitting at a table at the far end of the café's outdoor area.

"Hi, Mustafa! You came here fast! Are the flowers for me?"

Mustafa looked at the bouquet.

"Erm, no, but you're going to get some later."

Fatima smiled.

"I'll look forward to that day. Have a seat."

Mustafa stared first at Fatima, then at the chairs around the table. He took a seat after a few seconds of staring.

"What's the matter, Mustafa? You seem so... stary."

"You are quite right I am. Mum is going to sell me out to the Swedish press like some piece of meat! Aftonbladet, Expressen, and she went on bladdering about some Josefsson who's going to save us from the crocodiles! I've said it before, like 'mum's going mental', but then I was only joking. But now she's really crazy."

Fatima and her mum were best friends and they backed each other up. Fatima kept quiet to Mustafa about Merjam's plan.

"So you said."

"Yeah, so I said! She should be locked up, that's what I'm saying! Don't you realise what this means? Imagine if the papers wrote that a Tunisian, and a Muslim at that, has ripped off a temperance society and wasted all their money on Stureplan! What a scandal!"

Fatima looked up at the sky dreamingly and aimed with her hand as if she was going to set a headline on the clouds.

"Yes, I understand. This Tunisian is known as 'Mr Happy Hour' at the Stureplan hot spots."

She looked at Mustafa, satisfied.

"Don't say that, Fatima! You're supposed to back me up here!"

"Sorry, Mustafa. To be honest, I don't know what to say. It might be just as bad as you portray it, or worse."

"Why is mum doing this to me? Why? The press will write about this for years."

"Do you think so?"

"Of course they will. This is the best idea for a script that Hollywood has ever seen! A Muslim rips off a temperance society and drinks up the money. The CIA boss is going to quit his job to write the script, and Netanyahu and his party will produce the movie. You know, there are two things that sell these days: SEX AND ISLAM."

"No, Mustafa, you're exaggerating."

"It's true. And the problem is, I'll never be able to go back to Tunisia."

"Perhaps you can make mum change her mind?"

"How am I going to do that? She's off to crocodile

country! And by the way, she's stubborn as an old donkey."

Fatima's mate Claudia showed up.

"Oh hi, Mustafa!" she said. "So you're here!"

She spotted the bouquet in Mustafa's hand.

"Hey, Mustafa! Who's the lucky lady?" she wondered.

"Oh, it's for no one special. Well, I have to go. Nice seeing you, Claudia. See you at home, Fatima."

Mustafa set off in the direction of Sergels torg.

"My, he ran away quickly", said Claudia. "Have I done something?"

"No, Claudia", said Fatima. "You haven't done anything. Mustafa has problems. Big problems."

Refuge in Café Opera

Mustafa raced on. He passed Sergels torg and the House of Culture, continued down Hamngatan and turned right at Kungsträdgården. A visit to Café Opera seemed to be the only reasonable thing to do now. A drink and Diana's comforting words by the bar would be his medicine for his rising temperature. It was for her that he had bought the flowers in the first place. He politely said 'Hi' to the bouncer and was let in. Inside he walked straight to the bar. He spotted Diana mixing a drink with her back against the bar counter. He put the flower bouquet behind his back and sneaked up to the bar. Diana turned around and looked at him.

"Hi, Mustafa! Why didn't you come last Friday? You were going to have a party here! My friends were waiting for you".

"Sorry, Diana, but something came up. But it was bad of me to announce a party and not show up."

"Yeah, that's not the Mustafa I know. What happened – were you ill or something?"

Mustafa smiled.

"It's a sad story, I'll tell it to you some time. Listen Diana, I came here to pay for the limo. How much is it?"

"They've told me they charge four thousand for such a trip."

"Wait."

Mustafa stretched his hand down his pocket and twisted his body just enough to expose to Diana the flowers behind his back.

"Oh, what am I glimpsing behind your back, Mustafa?"

"Damn, I was supposed to give you the cash first and THEN the flowers. As a bonus, you know. Well, well. For you, my dear."

He gave her the bouquet.

"Oh, Mustafa! How sweet, thank you!"

Diana blushed. A somewhat tipsy man next to Mustafa in the bar started applauding.

"You were so nice and set us up with a limo, and I felt I had to cheer you up with some flowers. I've heard that girls like flowers", Mustafa said.

"You know exactly how women work, Mustafa", said Diana and twinkled her eye.

"So they say."

And what does the charmer like to drink?"

"A bottle of red would be nice."

"Oh, a bottle of red, how romantic."

"Get lost, Diana."

Mustafa stayed at Café Opera the rest of the night.

The Red Cross in Skärkolmen

At twelve o'clock the following day the door bell rang at Babuba's in Skärholmen. It was representatives from the Red Cross: Lars, Linda and Janne. They had come to collect money from a fund raising. Both Merjam and

Elisabeth knew them from before, since "Help Africa" and the Red Cross had been working together. Merjam led them into the living room and asked them to sit down around the big table, where Elisabeth was counting the money.

The banknotes were lying on the table. On the floor around the table there were six buckets filled with half-crowns, crowns, five-crown and ten-crown coins.

"Hi, Elisabeth!" said the representatives from the Red Cross.

"Hi!" Elisabeth replied.

"I have to say that I think it's simply amazing that a small organisation, consisting of you, Merjam, Bibbi and Linnéa, can raise so much money. You really are clever", Linda said.

The two other Red Cross representatives nodded and said hello to Elisabeth's dog, Timo, a proud male Alsatian which she had brought with her.

Merjam went into in the kitchen and came back with freshly brewed coffee.

"OK, let's get started", she said.

"With what", said Lars. "The aid or Mustafa?"

"I've finished talking about Mustafa and his affairs", Merjam said. "If someone has something to add, do it now, otherwise I suggest we move on to the aid part."

"Are you sure he's coming then?" asked Linda.

"Believe me, he'll be here at 2, but I'm not sure his friend from the temperance society will show up. Well, let's move on to the aid issue."

Merjam turned to Elisabeth.

"Could you please tell them a little about our fund raising first."

"We've collected over 900 000 kronor, but we're not clear about how much it is exactly, so we better go on counting."

Merjam poured out the first bucket onto the table,

and they started counting.

At twenty-five minutes past twelve a nervous Peter stood outside Skärholmen underground station. He looked towards the ticket gates wondering if Mustafa was going to show up at all. Suddenly he saw Mustafa walking through the ticket barrier.
"Hi, Mustafa!"
"Hi, Peter!"
They walked through Skärholmen shopping centre and found a secluded spot. Peter stopped.
"OK, do you have the cash?"
Mustafa nodded.
"Great! Then we can breathe easily, both you and I. Give it to me and all of this will be history."
"But I only have 30 000", said Mustafa in a regretful voice.
Peter exploded.
"What??? You promised us at least ninety thousand! What the hell am I going to tell the press? Where's the rest of the money? I'm worried about this. It could be a big scandal"
"OK, calm down. I'm in the shit as well, even more than you, as a matter of fact."
"That's impossible, I've got shit running out my ears!"
"Stop whining, Peter. If we continue fighting we'll both be in Aftonbladet and Expressen tomorrow. I have a brilliant idea that might just save both of us."
Peter sighed. "OK, let's hear it."

Beef Wellington à la Jacques Chirac spiced with ex-foreign minister de Villepin

One of Mustafa's favourite characters to imitate was Jacques Chirac. Mustafa had picked up all of the French president's manners: his voice, his gestures, his presence. Mustafa's eyes glowed as he presented his plan to Peter.

"We have to act smart, like Jacques Chirac", he said.
"I don't know what you're talking about", said Peter.
"OK, you know who Jacques Chirac is, right?"
"Yeah. But he's not my favourite Frenchman."
"Who's that, then?"
"There are two: Zidane and de Villepin, the French foreign minister."
"Zidane", Mustafa said, "is intelligent when it comes to football, and de Villepin is as intelligent, gifted, wise and tricky as Chirac. But Chirac has special attributes that make him a snake in politics. He's a master. Do you follow?"

Peter interrupted.
"Just tell me your plan, Mustafa!"
"You have to be a real snake like Chirac. Just chew up Aftonbladet and Expressen!"
"But how?"
"Make mum feel ashamed in front of Aftonbladet and Expressen."
"She must be a crazy, your mum, to sell her own son to the tabloids."

Mustafa told Peter about his plan while walking around Skärholmen centre. When he was finished telling about the plan Peter stopped.
"OK Mustafa, that's a deal!"
Mustafa smiled, content.
"That's my boy, Peter!"
They took their "Beef Wellington" under their arms and carried it up to the Babuba residence, where Merjam was waiting for them. She had just finished preparing her "Beef Wellington à la Aftonbladet and Expressen, spiced up with Janne Josefsson from Swedish television."

Mustafa was nervous. He and Peter went to the stable to

get Besbussa. But Besbussa wasn't there.

Merjam and the others hadn't finished counting the money when they heard the entrance door open. They nodded in concert. The show was about to begin.

Peter and Mustafa came into the living room, and everyone, except Elisabeth, stopped counting money. Instead they looked at the two with inquiring eyes.

"Good afternoon, everyone", Peter and Mustafa said.

"Good afternoon", the others said politely.

"This is my son Mustafa and his friend Peter", Merjam said and turned to the boys. "I told you to be here at two o'clock!"

"Yeah, I know, mum, but you can smell your delicious food all the way from Skärholmen shopping centre!"

"Really?"

"Yeah. Where's Besbussa?" Mustafa wondered.

"Besbussa has been traded for Timo! Me and Elisabeth decided to do 'the switch'. She got Besbussa and I got Timo."

Mustafa looked at the gasping dog, roaming about in the living room. He couldn't believe it was true.

"What? Why did you do that?"

"I'll explain later. But Mustafa, I didn't know that you had become a religious abstainer, when did you become that?"

He looked at Merjam and didn't know what to say.

"Ah!"

Merjam turned to Peter.

"Glad that you came, Peter! Are you going to admit to the press that you and Mustafa ripped the money off the temperance society?"

"We haven't ripped anyone off. We want to say that we appreciate your work for the starving children and take the opportunity to make a contribution. The temperance society wants to give an additional 30 000 kronor to the Red Cross."

He gave Merjam the envelope with the money. She looked back surprised at him. She wanted to say something but couldn't get a word out of her mouth. Instead, Mustafa took over.

"Dear mum, this means we've invested 90 000 kronor, plus these 30 000. Our members think it's better to give the money to people in need than to build a glamorous meeting place for the temperance society. The one we have now is good enough."

By now Merjam had understood that this was a "Beef Wellington à la Mustafa".

"You're not stupid, Mustafa. But I haven't received any 90 000 from you, dear son."

Mustafa knew that Imam Jibril had taken the 90 000 that was intended for the temperance society and invested it in a membership at "Stockholm Je t'aime." He looked with a frown at Merjam.

"But you know where those came from", he said and pointed at the money Elisabeth was counting on the living room table.

"You should thank me for all these thousands of crowns. If I hadn't been out learning 'THE MEANING OF LIFE' at the Stureplan clubs, you'd be washing and ironing until your arms were hurting. You would have made a couple of thousand crowns, at most. But thanks to me, you've collected massive sums of money. It's I who started all this."

"You're just imagining. Mustafa."

"Let me explain, mum, your son has fought hard for this money", said Mustafa. "I met two students from Qatar at the night club "Sturecompagniet" and they gave me some ideas and helped me with this."

"Wait a minute. You said that you had an Iraqi friend

here in Sweden who had helped you. Make up your mind, Mustafa, how's it going to be?"

"Yes, he has helped me! But it's not just like pushing a button from Sweden, and then everything works fluently down in Qatar. These students recommended me, they've walked around the mosques in Qatar and told people about the temperance society's project in Stockholm, in this way people know about us now, and they've donated money."

"But how could they recommend you?"

"Because I helped them! I dragged them around Stockholm in a wheelbarrow. Ruined my back and arms."

"Get out, Mustafa! If your back hurts it's because you've carried too many bottles of wine from Systembolaget (the Swedish alcohol monopoly)!"

"I wish it were! But seriously mum, one of the guys is lying on the ground outside the restaurant! No taxi wants to pick him up. And my delivery bike has got a flat tire so I had to borrow a wheelbarrow from the restaurant."

"To take him to the hotel or to the hospital?"

"No, he was looking for a girl."

"He was looking for a girl?" Merjam looked sceptically at Mustafa.

"He was dancing with her at Sturecompagniet and after that the race was on. But unfortunately she disappeared. He won't leave the country until he's found her!"

Merjam shook her head.

"What was so special about her?"

Mustafa continued.

"She looked like Anita Ekberg in 'La Dolce Vita'! She wore a tunic made of camel hair, and two big humps under it (in Arab countries, and in the Babuba family, the word "breasts" is taboo). Anyway, he danced with her, and then she just disappeared with his wallet! So I took him for a ride around Stockholm, looking for that girl, and he kept screaming 'I want to ride a camel' over and over again. We met a police officer and I asked him if he'd seen the camel lady. He bent down and looked straight into my friend's eyes. Then he said 'Turn to the right and then go straight ahead, I think I saw her at Slussen'. So we went there, of course. When we came to Slussen we met a new cop, and we asked him about the camel lady. He looked him straight in the eyes. 'Turn right and then go straight ahead to Mariatorget' he said. We followed his advice, and all of a sudden we were at the Maria clinic (a clinic for alcohol and drug abusers)!"

"Didn't you understand that the poor guy was drugged?" asked Merjam.

"I wish I did, but it led me to another insight. Now I understand why the Swedish police don't use batons, they use iris diagnostics to solve problems. I wish police forces all across the globe could learn from the Swedes, and use this iris diagnostics instead of waving their batons around all the time."

"Fantastic, Mustafa, you're so thoughtful", said Elisabeth.

"Mustafa, don't try and mislead me", Merjam said. "Go on with your story!"

"OK", said Mustafa. "The poor guy had no money and no ID. And then I understood. You see, I happened to dance with the camel lady's friend, a very cuddly girl, perhaps a little bit too cuddly. She tried to get near all the time, and now I can see why. I had my wallet in my chest pocket, and I think she wanted to be cuddly with my wallet rather than with me!"

Merjam looked straight into Mustafa's eyes.

"So you went out with a hoaxer?"

Mustafa nodded. Merjam went on.

"A hoaxer became hoaxed! Hahahaha, you're all the same over at Stureplan, scams everywhere you look!"

"It's not funny, mum. And by the way, the story's not finished there, it became worse! When I stood there at

Mariatorget, the other Qatar guy called me up from Grand Hotel. He couldn't sleep, he was devastated."

"Why couldn't he sleep?" Merjam asked.

"The girl that he had found at Sturecompagniet had left his hotel, leaving him all alone."

"Poor little guy", Merjam said with irony in her voice.

"Actually I felt sorry for him, he really couldn't sleep. So I left off the first guy at the Maria clinic and went straight to the hotel. When I got there, I told him that the best cure for sleeping problems is a morning walk, just as the sun rises. I mean, there's nothing better in this world than Stockholm on a summer morning. So I took him for a ride in the wheel-barrow, we went around half the city.

"Was he also drugged?" Merjam asked.

"He was devastated, he had followed my pick-up advice, but it went straight to hell anyway, that big trauma had left him sleepless."

"Hold on here, Mustafa. I'm curious, what pick-up tricks do guys use nowadays?" Elisabeth asked.

"Yeah, I gave him some advice about how to pick up a girl."

"Oh, really?"

"Yeah. Just some advice from the coach, you know."

Elisabeth shook her head again.

"I explained to him about the famous 'three-step tactic à la Mustafa'. 1 Treat mademoiselle with a filet mignon with a nice dessert. 2 This is a very important one. After you've eaten, treat her with champagne in the bar at Grand Hotel. 3 Take your lady by the hand and take the elevator up to the hotel room."

"I see. And he took your advice gladly, I suppose."

"Yeah! He succeeded with every step, but then something went wrong. They came up to his hotel room, and the guy was just going to pick up his Arabic slippers. But he couldn't find them! He really looked everywhere, he was even down to the reception and asked for help, but no one could find them, they were just gone! He searched for them for a good while, and eventually, the girl was gone! She couldn't wait any longer. Poor guy, that really got the best of him."

"Of course she left", said Elisabeth. "A guy that prioritizes a pair of Arabic slippers in favour of a Scandinavian girl, that's not much to cling on to."

"That's just your opinion, Elisabeth. Anyway, I had to drag him around in the wheelbarrow for quite some time until he fell asleep like a little baby! And these guys from Qatar have promised me to support my fund raising. Without them, no money would have been gathered."

"Listen, Merjam", said Peter, "your son had fought hard to bring in all this money. Someone in the Swedish tourist business should hire him! Sightseeing in a wheelbarrow, I mean, that's just unique!"

"Mustafa shouldn't work in the tourist business, he should be a PR officer instead! He could defend any hoaxer!"

"You think so?"

"I'm sure. But the thing is, my son has a weakness."

Mustafa looked at Merjam, clearly irritated.

"Tell me then, mum, what weakness are you referring to?"

"You tell lies by the dozen! And THAT is a weakness!"

"Really!"

"I don't believe a word of that story."

There are no crocodiles in Sweden

"What's the matter, mum? You're accusing me of lying! You're trying to stifle your own son, hang him out in the tabloids, trade our favourite donkey for a dog... what's going on, mum?"

Mustafa put his hand to his forehead.

"I traded Besbussa for a shepherd dog because we need a good friend that can protect us from the crocodiles."

"What's all this crocodile talk? I'm really getting scared now, mum, have you lost your mind completely? There are no crocodiles in Sweden!"

"No? I'll tell you this: here in Europe, or in America, you'll find the worst kind of crocodiles! Crocodiles ready to eat us all!"

Mustafa knocked on his head with a finger to demonstrate how screwed up he thought his mum was.

"OK. Let's say these horrible crocodiles attack our family. What will this dog do? Slap the crocodiles with his tail?"

He looked at the dog, which scratched the floor with his paws and barked at him.

"No. Listen here, Mustafa, A female crocodile lays up to 60 eggs at a time. The dog will eat 55 of them."

Merjam looked around in the room. The Red Cross representatives wrote frenetically in their notepads, just like journalists about to stumble across a major scoop.

"It means, you fool", Merjam continued, "that without media the world would be full of crocodiles like you."

"I'm no crocodile", said Mustafa.

"You are, in fact. That's exactly what you are! We're lucky to have the media, to scrutinise the world's crocodiles. If they hadn't done that we'd be in big trouble."

"OK, mum. Just one question. Why do the dogs only eat 55 eggs and not all 60?"

"Because a small percentage of hoaxers, and I'm talking about all kinds of categories, I'm talking about politicians, businessmen, mafia bosses, Wall Street swindlers… this little percentage gets away with it, they escape the dog, and you know why? Because they're experts on 'Beef Wellington à la Mustafa'. Just like you! THAT's the NEW POLITICS! Do you understand now?"

Mustafa felt as if he's been punched in the face. He didn't answer. Merjam turned to Peter.
"Peter, can I speak to you for a while?"
"Sure, but no crocodiles, OK?"
Merjam didn't like Peter's little joke.
"Follow me, we'll handle this in Fatima's room."
They walked into Fatima's room and Merjam closed the door behind them. She looked Peter straight into the eyes.
"How could you give Mustafa 90 000 without speaking to the rest of the temperance society? I mean, how did he manage to persuade you?"
"Mustafa is unbeatable in his own way. He's like a mixture of Chirac and Letterman. He can convince people, and he does it in quite an entertaining way. He seduces you, sort of. I was seduced. I believed him."
"I've heard this one before, sadly enough. Go on…"
Peter scratched his right foot nervously against the parquet floor.
"OK, I'll give you the truth. I had this idea. You know, Merjam, summer's a hard time for many people: alcoholics, young kids with nowhere to go, lonely people… When your son told me how much money we could get from the mosques, I thought that I could deposit 90 000 and have some fun with the rest of the money. Then a new idea took shape in my head. I wanted to take the 40 members of the temperance society on a boat trip to the Norwegian coast, I've actually worked at sea before. I have a mate who had a big boat on the west coast, and I thought about renting it for the money we were about to receive, you know, just let it float up the Norwegian coastline for a month. Such a trip costs at least 100 000, but with the money from Qatar we might be able to afford it, at least

that's what I thought. Mustafa made me believe that. I would afford the boat trip and I would be able to put 90 000 back into the temperance society .That was my plan."

"You have a warm heart, Peter."

"It's the least I can do. I know well how it is to be lonely in Stockholm during summer time. I'm a recovering alcoholic."

Merjam gave him a warm look.

"You're good, I love volunteers."

"Some people nowadays just become more and more egotistical."

"I know, but there's hope and you're part of it! I'm sorry for all that's happened. Here's your money, Peter."

Merjam gave him two envelopes, one with 150 000 crowns in it, and the other with 30 000 in it. Peter opened the envelopes and saw the money.

"Wow. Merjam, this is fantastic, but I have to ask you… where does this money come from?"

"Doesn't matter. And by the way, you don't need to worry about making headlines in Aftonbladet or Expressen. Thanks for all your help."

Thank you, Merjam, thank you so much. I never thought we'd get the money back and more so!"

"Sometimes you're lucky", Merjam said and hugged Peter.

"Absolutely."

"Throw a proper party on the boat for those 150 000, and give the rest to the temperance society."

Peter smiled.

"That's what I'm going to do! And you're invited to the party, Merjam."

"Thanks, but I don't think I have time for that. Hey, Peter?"

"Yeah?"

"Only non-alcoholic beverages at the party, OK?"

Peter smiled.

"Of course. Bye, Merjam!"

Peter turned around, walked out of Fatima's room and left the flat.

Merjam walked out to the kitchen. "What do you say, Elisabeth?" she shouted. "Do you want green or red tea?"

"I'll have green", Elisabeth shouted back.

"Janne, can you come over here and choose a brand of tea, we have lots of different brands."

"Sure", Janne said and walked out to the kitchen.

"It's time now", Merjam whispers to him.

Janne headed back to the living room, while Merjam stayed in the kitchen and made tea and coffee. A nervous Mustafa, who was convinced that Janne, Lars and Linda really were journalists from SVT, Aftonbladet and Expressen, tried desperately to re-establish himself after being elegantly outplayed by Merjam.

"Please, dear journalists, listen to me. I'm not a crocodile, not even the kind of crocodile that the media is after. I'll tell you again, so you have time to write it down. I've opened this fund in Qatar, we have put in 70 000 and used 20 000 for advertising. Thanks to the fund raising, mum had received all this money. I know you want to write the truth, so write the truth!"

Janne looked at Lars who nodded to him in approval.

"OK, Mustafa", Lars began, "we're no journalists, we come from the Red Cross. I don't know what's going on here, but I promise you, we won't write anything about you in Aftonbladet or Expressen."

"WHAT?"

Mustafa fell into pieces, down to the floor. Lying in his back he held his hands in front of his face and kicked wildly with his legs, just like he did when he was a little kid.

"My 30 000! My 30 000! Damn it! Mum fooled me! I could have had so much fun at Stureplan for that money, with Diana, Eva, Sara, Mona, Victoria and all the other cute blondes!"

Force and counterforce

Merjam came out to the living room, happy and content. She spotted Mustafa lying on the floor, walked up to him and put a foot on his stomach.

"Ouch, ouch, ouch", said Mustafa. "It hurts!"

"In physics they say that for every force there's an opposing force", Merjam said. "And for every 'Beef Wellington' there's a 'counter-Beef Wellington'!"

"I'm an illiterate, I don't understand physics!"

Merjam pushed with her foot on Mustafa's stomach.

"So you don't understand physics? What about politics?"

"That I understand! Politics is comedy and comedy is politics!"

"Good, Mustafa! Then learn this: for every Bush in North America, there's a Chirac and a de Villepin in France, a Schröder and a Joschka Fischer in Germany. And a Chavez in South America. You understand? Idiot! Idiot!"

"Now I get it, mum! When you said Bush, Chirac Chavez and Schröder , I understood, because they're my mates. They're the true comedians!"

"How can you say that?" Elisabeth said.

"Sure, in lack of real comedians the politicians are our comedians!"

"Oh, is that so?"

"Politicians and comedians are the same, they want to be loved."

The atmosphere eased in the room and everyone laughed. The Red Cross people applauded, the show seemed to be over. Merjam lifted her foot from Mustafa's stomach and he rose.

"30 000 kronor" he mumbled and walked over to the vestibule. "I lost 30 000."

A couple of seconds passed. Then the entrance door closed with a slam. Merjam turned to Elisabeth and the Red Cross people.

"Thank you all for being in for this", she said.

"If it's for a good cause, I can play journalist seven days a week", said Lars.

"You were good too, really good". Elisabeth laughed and then looked at Janne and Linda. "And you too."

"It wasn't that hard, just sitting there looking shocked", said Janne.

"Well, at least you're good at that" Linda said.

Merjam looked doubtful.

"I have to put my foot down sometimes. Teach him. I get so mad at him when he does this."

"He'll survive, Merjam. You taught him a lesson", said Elisabeth and turned to the Red Cross people.

"Believe me, I know Mustafa, he'll come out of this alive."

"Well, maybe we should take care of the finances now", Merjam said.

They continued to count the money. When they had finished they were up to one million one hundred and thirty thousand crowns altogether. The Red Cross people said goodbye and left.

Merjam and Elisabeth looked at each other for a moment, then they hugged.

"What a story. This will be a tale to tell the grandchildren", Elisabeth chuckled.

"I don't know about that, at least we shouldn't tell Mustafa's kids, if he has any", Merjam said.

"Did you know what your father did when he was young?" Elisabeth began. "He stole 90 000 from a temperance society and boozed it all up at Stureplan…No, you're probably right. We have to spare them that."

Elisabeth turned to the dog.

"It looks as if Timo wants to go home and I'm sure

that Besbussa wants to go home too".

The story of Bibbi and friendship between cultures

The evening after was Sunday evening. Our four heroines met at Babubas' to celebrate the money that they collected for "Help Africa." They had all played leading roles in the story: Merjam and Elisabeth had got the Imam to become a member of "Stockholm Je t'aime" and Linnéa had seduced him so that Bibbi could "arrest" him on Kungsgatan and force him to leave the country. Merjam had with some help from Elisabeth taught her hoaxer of a son a lesson he wouldn't forget.

Merjam had cooked a big dinner, and they sat down at the living room table. They discussed and discussed, about all that had that's happened, about the crazy Imam, about Mustafa's shamelessness, about strategies for "Help Africa" in the future. They were getting closer together. Merjam and Bibbi were more or less related, and through Bibbi, Merjam had got to know Elisabeth. But Linnéa was new in the crew and the curiosity that usually appears when you meet new people was still there. Bibbi and Linnéa had just met a couple of times the last few days, during their little coup against the Imam.

"Cheers, girls!" Linnéa shouted.
"To us!"
"To 'Stockholm Je t'aime'!"
"To Imam Jibril's money!"
They continued to eat, drink and discuss.
"I have to ask you one thing", said Linnéa. "How did you two get to know each other? Excuse me for asking, but I'm just so curious, a Swedish policewoman and a Tunisian superwoman, I mean, such friendships are rare."

"I see what you mean", Merjam said calmly. "It's a long story."

"Yeah", said Bibbi, "as the kids say, we go way

back!"

"I've known Bibbi since she was this tall", Merjam said and held her hand about one meter above the floor.

"Oh, how interesting", said Linnéa. "How come?"

Merjam cleared her throat.

"OK, this is how it happened: when Bibbi came to the island of Djerba in Tunisia for the first time she was ten years old. She was there on holiday with her mum Jeanette. They stayed at Abounawas Golf Hotel, where I used to work as a room cleaner. I was 33 years old then. The first time I saw her was when I was on my way to the storage room to change some towels. I passed the reception and there was Bibbi. She sat on a chair with her mum next to her. Bibbi was incredibly cute. To me she was a goddess, I had never seen anything like it. She had blonde hair, big blue eyes deep as the sea, you could drown in them. She looked like she does now, just smaller."

Bibbi gave Merjam a tender look. She knew Merjam loved her more than anything, that she was like a second daughter to her.

"I couldn't help but stay there for a while and talk to her, in my bad English. I managed to say 'Oh, you are beautiful'! I remember she let me touch her long hair. It went all the way down to her bottom. Then I remember asking her 'Where do you come from'? 'From Sweden', she answered. I asked which room they had at the hotel, and Jeanette said 'Room 16'. I laughed and said 'That's on my floor'! We shook hands. Then I couldn't help but ask Jeanette one thing, and I remember exactly what I said. 'How do Swedish, Finnish, Danish, Norwegian and Icelandic women do it when they make babies? Do you have a tiny little surgeon in your stomachs fixing the nose, the mouth, the eyelashes.... your kids are so cute'."

Bibbi was filling in the words at the end of the sentence, she had heard the story before and knew it by heart. Everyone laughed.

"I remember that day very well", she continued. "That moment has stuck with me."

"It has stuck with me too", Merjam said. "I remember how everyone smiled after I said that thing about the tiny surgeon in the stomach. After that, not much more was said, since I had to continue working, I couldn't stand and talk to hotel guests for long, I could get fired if I did. I walked up to the second floor and started to clean the hotel rooms. As I was cleaning a room I saw my son Mustafa through the window. He was nine years old back then. He worked on the beach, selling jasmine flowers to tourists. I called for him, asked if he had any jasmine flowers in his bag. He had, and he came up to me and gave me some. I brought the flowers to room 16. Then I put the jasmine under the sheet on the bed and wrote in big letters: 'WELCOME B.B', that is Bibbi, which is pronounced Bebé in French, and also it was the initials of another beautiful lady, Brigitte Bardot. When I had finished I covered the bed with the sheets and sneaked out of the room."

Bibbi nodded.

"Do you remember the smell in the room when you got back, Bibbi?"

"Yeah, I remember it so well. That moment I'll never forget."

"You see, thing was that when I and mum came back to the room it smelled as if the bed was placed in a herbarium! Of course we had no idea where the smell came from, but I remember that room service knocked on the door, they where re-filling the minibar with liquids. Mum asked the room service boy 'Where does the jasmine smell come from?' The room service boy started walking around the room, sniffing. At last, he lifted the sheets, and there it was, Merjam's message to me, written in jasmine."

This part of the story was a very sentimental one for Bibbi. "Didn't you ask who had sent this jasmine message?" Elisabeth asked.

"Of course", Bibbi said, "so we they asked the room service boy. He said that the only one who could have done it was Omi Merjam. She was responsible for cleaning the rooms on that floor. My mum Jeanette asked him 'Is her name Merjam or Omi Merjam'? The boy said 'there are two Merjam at the hotel. One is tall and thin and one is short and chubby. We call the second one Omi Merjam, it means Mother Merjam in Arabic. We call her that because she's warm and good-hearted, helps and supports. She has a lot of humour and she loves to make people happy'."

Linnéa and Elisabeth smiled. Bibbi went on:

"My mum and I were of course touched by the gesture with the jasmine flowers, so we asked the boy where Omi Merjam was. 'She's finished work for today', he said. My mum asked him where Merjam lived. Apparently she lived in a house in the countryside, but he didn't know exactly where the house was situated."

Elisabeth and Linnéa listened with interest.

"I became really curious when he said that, I remember that I really begged her to go down to the reception and ask where Merjam lived, so that we could go there and thank her for the 'jasmine gesture'. Mum gave in after a while, to be honest I think that she was a bit curious too. At the reception they said that Omi Merjam lived far away. There were two buses going there, but both stopped almost a kilometre from her house. It all seemed really difficult, and we were told to look for her the day after instead, she was going to start work at six in the morning…"

Merjam shook her head.

"The working hours, the conditions", she said in a lamenting voice.

"You must think that working at Stockholm University is like a walk in the park", said Linnéa.

"Oh yeah", Merjam chuckled, "it's a different

world."

"Go on, Bibbi", said Linnéa, "I want to hear more!"

"OK, where were we… yeah, we were standing in the reception. Then suddenly a little boy my age showed up. He was dressed in Arab clothes and sold jasmine flowers. I didn't know then that it was Mustafa, but I remember that I thought he was cute, so I smiled at him. 'Here's Omi Merjam's son', said the receptionist. 'He's selling jasmine flowers down on the beach'"

"You were starting to sense where the jasmines on the bed came from then, right", said Elisabeth.. "Yeah" said Bibbi. "I thought we could follow the boy, Mustafa that is, home to his house, because surely he lived with his mum. I begged my mum a little bit more, and she gave in."

Merjam took over.

"It all ends with Hotel Abounawas arranging a car and Bibbi, Jeanette and Mustafa being driven out to my house in the country."

Bibbi took the storyteller's role back.

"Mustafa didn't stop selling jasmine until nine o'clock in the evening, it was quite dark when he left, it must've been around nine o'clock. I remember that it was dark but still really hot outside."

Bibbi took a sip of Coca-Cola and gestured to Merjam to take over.

"I sat with Fatima and Ali under the olive tree where the breeze came in from the ocean, we drank tea and ate watermelon. I told my kids about the Swedish girl at the hotel, who was of the same age as they were and had this strange name, but I called her B.B after my favourite actress Brigitte Bardot. And I told them about how beautiful I thought this B.B was, gorgeous as a goddess. Fatima of course became really interested. She said to me 'I want to meet this girl, mum'! And just a second later a car came rolling up to our house. Then Mustafa came running. He cried 'Mum, mum, you have visitors from

Sweden'! I thought that it must be them, I became so glad I just cried out RRA, RRA, RRA."

Elisabeth and Linnéa looked at each other and smiled. Bibbi continued.

"I have to take over from here, Merjam, I just have to tell about how I felt then, because I remember it so well. The white-painted house, with all these olive trees around it, and that strange sound, we wondered where it came from. Mustafa had run off ahead of us, but he told us to stay there and wait. There were all these olive trees in front of the house, so we couldn't see what was behind them. And then that sound again, 'RRA, RRA...' I thought it sounded like Indians, but mum told me there were no Indians in Tunisia. Then Mustafa came back and took us down through the olive trees. After about ten metres I saw Omi Merjam."

Merjam went on.

"I guess it must've been a little scary for you, late in the evening and then that sound, 'RRA, RRA'...."

"Yeah, but then when I saw you I wasn't afraid anymore."

"We gave our guests watermelon and green mint tea, then we sat there under the olive trees and looked out on the Mediterranean, the moon lit up the water in such a beautiful way. I could speak a little English, so that we could understand each other. The kids didn't speak English then, so they and Bibbi could only communicate by sign language. Mustafa played the clown and tried to communicate as best he could, while Ali just sat looking at Bibbi and Annette. We let Bibbi take a ride on Besbussa, who was young then..."

"Yeah, I remember I thought it was wonderful, since then I've always loved that donkey."

They all looked at Besbussa, who had fallen asleep on the floor.

"Yeah, you really liked it. And then your mother

Jeanette wanted to bathe under the full moon, because it was so hot outside. I said 'Sure, we can arrange that', so I brought swimsuits and four towels. Ali and Mustafa remained while we girls went down to the beach. It was lukewarm in the water, lovely."

"Yeah, to me it was magical, I had never experienced anything like it. The sand was so soft, it was like walking on icing sugar. The moon stood high and we bathed and had a good time."

Merjam interrupted Bibbi.

"Good time, good time, to bathe in the sea the Scandinavian way."

Bibbi laughed.

"My mum had borrowed Merjam's large swimsuit and as soon as she got into the water she took it off and hung it around her neck. Merjam was very surprised when she saw my mum bathe naked. And I did the same, it was wonderful! I had never thought that I would experience this. We had left a rainy Stockholm that morning and a couple of hours later we were taking this fantastic night swim. When we had finished bathing we went back to the house and Merjam treated us with Tunisian salad, salad mechouia (grilled salad) with French baguettes. After that night, I didn't want to go back to the hotel, so mum let me stay at the Babuba's for the rest of the vacation. I slept on a small mattress on the floor, with Besbussa's back as a pillow. For two weeks. It was fantastic, but the strongest memory for me is this first day and night in Tunisia, when I got to meet Mother Merjam and her family, I'll never forget that."

It became quiet around the table. Elisabeth and Linnéa looked at each other. They had been sitting like spectators at a game of ping pong, watching Merjam and Bibbi throw the story to each other over the table. And what a story!

"Unbelievable" Linnéa said at last. "You're like

twins, one continued where the other stops. Were you sisters in a past life?"

"We must've been", said Bibbi. "And in this life too!"

"I thought you were my daughter!" Merjam exclaimed.

"That too", said Bibbi.

"Continue, tell us more about Tunisia", said Elisabeth with excitement in her voice.

"You go on, sis, I have to go to the toilet", said Bibbi and winked to Merjam.

"It was such a sad day when Bibbi and Jeanette left", Merjam said. "I can still recall it, it's like a photograph that's stuck in my brain. Bibbi and Fatima standing there holding each other's hands in the hotel reception, two little girls from two sides of the planet, they were so sad, but I thought it was beautiful in a way. The airport bus arrived. I gave them some presents, one for Bibbi and one for Jeanette, it's a tradition among us Tunisians. I know that Mustafa and Ali were sad too, but didn't show it like the girls, boys are like that. Mustafa handed over a cooler filled with Jeanette and Bibbi's new favourite salad, mechouia, and chaplets with jasmine flowers. Jeanette was moved to tears when she looked down in the cooler. Ali handed over a birthday present to Bibbi from the Babuba family, she was going to be eleven the day after they came home, the 11th of August."

"What was the present?" Linnéa wondered.

At that moment Bibbi came back from the bathroom. Merjam looked at her.

"Bibbi can tell you."

"Tell what?"

"I'm telling them about the day when you were going home."

"Oh, it was so sad, but yet beautiful in a way."

"Do you remember the water thing?"

Bibbi laughed.

"How could I forget?"

Linnéa and Elisabeth looked at each other, puzzled.

"What 'water thing'? Keep telling your story instead of sitting and giggling as if you had a mutual secret", said Linnéa.

"OK. The time had come when Bibbi and Jeanette had to get on the bus. We said good bye, many tears were shed, and there were many hugs. The bus driver was almost angry with us. Of course he had to drive the bus according to schedule. Bibbi and Jeanette stepped on the bus, and walked all the way to the back of the bus to be able to keep eye contact for as long as possible when the bus had started, wasn't it so, Bibbi?"

"Just like that, Merjam. And it was then I experienced the first cultural clash in my young life. A real frontal crash, like a sport car driving at 150 km an hour straight into a mountain." Bibbi made a dramatic pause and looked at Linnéa and Elisabeth with secretive eyes.

"Aren't you going to continue? If you say A you have to say B", said Elisabeth.

"I take over from here", Merjam said and took a sip of water.

"The thing is, Ali and I had brought buckets filled with water. When the bus started rolling Ali and Mustafa took one bucket each and threw water on the bus…"

"I sat right at the back of the bus", said Bibbi. "I looked through the back window, down on those sweet little Tunisian boys who splashed water on the bus. I didn't understand anything. Why were they throwing water after us? Were they mad at us because we were leaving their country? I did what every curious kid does, I asked mum, but she didn't know either. She just told me that every country has its own culture. Of course there were people from lots of different European countries in the bus, Germans, Swedes, Frenchmen and so on. Mum asked a tourist sitting in front of us, but he didn't know why either. I just had to walk up to the bus driver, my last hope. His English was all right, and he said that if I only walked back to my seat, he would tell me later. After a while he put on the loudspeaker and started talking, it was the regular talk, 'Dear passengers, bla, bla, bla', you know how they talk?"

"Sure", Linnéa said, "I've been to a charter trip or two in my life."

"But then the bus driver told us: 'For those of you who asked about the Tunisian boys throwing water on the bus when we left Abounawas, I just want to say: take it easy, they mean well, in fact, it was a gesture of love, they were hoping that you would come back soon. I happen to know the boys behind this little prank, and I know that it's a tradition in their family. My family doesn't do that, but for some Tunisian families it's a tradition. They throw water after the bus to show their love for those going away. And we all saw who were hugging them before we left, didn't we? Everybody in the bus cheered. The driver continued. 'I think the boys were a little fond of the Swedish girl in the back of the bus, they told me that she was so beautiful, they call her the Cleopatra of Sweden. They told me to say to you, that you and your mum are more than welcome back to Djerba, that you have to come back soon'! And then came a long applause from the people in the bus. I was embarrassed, but at the same time a little proud."

"Mmm, what a story, delicious!" Elisabeth burst out.

Friendship between continents and cultures

"Yeah, that was the story. The start of our friendship", Bibbi said. "Let's toast to that! To our friendship! Friendship between continents and cultures!"

They toasted.

"What a trip it must have been for you", said Linnéa and looked at Bibbi.

"Yeah, it was cool. I remember as if it were yesterday."

"Wonderful story", said Elisabeth. "But you forgot to tell one thing. What did Bibbi get as a birthday present?"

"Good question, Elisabeth. That leads us to the next big surprise from the Babubas. Of course I had already announced the Big Birthday Party before we went to Tunisia. Before we went, it was all about the my birthday, you know how kids are at that age, birthdays are sacred. But then when we came back, all I could think about was Tunisia. Anyway, we held the birthday party in our flat in Stockholm, I got lots of presents from my friends. We had waited with opening the present from the Babubas until the birthday party. When I opened it I saw that it was a big ceramic plate, one of those you put up on the wall, with a painted portrait of me on it. And the under the portrait a text: 'B.B. Cleopatra of Sweden'."

"Wonderful" Elisabeth yelled.

"Right? I laughed hysterically when I saw it, because I knew how they managed to fix it. The thing was, one day, we were walking through central Djerba, me, Merjam, Fatima and Ali. We had our picture taken by a photographer on the market square. Merjam bought the pictures. Then we passed by a potter who had plates that he had made on the walls in his store. Merjam asked me which plate I liked best. Then they started talking in Arabic with the potter, I didn't understand a thing, of course. Then Fatima started gesturing wildly, pointing at the ice cream store, 'Come on, let's have an ice cream'! The strange thing was, Ali didn't come with us, he stayed at the potter's. When I looked at the plate back then, at my birthday party, I realised how it must have been arranged."

"It must have been very touching for you when you

saw the plate", said Linnéa.

"Yeah, definitely. There are so many things from that trip that have stayed in my heart.

"After that I went to Tunisia every summer holiday, directly when school finished, just 'schwupp'!" Bibbi tried to imitate the sound of an airplane. "Off to Djerba! I stayed at the Babuba's for three months every summer the rest of my childhood."

"Now I understand why you call her your 'second daughter'", said Linnéa.

The Fabizaists

"I have a third daughter as well, an American girl, Zaza. She lives in Los Angeles. She's like a half-sister to Bibbi. Wonderful girl, super-charming."

"Unbelievable" said Elisabeth. "What are you, mother Earth or what?"

Merjam smiled.

"I love people, that's all. Anyway, these three girls, Fatima, Bibbi and Zaza, they became best friends after a couple of summers on Djerba. Then, when they were kids, they dreamed about peace on earth between all people of all religions. And about five years ago, they founded 'The Fabizaists'."

"'The Fabizaists'?" Elisabeth wondered.

"'The Fabizaists'. **Fa**tima. **Bi**bbi. **Za**za. Do you follow me?"

Bibbi smiled.

"Good name", said Linnéa.

"Yeah, catchy" Elisabeth filled in.

"The thing is, Fatima had grown up with Islam, Bibbi with Protestantism and Zaza with Judaism. They wanted to build bridges of friendship between people of different religions. The message was that all of us are human beings, no matter what religion we have. It seems as if people today don't understand each other, Christians, Jews, Muslims… and all the other religions. I can't accept that going on. And not my girls, either."

Bibbi smiled, abashed.

"I agree", said Linnéa. "Great idea. Sounds like a movement I would like to be a part of."

"Me too", said Elisabeth. "If it wasn't for the fact that I work hard for 'Help Africa' already, and have a child, I'd be an active member of every help organisation there is. I would work for free, every day, all the week. Then I would really deserve the name 'Madame Volunteer'."

"You deserve that name just the way you are", Merjam said.

Suddenly the donkey got up and went to the door.

"What happened to Besbussa?" Linnéa asked.

"She needs to relieve herself", Bibbi said, "she wants to get back to the stable."

"What a clever donkey!"

"OK, maybe it's time to go home", Bibbi said.

Bibbi, Linnéa and Madame Volunteer said thank you for the food and took the donkey to the stable.

The impatient imam

After three weeks Imam Jibril started losing his patience. He constantly called the Millenium Hotel in Doha to reach the couple who were going to convert to Islam. He felt as if he had been fooled and he became more and more upset and angry. At last, he decided to give Merjam a call.

Merjam was sitting with Elisabeth drinking coffee when the Imam called her.

"Hello, this is Merjam."

"It's the Imam."

"Oh, hi, Jibril! Is everything OK with you?" Merjam asked in a friendly voice.

"Nothing is OK! You promised me a woman, she was supposed to arrive here a week ago. Either you send the woman down immediately or you give me my money back!"

"Listen, Jibril. First and foremost: it's not your money. It's money that had been collected from the mosques in Qatar, and now they've been redistributed to Africa. They're going to help hundreds of children. That's good, isn't it?"

"Are you kidding?! Listen here, if the money's not returned at once, I'll report this to the Swedish embassy in Qatar!"

"Do that, Jibril, do that", Merjam said in the same friendly tone as before. "But then I'm going to put some pictures on the website www.godblessaljazira.net, and they're not nice pictures, I'll tell you that…"

The Imam became worried. What kind of threat was this?

"What do you mean by that?"

"Well, there are some pictures of a certain Imam kissing a certain Linnéa Blixt in the middle of Kungsgatan in Stockholm, in the middle of the day. There was a report of someone buying sex there, wasn't there?"

The Imam became completely furious.

"I never thought this of you, Merjam!"

"And I never thought that an Imam would accept a gift from several mosques and put it in his own pockets! Now I say thank you and goodbye!"

Merjam hung up.

"Bravo, Merjam", said Elisabeth. "You've really cracked down on him"

They continued to drink coffee and talk about all kinds of things. After about twenty minutes Elisabeth got a call on her cell phone.

"Elisabeth."

"Hi, this is Imam Jibril from Qatar."

"Hi!" said Elisabeth. She wrote "Imam" on a piece of paper and showed it to Merjam who nodded.

"Are you busy?" he asked.

"Yeah, I have a patient in front of me, but hey, what's on your mind?"

"You know, the money that I invested in 'Restaurant Stockholm je t'aíme', I want to give it to poor people."

It became silent for a while.

"Eh… that's good", said Elisabeth.

"Good, and say hello to Merjam from me and tell her to 'forget the money and al-Jazeera'."

"Sounds good, I'll tell her. Thank you, Jibril, and goodbye", said Elisabeth, switched off her phone and turned to Merjam.

"Unbelievable, 'forget the money and al-Jazeera' Jibril said."

Merjam nodded.

"You know Elisabeth, al-Jazeera is the Arab atomic bomb. It has such respect in the world. There's a saying: 'Don't harm your friend, Mother al-Jazeera is watching you!'."

"And what does that mean?"

"It means that al-Jazeera is like a vacuum cleaner. It sucks up everything that moves."

"Ah, now I see. He must be very scared."

"He knows that al-Jazeera would spread it across the world in no time, but they have to have proof first."

"You really mean that, Merjam?"

"Yeah, they have to have hundred per cent proof before they spread any news."

"Interesting, Merjam, but you have to excuse me, I must go now, thanks for the coffee!"

"Not at all."

"By the way, how are things with Mustafa? Any comedy show going?"

"No, he's back to square one with the bucket and the broom."

"Sorry to hear that, but things will work out for him, don't you think, Merjam?"

"He has no reason to complain, he has a job!"

"You're a wise woman, Merjam, I like you", she said.

They hugged and Elisabeth left. Merjam was left standing in the vestibule.

"We have to show that we're cultural people!"
"I want to ask journalists from all over the world: what is a cultural person? Is it someone who understands his fellow citizens, like Mustafa? Or is it a person who hides his egoism and frustration behind words and phrases?"

"Sweden is an open society and the ministers like being among people. This proves that we have a democracy! I wish that all ministers in the whole world would imitate Anna Lindh."

CHAPTER 3

SWEDEN IS FANTASTIC

It was a cold winter day and there was a snowstorm outside, but that didn't stop Merjam from taking Besbussa for their daily walk. She went out with the donkey already at 6.30 in the morning. She was going to start work at one o'clock, so there was plenty of time.

After the walk, she woke up Fatima, who was going to work at the day care centre and then study Swedish and English at the adult education centre in the afternoon.

Ali and Mustafa were already at work.

Merjam was sitting in the kitchen smoking a water pipe. Fatima was in her room. She looked out the window every now and then, while doing her make up in front of the mirror.

"Fatima, Fatima, breakfast is ready!" Merjam shouted.

Fatima first walked to the living room and gave the donkey a morning hug.

"I'll be right there", she said. "Good morning, Besbussa!"

She continued towards the kitchen.

"Good morning, mom", she said and kissed Merjam on the cheek.

Merjam was ironing children's clothes that she had collected. She was going to sell the clothes and give the profits to Help Africa.

"Good morning, my sweetheart!" she said to Fatima.

"Oh, how cute these baby clothes are!"

"Do you think that you could sell some to the parents at the day care centre?"

"Yeah, come by today between four and six."

"I can't between four and six, I'm going to work from one to nine in the evening, but maybe tomorrow?"

"OK, we'll do it tomorrow then. By the way, mom?"

"Yeah?"

"Seems as if someone new has moved into the house across the street."

"Really? Well, that's nice, isn't it?"

"Not at all. This newcomer stands the window and stares at me through a telescope all day long."

"What? What a moron! That's not allowed, staring at your neighbours like that."

"I know, and it's starting to upset me."

Merjam grew angry.

"Tell me his name and where he lives, I'll walk over to him and slit his throat!"

"HER name, it's a girl! Birgitta Johansson. Lives on the second floor."

"No, not a girl!"

"Yes, really, mother, a girl."

Merjam shook her head.

"Sweden really is a land full of surprises. When I came back with Besbussa today there was a bouquet of flowers hanging on the door handle."

Merjam gave the bouquet to Fatima. It was wrapped in wrapping paper. Fatima opened it and looked at the flowers. There was a little card with the flowers, it said, "I think of you all the time", signed only with the letter "B". Fatima put two and two together.

"Let me handle this. I'll be back soon."

She went back to her room and picked up the phone. She called the voyeuse Birgitta, a woman in her thirties with a shaved head and big rings in her ears. She was sitting at her kitchen table with a telescope when she picked up the phone.

"Hi, I'm Fatima Babuba, I live across the street."

"Hi, Fatima", said Birgitta. "I think about you all the time."

"Yes, I've noticed that. You have called my cell phone a couple of times."

"You're so gorgeous."

"You really do keep track of me. Did you see where I put my nightgown yesterday?"

"I believe your pink see-through nightgown is under your pillow."

"Thank you, Birgitta, it's good that you know where I put my stuff, but…"

"How come you buy so many nightgowns?" Birgitta interrupted.

"Pu pu, pu pu, I'm forgetful, I never remember where I put them", Fatima exaggerated.

"Mademoiselle pu pu, it seems exciting!"

"Why are you spying on me like this?"

"Because I think you're cute! I think you should be a Lucia candidate. I happen to be a member of the Lucia committee." (Lucia is celebrated on December 13 each year.)

"I don't think I have a chance, I'm a short, black-haired Tunisian, I don't have anything to put up against tall, thin, beautiful Swedish blondes?"

"Don't say that, Fatima! You're beautiful!"

"Really? I´ve got to go now, Birgitta", said Fatima and pulled down the window blind. "I'm going to work."

"Wait, Fatima, wait! What do you think about the flowers?"

"They are from you?" Fatima said with feigned surprise.

"Yes! Are you surprised?"

"No, no, not at all, I'm glad", Fatima said with a smile. "My brother used to tell me that I couldn't even get a Tunisian donkey for a husband, and now I have a nun as a fan! But Birgitta, you really have to stop chasing me now.

If you call me again, I'll report you to the police!"

It got quiet, all Fatima could hear was some heavy breathing. She hung up, she didn't want to talk any more. She went out to the vestibule, put on some warm winter clothes and shouted to Merjam in the kitchen:

"I think I solved the problem with the voyeuse"

"That's good. But if you see her staring again you must tell me, promise me that, Fatima!"

"I promise. Bye, mom."

A Volvo in the snow

This month Ali and Mustafa had been sent to the Volvo Showroom in Kungsträdgården by their cleaning firm, "Keep Stockholm Clean." They really enjoyed it there, everyone who worked there was so nice. They were good people. When Ali and Mustafa had finished their first week at Volvo, they decided to go to a sports bar to grab a beer and watch Champions League with Pedro. On the same day a big snowstorm swept across Stockholm. As the boys were on their way up to Vasagatan , they saw a desperate middle aged man and an immigrant screaming and gesturing at each other.

"Why are you blocking me, I can't back out!" the Middle Aged Man screamed.

Mustafa saw a little Fiat parked right behind a Volvo, blocking the way out. He assumed that the Volvo was the Middle Aged Man's, and the Fiat was the iimmigrant's.

"I'm not blocking you", said the immigrant. "It's the car in front of you! Look! He hasn't left you an inch!"

Mustafa cut into the discussion.

"Hey, mate, what's happening?" he asked.

"Hell's happening, I can't start my car, and Mr Volvo here can't get out", said the immigrant.

"No problem, mate, we have these kinds of problems all the time back home in Tunisia!" Mustafa, Ali and Pedro helped lift the Fiat to the side so that the Volvo could get out.

"Hey, mate, perhaps you don't have any fuel left in it", said Mustafa.

"I have, mate, I filled her up up with 20 litres yesterday and I've driven three kilometres at the most. I don't know what is wrong with this car."

"I see, mate. Your car has the same habits as our Tunisian camels. They drink like hell, and they can't wake up in the morning!"

Everyone started laughing at Mustafa's joke.

"So you say? Then my son Adam must have the habits of a camel."

"Not just your son, millions of men across the globe have the same habits as camels."

The middle-aged man got into his car and drove away to the north on Vasagatan. They didn't know that the middle-aged man was head of advertising at Volvo where Ali and Mustafa worked. They hadn't seen him during their first week at work.

"Thanks, boys", he said and waved.

They waved back and started to push the immigrant's car. It rattled a little at first, but then it started.

"Thanks, boys! You're more than welcome to 'Ringens Grill och Kebab' at Skanstull some day, I'll give you free kebabs!"

Cleaning for Volvo

The following day, Mustafa was cleaning the entrance at Volvo Showroom. He discovered a good looking girl, who to his excitement reminded him of the beautiful actress Cameron Diaz, just a little bit shorter and more buxom. She was dressed in an expensive looking coat and wore tall high heeled boots. She passed him and walked to the staff elevator. Mustafa picked up his small vacuum cleaner and followed her, but he was too slow, and the elevator door closed just as he came up. An hour later he saw her again, now wearing a tight dress with a revealing cleavage. He could now see the shape of her body more clearly. She had enormously big breasts. He could see that she had Jennifer Lopez's body and Cameron Diaz's face. Mustafa wanted to find out what section she worked at, so he stayed close to the elevator to do his cleaning just there. When the girl finally went out to the elevator, he followed her.

"Hi! So we meet again", said Mustafa.
"Hi. Have we met before?" the girl asked.
"Oh yeah! At a very rare artistic job for women. On a Saturday."
"Artistic job? For women?"
The girl studied Mustafa, saw his moustaches and realized he was joking with her. She played along.
"Was it at a gallery? Where they sold Dalí paintings?"
Mustafa fixed his moustaches.
"Exactly! Do you like art?"
"I love art! In fact, art's probably what fascinates me the most in the world."
"When you stood there at the auction with the club in your hand and yelled with a hypnotic smile..." Mustafa contrived, "I can't forget that, how do you do it?"
"You mean how do I yell while holding the club in my hand?"
"Yes! Yes!"
The girl leaned forward in front of the mirror, smiled and exposed her cleavage. She had a beautiful bust.
"Gentlemen! Gentlemen!" she shouted exaggeratedly. "Do we have a bid?"
Just as Mustafa was going to attack, he was interrupted as the elevator doors opened and two

gentlemen stepped in. The girl went out and Mustafa walked after her. He held out his hand to her.

"I'm Mustafa."

"I'm Merike."

The girl walked into her room, and Mustafa walked, imitating Charlie Chaplin, down to the end of the corridor where he saw Pedro and Ali with the cleaning wagon. Mustafa grabbed Pedro's collar.

"Move me to section five or die", he said.

"Ah, so you're interested in the girl that looks like Cameron Diaz with Jennifer Lopez's ass?" Pedro replied.

"Yes I am. You're not as stupid as you look."

"Seriously, Mustafa, are you mad?"

"Why?"

"This is an upper class girl, she comes here every day with new designer clothes, and every day when she leaves there are handsome men with beautiful cars outside waiting for her. Do you really think she would choose a cleaner? Idiota!"

"Well, love is blind!"

"Don't even try talking to him, Pedro", interrupted Ali. "In Tunisia, they used to call him 'Le Saharien Imaginaeux'!"

"What does that mean?"

"The Imaginative Saharian."

Pedro laughed.

"They were right! Let go of me Mustafa, we can discuss this. What do I get if I move you to section five?"

"A lunch, beef steak with French fries and béarnaise sauce. But just her office!"

"Ok. You can switch with Assil. She will be happy if she doesn't have to clean that office."

"Thanks." Mustafa said

"You're welcome", Pedro said and turned to Ali.

"How many names does your brother have?"

"Many, many, can't count them all. 'Le Saharien

Imagineux', 'Mr Happy Hour', our mom calls him a crocodile, others call him The Happy Saharian. Can you invent a South American name for him?"

Pedro smiled and patted Mustafa on the shoulder.

Merike

The next day Mustafa switched sections with Assil, who worked at section five.

This would give Mustafa the chance to get close to Merike. Mustafa went into her room and cleaned it thoroughly. After he had finished he put a little note with funny stories on her desk. Since he was illiterate, he had made Ali write down the stories for him. At the bottom of the note he had painted a caricature of himself with the Dalí moustaches. Along with the drawing there was a message: "Spice your every day life with humour. It's the best cure for stress!" The note was signed "The Happy Saharian".

When Merike arrived at work in the morning, she discovered the note from Mustafa. She read the stories and laughed at all of them. Throughout her workday she looked for Mustafa, in the corridors, in the lunch room, on the other floors. She didn't see him.

With a little help from Ali, Mustafa continued to produce funny notes for Merike. He put a new one on her desk every day. Merike loved Mustafa's sense of humour. The highlight of her working day was coming to work to find a new note from "The Happy Saharian." After a while, she didn't even bother to take her coat off when she arrived, she was so curious about what Mustafa had to say in the note of the day. She became more and more interested in "The Happy Saharian", but she couldn't find him anywhere at work.

Volvo advertising

After another week, the head of advertising, Bengt Sjöström, returned from his business trip to Germany. When he arrived in the morning, he first went to his office and then to Merike's, which in fact adjoined his own office. He went in there to pick up his mail. He spotted a note on her desk and picked it up. It was a note from "The Happy Saharian".

Sjöström laughed and Merike explained to him: the cleaning company "Keep Stockholm Clean" had sent a clever and funny cleaner who left her notes with funny stories on them, a new one every day.

"Are his ears really this big?" Sjöström asked.

"Yeah, and he can move them too, it looks so funny, never seen anything like it", Merike answered.

Sjöström wondered if it could really be that guy with the Dalí moustaches, the guy who had helped him with his car on Vasagatan, just before he went to Germany. He went to his office and after some thinking he asked Merike to find the guy. Merike didn't dare to ask him why he wanted to get hold of "The Happy Saharian."

After some detective work she managed to find Mustafa and brought him to Sjöström's office.

"Thanks for all the funny stories you send me all the time. You are 'The Happy Saharian', right?"

Mustafa smiled broadly.

"The truth is out. I just wanted to cheer you up a little."

"That's really sweet of you. My boss wants to speak with you."

"What does he want? I haven't done anything wrong, have I?"

"I don't know, but I'm sure it's nothing important."

Merike opened the door to Bengt Sjöström's office. Mustafa almost went into shock when he came in and saw the man whom he had helped in the snowstorm just a week before.

"So there you are, 'The Happy Saharian'", said Sjöström. "Pepper your every day life with humour. It's the best cure for stress!"

That took the heat off Mustafa a little bit, he breathed out heavily and smiled.

"You remember!"

"How can I forget? I want to thank you again, Mustafa. Without you and your friends I wouldn't have made it to the airport and to my plane last week."

"Ah, that was nothing."

Sjöström had already then understood that Mustafa was a person who spread joy around himself.

"How could you be so happy, the weather was awful?"

"You know, in all kinds of weather, when you're stressed and troubled, you have to spice your day with humour, in order to get by!"

"Maybe you're right… Look, your friends who were there with you, do they work here as well?"

"Yep!"

"OK. Mustafa, I would like to thank you and your friends. We're having an office party on the 11th of December. Normally, only people working for Volvo or its collaborators participate, but I'm going to make an exception this time. What are your friends' names?"

"Ali Babuba and Pedro Gonzales."

"And your full name is Mustafa Babuba?"

"Yep!"

"Write that down, Merike!"

"I must thank you for the invitation!"

"It's the least I can do! Before you go, how did you come up with that idea?"

"What idea?"

"To colour your moustaches in the same colours as

the Swedish flag!"

Mustafa smiled triumphantly and replied:

"I'm honouring Volvo, you know, my moustaches are my accessories."

"How long have you lived here in Sweden, Mustafa?"

"About three and a half years."

"You speak good Swedish, do you study Swedish after work?"

"Sure", Mustafa lied. "Last week my teacher told me: 'Mustafa, if all immigrants were like you we could shut this school down straight away'!"

Sjöström laughed.

"Now I have to work. See you at the party, Mustafa. Bye!"

After the Volvo party

Ten days later, Ali was feeling bad, his stomach wasn't in the best shape. That, in combination with the fact that his favourite team Real Madrid was playing Barcelona late the same evening, made him and Pedro turn down the party opportunity. Mustafa went alone. That night after the party he didn't sleep at home, he was too drunk to dare coming home to Merjam in Skärholmen.

On Monday, the first working day after the party. Ali went into the secretary Siv's room with a bucket full of water. When he came into the room, he saw Mustafa there, cleaning.

"Aren't you finished yet?" Ali wondered.

"Almost. Can you wipe the batten with a cloth?"

"Sure."

Ali went down on his knees and started to wipe the batten.

"I can't understand why you turned the office party

down", Mustafa said.

Ali lifted his head and looked at Mustafa curiously.

"What's so special about an office party, then?"

"Office party? I'll explain to you, Ali. Here in Sweden, every company arranges a party for the staff once a year. Everybody working for the company eats and drinks and gets to know one another. It's a unique Swedish concept."

"Really? And what's so special about it then?"

"Don't you get it? In what other country does the head of the company drink a toast with the guy working on the floor?"

Ali shrugged.

"I can tell you", Mustafa continued, "that I've shaken hands with Volvo's Chief Executive. Very nice bloke!"

"Ah, run away! The Volvo's Chief Executive works in Gothenburg, where they make the cars! Here in Stockholm there is just the advertisement section!"

"But he was there at the party! Promise you!"

Mustafa felt proud, but Ali didn't believe what he said one bit. Then suddenly Siv, the secretary entered the room.

"Oh, it's so neat and clean in here, I almost don't dare to walk in with my shoes! Can you give me the white file?"

"Voilà mademoiselle!"

"Thanks! You guys do such a good job!"

"Thanks mademoiselle, thanks!"

Mustafa sneaked out of the room and followed Siv with his eyes as she walked through the corridor. She wore high heeled shoes and wiggled her bottom as she walked. She had a nice bottom within Mustafa's range of approved bottoms.

Then suddenly he heard a loud crash. The wall-clock had fallen on the floor. Mustafa who stood outside the room put his hands on his head and started jumping like a monkey when he heard Ali screaming.

"Ouch, ouch, ouch! That was close!" Ali yelled.

Mustafa went into the room to Ali, who looked shocked. He looked at the clock on the floor.

"I nearly got this damn clock in my head!" said Ali, terrified.

"Ouch, ouch, ouch. Haven't I told you that this clock goes too slowly, little man?" said Mustafa with irony in his voice.

An irritated Ali threw the batten-brush at Mustafa.

"Idiot. Would it have been better if the clock had been right and I had been lying here on the floor with a hole in my head instead?"

"Easy, I was only kidding."

Then Pedro came by and called for the boys.

"Ali, Mustafa, coffee break!"

"We're coming!"

Mustafa turned to Ali.

"Hey, brother, let's drink some coffee!"

"I don't want to drink anything that you drink", said Ali angrily.

Mustafa threw himself over Ali, who was still sitting on the floor. He started tickling Ali so that he swung around and ended up lying on the floor. Mustafa then grabbed his legs and started pulling the helpless, jiggling Ali through the corridor towards the coffee machine.

"This one's on me, little man", said Mustafa. "Coffee and pastry."

"No, no, I don't want to have anything to do with you, you're mean! Stop it, stop it!"

"You're not getting away!"

Nathalie

Nathalie, a thin middle-aged secretary at Volvo, stood in front of the coffee machine to get a cup of hot chocolate.

"What's the matter with him?" she asked.

Mustafa didn't want to show that he had hurt his brother. Instead he came up with a little lie.

"He's so obstructive. One must drag him to the coffee machine. He is as stubborn as my old grandfather! Refuses to eat lunch or go to the restroom, takes no breaks… he says that he is here to work!"

"But Ali", said Nathalie," there is time for both work and breaks, one must take it easy sometimes in order to work well."

Ali did not reply. He sulked and looked down at the floor.

"Exactly", said Mustafa. "Listen to this wise woman, Ali!"

Nathalie wanted to continue the discussion and turned to Mustafa.

"So, your old grandfather does that when one invites him to coffee?"

"No… or yes, but in another way."

"How?"

"Did. He is dead now."

"Oh, I'm so sorry!"

"It's OK! Anyway, my grandfather used to go down to the beach, each morning after his kids had gone to work. He packed food in a bag, brought a deck chair and went there in order to watch buxom women. He was obsessed with curves, especially tourist curves."

Nathalie looked puzzled at Mustafa.

"His sons, that is, my uncles, they used to go down to the beach after work to retrieve him. There were three of them and they had to work together because grandfather never wanted to go home. So they had to drag home him through town, just like I had to do with Ali now. But down there it was 45 degrees in the shade!"

"Oh dear!"

"Yes, you might say that! After a while his sons

started to get tired of dragging grandfather off the beach every day. So, one day they locked him inside the house. It was on a Sunday. One day later they found him dead."

"Oh, that's terrible!"

"Yes, you might say that! The doctor thought so too. He said to the sons, that is to my uncles, 'Why have you prevented your father from living? A life without curves to look at is no life'!"

Nathalie laughed a little. She didn't know if Mustafa was telling a true story or if he was pulling her leg.

"I have to say, you have a different culture down there!"

Nathalie took her chocolate cup from the coffee machine.

"No, why are you saying that?" Mustafa asked. "I saw three men dragging an old geezer along Drottninggatan yesterday!"

"Go on!"

"No I didn't, just kidding."

"Let's be serious for a moment", said Nathalie with a low voice.

"I'll try", said Mustafa.

"You know, last Friday... I got a bit drunk after a while, and now my friends are telling me that I was chasing you all the way to the men´s room! I'm so sorry, hope I didn't do anything bad to you."

Mustafa lied, he didn't want to hurt Nathalie. "No, not at all! You were drunk all right, but you were in an excellent mood the entire time! The only thing you chased that night was drinks!"

"Oh, thank you so much, Mustafa, I'm so relieved! What do you do to cure hangover anxiety?"

"You just have to gloss over when you know that you've made a fool out of yourself! It's not easy, but do like Mustafa, laugh and make jokes when you've done silly things!"

"Yeah, one always sees you with a smile on your face! And you're always playing with your moustache!"

"Oh, you know a thing or two about me!"

Nathalie laughed and hugged Mustafa, relieved. She had shaken off the worst of the hangover anxiety by now.

"I have to move along. Good to straighten this out with you, Mustafa. See you around!"

Nathalie walked away. Mustafa took his cup of coffee and turned to Ali.

"That was a major lie I just told her. Truth is, she was hammered and chased me all night long."

"What are you saying?" said Ali.

Mustafa imitated Nathalie, with a sluggish voice. He acted as if he were drunk.

"Sure", he said. "She said she gets turned on by two types of men when she drinks wine, Indians and Saharians. And then she sat down on my lap and told me, 'You can steal an open mouth kiss from me if you like'."

"What did you do then?"

"Well, what do you think? I have my principles. Firstly, she has no bottom whatsoever, her bottom should be reported missing on 'Efterlyst' (a Swedish television show where the viewers can help the police in finding missing persons)! Secondly, she's married. I respect married women."

"So, how did you escape from her, then?"

Mustafa was tipsy at the party, not wasted.

"I simply told her that I was going to the toilet, and then I crawled away from her under the table!"

"Under the table? Were you drunk?"

"Well, almost. But most of all, I enjoyed the view from down there!"

Ali now became even more amazed. He stared at Mustafa with wide eyes.

"Don't you believe me, Ali?"

"You come up with so many stories I don't know what to believe. One thing I definitely don't believe is you shaking hands with the Volvo's Chief Executive! Do you really think I'm that stupid?"

Ali took his bucket and went to the cleaning room to change the water, when Pedro came to the corridor.

"You have to start cleaning the windows", he said.

"Aye, aye, captain" Mustafa answered.

"Ey, man, the Tunisian Casanova! How did your little Volvo project go at the party?"

Mustafa looked puzzled at Pedro.

"Merike, the Cameron Diaz lookalike", Pedro clarified.

"Oh, OK. Well, who am I to tell? I don't think so, but you know, I was drunk!"

"Not good Mustafa, that's your weakness as a chick-hunter. You fall more deeply in love with wine than you do with women! You can't go on like that!"

Mustafa couldn't help but laugh.

"I know, have to work on that."

"So, how has it been going with Cameron Diaz, then? I mean, you were mighty positive last week!

"As we say in Tunisia, 'I'm grilling her slowly'!"

"What are you saying? She's not a chicken, is she?"

"That means I'm working on her. Think project!"

"OK, now I understand. Got to go to work now, take it easy, grillmeister!"

Ali and Mustafa started cleaning windows in the corridor.

"So, where did Casanova sleep last Friday, then?" Ali asked.

"At a girlfriend of your favourite girl, Kerstin!" Mustafa replied.

"What, was Kerstin at the party?"

"Yeah, she asked after you, and I told her that you were at home, watching football. I can't believe you preferred staying inside like some eighty year old!"

Kerstin

Ever since Ali had started cleaning at Volvo, he had had eyes for Kerstin, a 27 year old economist from the north of Sweden, with long beautiful blonde hair, built like Queen Latifah and with a nice big bottom, just as Ali preferred. All of a sudden, she passed the boys on her way to her room. Ali went cross-eyed when he saw her.

"Hi, gorgeous", said Mustafa. "Good party last Friday!"

"Oh, hi guys! Yeah, it was really great, shame you couldn't be there, Ali."

Ali was really shy in front of his dream girl, oh "yeah, shame" was all he could come up with.

Kerstin continued towards her room in her high-heeled shoes, waving her bottom. Mustafa then poured out washing powder and water on the floor, slid over it like James Brown and started to sing "I feel good", but with changed lyrics: "Ali feels good!" He pushed Ali towards Kerstin's office while talking.

"Have you seen the curves on her? Just like you like it! You like buxom girls, there you have her, your dream girl! You just have to make your attack now!"

"I don't dare do a thing, she's educated and beautiful. I don't stand a chance."

Mustafa wanted to encourage Ali..

"Don't say that, Ali, in Sweden people don't care about titles, it doesn't matter if you're a cleaner or an economist, doesn't matter! All that matters here is being a good person."

"I don't dare do anything!"

Mustafa then found a bottle of Greek wine close to the waste basket. It must have been left over from the office party.

"You have to…", he said. "To dare to lose your foothold for a little while. Not daring is like ending up in the Sahara desert and getting lost for ever. Take a sip and lose your shyness! Wine is a tool for picking up chicks!"

"No way! Drink at work? Anyway, I'm an abstainer, you know that. No, no, I don't dare! What would I tell her when I got in there?"

Mustafa started imitating John Travolta in "Saturday Night Fever", with the bottle in his hand.

"Confuse her by watering the flowers with the wine. Then she'll become curious. Go à la Travolta!"

"I can't do this. I won't be able to say one word."

Mustafa then started to imitate Michael Jackson, pushing his abdomen forward with one hand over it.

"Just push ahead like monsieur miracle Michael Jackson, then it'll come out, the talking. Go on now, push my son, push!"

Mustafa put the wine bottle into Ali's bucket and pushed him towards Kerstin's office.

Ali knocked on Kerstin's door, very nervous.

Beef Wellington à la Vásia Trifili

"Come in", Kerstin shouted from inside the room.

"Hi again", said Ali nervously. "I'm going to water the flowers."

"Be my guest! I have to ask you, how do you keep the flowers so strong and beautiful?" she asked and looked at all the vases that were filled with beautiful flowers.

"The secret is here", said Ali with a smile, and produced the wine bottle from his bucket.

Kerstin wrinkled her forehead and smiled when she saw how Ali started to water the flowers walking with exaggerated shoulder gestures à la Travolta.

"What are you doing? Are you watering the flowers with wine?"

"Yeah, Greek wine makes them feel good."
"Go on! Is it true?"
"Yeah, a hundred per cent, promise you."
"What are you, some kind of flower expert?"
"Yes, as a matter of fact I am."
"So, why don't you work as a florist?"
"I can't because everyone wants to see a job certificate from my last employer."
"So why don't you get it?"

Ali pulled a joke and made a sweeping movement with his hand to symbolise drinking.

"It's difficult! My last boss was called monsieur Bug". Ali pretended to put a bottle to his mouth and drink with a gulping sound, 'Bug, bug, bug'. "He died three years ago, down in his wine cellar!"

Kerstin caught up on the word game.

"That's sad", she said. "Anyway, do you want some deg, deg, deg?"

"Deg, deg ,deg… what's that?"

"Deg, deg, deg. It's dates from Algeria, Morocco, Libya, Egypt, Iran, Jordan, Iraq, Syria, Tunisia."

Kerstin opened her drawers, one after another. They were all filled with dates from different countries. Ali looked at the dates, surprised.

Kerstin put the dates on a plate and handed it to Ali. He sat down across from Kerstin and tasted them.

"Oh, this is really good, where are these from?"

Kerstin took up a date plum from the same plate.

"These ones are from Iraq", she said.

"You're a specialist in dates, that's unusual! Never would have thought of a Swedish blonde with dates from all over the world in her desk drawer!"

"I love dates, couscous and Arab belly dance!"

"M… m… magnificent", Ali stammered.

"By the way, I've brought this hyacinth from home, it's not in top shape, maybe you can save it? Does the wine have to be Greek?"

Ali couldn't think of a thing to say. "Erm…"

Mustafa, who had been standing outside eavesdropping, knocked on the door.

"Sorry to interrupt, Ali, can you help me move a desk?"

Ali turned to Kerstin.

"I'll be back soon."

When they came out in the corridor, Mustafa gave Ali a kick in the bottom.

"Ouch, what are you doing?" Ali screamed while staring angrily at his brother. "Stop doing that! Where is this desk?"

"What desk? Haven't you understood anything? Idiot, you just mumble and mumble, 'erm', 'erm', you're making a fool of yourself! Listen to me and maybe you can save this situation."

Mustafa spiced up a "Beef Wellington à la Vasia Trifili" for Ali to serve. He also revealed to Ali that Kerstin didn't have her own apartment, she had just moved back to Stockholm after five years in Greece, and now she lived at her sister's place.

Mustafa went down to the big hall to help Pedro cleaning, Ali went back to Kerstin's office and knocked on the door.

"Excuse me", he said.

"No problem", said Kerstin. "Where were we, yes, why does it have to be Greek wine, and not Italian or French?"

Ali started serving his "Beef Wellington à la Vasia Trifili."

"Because Vasia Trifili recommends it" he said.

"You mean that Trifili, the Greek talk show host?"

"Yep!"

"Oh, I love him! He has such charisma and charm! But I guess he recommends Greek wine just because he's

Greek, right?"

"No, actually not. There's an explanation for this. Once upon a time, Apollo accidentally killed a son of a king, named Hyacintus. The blood from his body poured down into the soil, and a flower started to grow, the hyacinth. And it loves a shower of Greek wine every now and then!"

"Oh, how interesting", said Kerstin and smiled. "Do you speak Greek?"

"No, but I read an article about him in Paris Match", Ali made up while looking around in the room.

"So, where's the hyacinth?" he asked.

"Here!"

"Let me study it for a while."

Ali looked at Kerstin's hyacinth, pretending to be an expert.

"Hmm", he said. "On this one, wine will only help for a little while, then it'll die."

"Why?" Kerstin wondered.

"You can see on this flower that it has been exposed to compact living. One of the plants must move to another pot, no one benefits from living in too small a space."

"You're right, we really have no space at home! My sister and her kid moved back to her old flat, so now I have to move, and getting an apartment in this town is so difficult!"

"I can fix a three room apartment in a nice house for families with lots of kids, near Karlaplan!"

"Really? That sounds great! But I'm neither married, nor a mother. Can l still live there?"

"'Mademoiselle Single', my sister works at a day care centre. You can borrow five kids from there when you go to the landlord."

Kerstin laughed loudly. Then the phone rang.

"Wait, Ali, I just have to answer this. Hello, Kerstin… OK… I'll be right there", she hung up the phone and turned to Ali.

"You have to excuse me, I have to go and see the advertising manager, Bengt you know."

Ali rose up. He suddenly felt insecure and dizzy.

"Erm… do you want to take a cappuccino after work, at Kafferepet?"

"Kafferepet, where is that?"

Right across from Åhléns, on Klarabergsgatan, close to the Nils Ferlin statue. One of Stockholm's last culture cafés."

"Ah, now I know! Yeah, I'll be there if I can make it. If not we can always take a cup of coffee tomorrow morning? The Lucia parade is at 8.30 tomorrow, you know?"

"OK, that sounds great. Bye!"

Ali went out in the corridor, outside Kerstin's room, jumping and doing pirouettes, like Tomas Brolin, the Swedish football player, whom Ali had seen on TV in Tunisia. Then he went down to the big hall where Mustafa was cleaning.

"Can you believe it?", said Ali astonished. "I'm going to meet economist Kerstin after work."

"I know", said Mustafa.

Ali was nervous.

"How do you know that? Did you go back and listen outside the door?"

Mustafa held his hand over his nose and went to the window.

"No, but I can smell it on your breath and your under arm perspiration! I have to open the window."

Ali kicked Mustafa in the bottom out of pure joy, he was so happy to finally get a date.

"You asshole" he said joking.

"You see, Ali! You need self confidence to push it!"

Ali imitated Mustafa

"Push it, damn!, push it!"

After work, Ali and Mustafa went to Kafferepet and ordered two cappuccinos.

Caroline instead of Kerstin

"We've been here for one hour, and Kerstin hasn't showed up", said Mustafa lowly. "She's not coming, simple as that!"

"Maybe she had to work late, or maybe something has happened?" said Ali, concerned.

"Why didn't you invite her to Bux-Biou instead? Then you could have seen what her curves look like in a bathing suit, and I could have been looking at pretty girls. This is killing me slowly, looking at culture blokes drinking coffee."

"Are you nuts? You can't have your first date on Bux-Biou! It's not fitting, having your first date in bathing suits, don't you get it?"

A fashionably dressed woman in her forties, carrying an attaché case, came up to the boys.

"Excuse me, is this seat free?"

"Sure", said Mustafa and shone up. "Have a seat!"

The woman put her cup of coffee on the table and her attaché case on the chair. Before she had sat down, her cell phone rang.

"Björkman! Yeah? Oh, the journal, it's on X-ray… no, I can't check it now, I don't work at the radiotherapy department. Come by Liljeholmen health care centre tomorrow and we can talk about it. OK, we'll do that, bye."

Still standing, the woman called her daughter's new nanny.

"Hi, this is Kim's mom. May I speak to Jeanette?"

"No, she went out shopping, but she'll be back soon", answered a little girl, who sounded about eight years old.

The woman turned her back on Ali and Mustafa, looked out the window and continued talking. As soon as she turned her back on the boys they saw it right away. She had a wonderful bottom à la Marilyn Monroe!

"What's your address?"

"I'll ask?"

"I can't hear you", said the woman.

"Bergsvägen 235", said the other girl.

"Bergsvägen 235? Where is that?" asked the woman.

"I don't know", said the girl.

"OK, but say hello to your mom and ask her to call Caroline Björkman on her cell phone, I'm waiting at a café, it's called Kafferepet."

The woman, whose name was Caroline, picked up a pen and wrote down the address. She took her cup and went to get some coffee.

Beef Wellington à la Volvo

Mustafa understood that the beautiful woman who had left her attaché case at their table was a doctor. He also understood that Kerstin wasn't going to show up.

"Kerstin is not coming", he said to Ali. "Now, start your attack! Allah has sent you this woman as a replacement!"

"But her curves aren't big like Kerstin's!"

"Perhaps not now, but if you give her some of your Tunisian stews with pasta, then the curve problem will be solved."

"You think so?"

"Hell yeah, women gain weight fast if you give them some decent food!"

Mustafa started pondering how to make a "Beef Wellington à la Volvo with crème fraiche" which tasted of knowledge and intelligence. A rule of thumb for Mustafa's Beef Wellington was taking the person's status and position into consideration, and then using it to reach maximal effect.

"But she's a doctor", said Ali with doubt in his voice. "Do you really think I have a chance?"

"Why not? Let me just run 'the Sahara technique', and things will work out!"

One of Mustafa's best techniques for picking up girls was what he used to call "the Sahara technique."

When he went to a café or a restaurant with Ali, he sat down next to a girl he wanted to come into contact with. He simply pretended that she didn't exist, ignored her completely, and with Ali as support, he came up with all kinds of jokes, funny stories, used all kinds of moves, and suddenly he turned around and surprised whoever sat there listening. The girl, who had been listening all along, pretending to read a book or look the other way, became all surprised and started laughing hysterically, without being able to stop the laughter.

This was Mustafa's best way to get in touch with girls, and at the same time get approval for his comedy talents, nursing his dream of becoming a famous comedian. Now he wanted to help his insecure brother to get this Caroline woman.

"OK", said Mustafa and started teaching his brother. "You're an economist, working as a trainee at Volvo, that will sound good and trustworthy. I work as a designer trainee there. This is a woman with high social status, so we need a 'Beef Wellington à la Volvo'. Come on now Ali, push it, she's got beautiful curves!"

They started to speak Swedish while waiting for Caroline. Mustafa winked and made a signal with his foot when Caroline came back. The brothers continued quasi-discussing. Caroline sat down with her coffee. She picked up the latest edition of "Doctor's Magazine" and started reading.

"Well, well, that's life", said Mustafa, "but never

mind, why complain, things are going well now. How are things for you at Volvo, everything OK?"

"Very stressful. And how is it for you?"

"Fantastic. I'm so glad that I got this trainee post at Volvo. And there are so many exciting things happening there!"

"Interesting, tell me!" Ali said and pretended to be curious.

"Listen to this. Volvo has put all their resources into this new model, 'Volvo Respect', a grandiose project!"

"Really? Never heard of it. What will it look like, the car?"

"I don't know! This is a top secret Swedish project, foreign trainees won't even get near it!"

"So, Mustafa, why is the car called 'Volvo Respect'?"

"From what I've heard it's because this car respects pedestrians, respects red lights, respect traffic rules. The whole driving part is pre-programmed. There's a computer in the car, all you need to do is write the address, and the car will go there immediately." Caroline started giggling, trying to sip her coffee.

"So, frankly speaking, you won't need any driver's licence anymore?" Ali wondered.

"No, it'll be just like riding a camel", Mustafa went on. "You won't need any papers anymore. And the best thing of all, you can get drunk and drive anyway! The alcohol sales will sky rocket, Systembolaget (the Swedish alcohol monopoly) will start having their stores open 24 hours a day!"

"Unbelievable!"

"Oh yes, Monsieur Economist, they say that the Swedish Finance Minister is so happy that he has started laughing in his sleep."

"This is a sign that the Swedish economy is recovering!"

"Sure."

Caroline tried to hold her laughter back, but she just couldn't help giggling at Mustafa's merriness. Ali, who, unlike Mustafa, was an abstainer, played along.

"That really sounds fantastic! Imagine going out partying, then taking the car home, and the police can't do anything about it!"

"Oh yes, dear Ali, drivers across the globe will shout 'Go Volvo'! 'Go Sweden'!"

"Magnificent! Sounds like an old dream for the people of the world, no driver's licence, drink whatever you want, Volvo takes you home!"

"Voilà! But listen now, and this is between the two of us…"

Mustafa leaned forward towards Ali and continued.

"I heard that because Volvo doesn't have any money left, Systembolaget and Mediterranean countries like Tunisia, Algeria and Morocco have decided to finance the project!"

"What? North Africans? And Muslims too! Is it true?"

"It's business! Everyone has to survive! What will they do with all their grapes? Throw them into the sea and live on dates? With the new Volvo, there'll be plenty of jobs and more people drinking."

Mustafa noticed that Caroline was struggling to hold back her laughter. He also discovered the nice waitress Monikka, a Polish girl who always seemed to be in a good mood, and a friend of his and Ali's. When she was serving two lasagnas to the table next to Mustafa, he took his chance.

"Mademoiselle Warszawa!" he cried.

"My name is Monikka", she replied, still in a good mood.

"Oh, sorry Monikka, but I was just wondering… do you have that good chocolate cake here, the one that you ran out of in no time yesterday?"

"Yes we have", said Monikka and walked away. Mustafa turned to Ali and said in Arabic, so Caroline wouldn't be able to understand...

"Buy three pieces of chocolate cake, and two for her daughter. Put them in a small, neat box." Ali went to buy the cakes. Mustafa was fixing his long Dalí moustache, painted blue and yellow. He smiled at Caroline. "Sorry to bother you, it may be difficult for you to find peace and quiet to read that magazine with us babbling about. But you know, if you're from Sahara, you're from Sahara!"

"No problem", said Caroline. "You look like Salvador Dalí. Are you an artist?"

"Yes I am! I love painting. Dalí is actually my favourite."

Ali came with the chocolate cake, and Mustafa reached out his hand to Caroline and presented himself.

"Mustafa Babuba", he said.

Caroline reached out her hand.

"Caroline Björkman."

"This is my brother Ali", he said and pointed at Ali, who put his plate down on the table and presented himself.

"Ali Babuba."

"Nice to meet you."

"May I interest you in some cake? In our culture it's a crime not to treat a woman with a beautiful smile like yours", Ali said.

"Thanks, that is nice of you."

Caroline took a piece of the cake.

"Mmm... really good. Sorry, but I couldn't help but listen to your conversation earlier, this Volvo project sounds really interesting, that could help me programming my next car and take me straight to Bergsvägen 235."

"Absolutely", said Ali in a cheerful tone. "This project is necessary and will make life easier for people."

"And best of all, it's going to be the end of traffic

accidents", Mustafa filled in.

Mustafa then signalled to Ali with his foot under the table. It was time for the attack. Ali was insecure and didn't know how to start. He went back to the Volvo talk, trying to come across as an intellectual.

"Don't you think that Saab will beat Volvo in this new technological race?" he asked.

"Ah oui", said Mustafa. "It's quite possible, they have good technicians who've built the world's safest car, but I've heard they're busy finding a solution to the oil problem, you know, we'll be out of oil in 30-40 years, at the latest."

"But now we have ethanol at least."

Caroline looked curiously at the two intellectuals. Mustafa, who had learnt almost everything he knew from politics to climate issues from the TV channel Al-Jazeera – he used to call it his university - didn't want to continue talking about oil, but he had to answer his stupid brother..

"Ethanol means catastrophe and starvation!"

"What do you mean?" Ali asked.

"You know that they get ethanol from corn, wheat, sugar cane and so on. If everyone is going to drive ethanol cars, then the price of corn, wheat and sugar cane will sky rocket. People in many countries won't be able to buy bread anymore."

"So you say, huh?"

"Yes! People in the third world will once more go on an unintentional diet! We'll have more people with legs like drumsticks and bellies like footballs, and different shoe size on the left and right foot!"

"Go on!"

"It's cruel, but it's the truth! Believe me, the soldiers of the future won't fight, they will be guarding the food supplies!"

Ali tried to keep the conversation going.

"But what do you think about bio gas then? Maybe

Saab will conquer the world with that technique?"

Mustafa wanted to finish off the Volvo-Saab talk with something funny. He gave his brother a loose kick.

"Absolutely! It'll be like in the old days. Vikings are going berserk on the continent again. Let's hope they don't get hallucinations from eating mushrooms and start chopping people's heads off. Let's conquer the world in a decent way, and help all the women who dream of having blonde babies!"

Caroline laughed again, but then she was interrupted by the phone. She stood up from her chair and walked away to speak in private. After a while she came back.

"Thanks for the cake, guys! I have to fetch my daughter now."

Ali stood up and took the box with the chocolate cakes from the table and gave it to Caroline.

"Here you are, I know that kids like chocolate cakes."

"Oh, thank you, what a gentleman! But now I have to hurry."

"Erm, erm, I wish, erm… maybe I can, you know… erm… meet up with you… some time?" Ali asked nervously.

"Well, there's a possibility!"

"Can I have your phone number?"

"Hmm… you know what, maybe it's better if I… can call you at Volvo? What extension number do you have?"

Ali took a number out of the air, without thinking.

"Ah 666, can you remember that?"

"Oh yeah, that number is easy to remember! I'll call you after our Lucia celebration tomorrow, around eleven? Is that OK?"

"Sure! Bye!"

"Bye, boys!"

Caroline walked away. When she was out of sight Ali jumped up and did a pirouette à la Tomas Brolin, and landed straight on a customer.

A wrong number

"Sorry", said Ali. "When I was a kid I got so inspired by Tomas Brolin's way of celebrating a goal."

"OK, OK, no harm done."

Ali got up from the floor, started to play a fool.

"Charm-boy of Tunisia! What do you think, Mustafa, it worked, right?"

Mustafa gave Ali an angry look.

"Camel charm, Sahara charm, lying is an art form! Here I've been working my ass off to help you get this girl, and then you mess up everything yourself!"

"Mess up? What do you mean?"

"Idiot" Mustafa hissed. "Extension number 666 goes to Volvo's advertisement boss, Bengt Sjöström! Caroline is going to call and ask for an economist Ali Babuba, and Merike will tell her that there is no economist with that name... but we do have an Ali Babuba working here. For the cleaning company 'Keep Stockholm Clean'! Do you think you'll have any chance after that phone call?"

"Oh, damn it", said Ali slowly. "How could I get it so wrong. I had no luck."

Ali walked down the stairs, talking to himself, Mustafa remained seated by the table.

"How could I be so dumb?" Ali mumbled to himself.

He came out from Kafferepet, sad and desperate, and walked up to the Nils Ferlin statue (a Swedish poet). He looked to the left and to the right to see if Caroline was anywhere in sight. He didn't know what to do.

Kicking Ali's back side

A a beggar came up to Ali.

"Do you have a dime to spare, please?" he begged.

At the moment, Ali felt like a little piece of dirt, because he had just made a fool of himself.

"You know what?, You can have a hundred crowns if you kick my back side", he answered.

When the beggar heard about a hundred crowns he became greedy.

"A hundrdd to kick you? That's too little, I have to get at least two hundred. It.would be risky. I might be looked upon as a racist."

"Ok, I'll give you 200", said Ali. "But then you have to give me a proper kick, I deserve it."

Ali leaned forward and grabbed a hold of the Nils Ferlin statue. The beggar started kicking Ali hard in the butt.

"Ouch, ouch, ou, aaaa... encore, encore ('more, more' in French)!"

Ali enjoyed it even though his butt, his heart and his soul were hurting.

An angry woman passed by. She pointed at the wall next to Ali, with a poster showing European presidents and the message "Stop racism."

"Stop it, are you a racist?" the woman shouted. "Why are you hitting him? Look how Europe is struggling against racism and now you're standing here tormenting a poor immigrant."

"Stay out of this, old lady", said the beggar. "This is a job with bright prospects for the unemployed."

Ali continued screaming.

"Encore, encore, encore..."

Monikka saw what was happening through the window and she went upstairs to Mustafa on the first floor.

"I looked outside the window. Someone is kicking your brother hard in his bottom, he's screaming something in French, it sounds like 'NK', 'NK'."

"Maybe he's screaming 'Encore', encore'?"

"Yeah, exactly, that's what he's screaming! Shall I call the police?"

"No, you don't need to. He needs some punishment to be able to sleep tonight, he's really made a fool of himself today."

"I have never seen anything like it. Is it an Arab tradition?" Monikka asked.

"No, not nowadays, but wait another 30-40 years, when we're out of oil, then we're going to see a lot of this in the oil-producing countries. Then the grown-ups will lean forward and ask their children and grandchildren to kick their butts."

"Will the Arabs scream 'Encore', encore' then?"

"No, they'll scream 'al-Jazeera', 'al-Jazeera'. Why didn't we listen to al-Jazeera, to the doctors Faisal, Ahmed, Sami and everyone else who begged us to cut our oil consumption by half and save some oil for our grandchildren? But then it'll be too late, the oil will be gone, all that will be left will be rusted weapons under the sand, it will be too late... it's a shame." He was quiet for a while. "But I hope the Arab oil countries will change their minds, and start saving their oil" Mustafa continued.

Mustafa felt a bit down. He left Kafferepet and continued to Bux-Biou, went to the pool bar and watched women's bottoms to forget Ali's stupidity. Ali had left Kafferepet and the beggar a long time ago. After receiving some well-deserved kicks he felt better, even good. He started whistling an Arabic melody when he suddenly caught sight of a couple walking towards the underground central station. It was Kerstin hand in hand with a man!

Beef Wellington à la three musketeers of al-Jazeera: Faisal al Kasim, Ahmed Mansour and Sami Haddad, among the best debaters of the Arab world

The next day at Volvo Pedro came up to Ali and Mustafa who were cleaning in the corridor.

"Ali, Mustafa", he shouted. "Come, we're celebrating Lucia in the dining room between eight and half-past eight."

"We'll be there soon", said Mustafa.

"You go, Mustafa", said Ali in a low voice. "I don't feel like it."

"Come on now! As the Swedes say, things will work out!"

Ali was sad and desperate.

"How will I get the boss out of the office to answer the phone at eleven o'clock? Shall I make him believe that an important person is waiting for him down at the reception? And drop some water in the corridor so that he slips and falls and hits his head?"

"You should not do anything, just let me take care of this! If you buy me some drinks in the pool bar at Bux-Biou, then I'll settle this, OK?"

"OK."

A couple of hours later, Merike was standing in one of the corridors on the fifth floor. She was dressed in a very short skirt and high-heeled shoes. She passed Mustafa and Ali with a coffee tray and purposely dropped a lump of sugar onto the floor. The boys stood behind her in hopes of seeing her butt under the short skirt when she leaned over to pick up the sugar lump.

"Hi, guys", she said. "Can one of you be a gentleman and pick up that lump of sugar for me?"

"For you, anything", said Mustafa and picked it up. "Here you are!"

"Thanks! By the way, Mustafa, the boss wants to

speak with you."

"Really? What does he want?"

"No idea. But he's in an unusually bad mood. Did you do something stupid at the party last Friday, Mustafa?"

"Not that I can recall."

With a flirty smile Merike walked over to Sjöström's room.

"I wonder what the boss has to say", said Ali.

Mustafa suddenly felt nervous.

"I'll be right there, I just have to take the bucket to the cleaning room!"

Beef Wellington à la John Cleese

Mustafa took the elevator down to the cellar. There were no offices there, so no one could hear him. He went to the bathroom, looked into the mirror and started to imitate John Cleese. He laughed loudly and imitated John Cleese's grimaces over and over again, to shake off the anxiety and think more clearly. He created an exciting environment of his own which would make it easier for him when he met Sjöström and he started to plan a "Beef Wellington à la John Cleese."

Ali was waiting in front of the elevator. After a while, Mustafa came up again and they both went along the corridor to Sjöström's room. Ali looked at his watch.

"It's a quarter to eleven now. In 15 minutes Caroline will call. Do you think that you can get that old geezer out of the office before then?"

"Things will work out", said Mustafa confidently. "We have to improvise a 'Beef Wellington à la John Cleese' and get him out."

Mustafa knocked on the door. Ali was outside looking through the keyhole.

"Come in", said Sjöström.

Mustafa tried to confuse him.

"Good day boss. What the boss is thinking of right now, that's what I'm thinking of, and what the boss thinks is important, that's what I think is important."

"Well, that's good", said Sjöström surprised. He didn't understand a thing.

"You know, there's something I've been thinking about. Many times, actually. Why are car sales so low in the Arab world? So then, last night, I came up with this advertising slogan."

Mustafa picked up his cell phone, on which he had recorded rhythmic Arabic instrumental music.

He started the song and began dancing and singing about Volvo in Arabic. He had come up with the lyrics himself: "Drive Volvo, buy Volvo, Volvo is good, Volvo is fine" and so on. He danced enthusiastically to the music. Sjöström looked at him with surprise. He smiled and nodded to Merike, who was standing in the entrance to her room, watching.

When Mustafa had finished he looked nervously at Sjöström, who was scratching his head.

"Thanks for your thoughtfulness, Mustafa, that was a nice dance. But I'm still mad and upset about what happened at the office party the other day."

Ali, who had been listening, standing outside the door, had now left.

"Ouch, what did I do?" said Mustafa.

"Here in Sweden", said Sjöström, "companies arrange a big party every year so that the staff can get to know each other better. NOT to cause a scandal, that's not the point. I invite you to a party despite the fact that you don't work for us, and what do you do? How could you be so stupid to start groping Miss Nathalie Larsson? She's married and has kids. Even if you yourself don't care, you have to respect the rules of the Volvo group."

Mustafa started imitating Nathalie's drunkenness.

"I haven't done anything, Mr Sjöström! Give me a

chance to explain what happened. This is how it went: you stood behind Madame Larsson and held her hands, and you said 'Kiss her, Mustafa, come on'! And then I said, 'Please boss, I don't want to, I can give her a friendly kiss on the cheek at best, not more than that!'"

Sjöström had been rather drunk at the party himself and didn't remember that much. Suddenly he became concerned and insecure.

"What did you say I was doing?"

"You held her and said 'Kiss her'! I kissed her on the cheek and then she started rolling with her tongue, like this!"

Sjöström felt dizzy.

"No, why did she do that?"

"No idea!"

"So you say? What I've heard is that you tried to drink her under the table."

Mustafa acted drunk again.

"Ouch, no, that's not true, they gave me a glass of wine that tasted exciting and I asked Madame Larsson if she wanted to taste it, and then she said, 'You don't need to get me drunk, Mustafa, we can go to your place and go to bed straight away'!"

"Did she follow you home?"

"No, she went to the toilet. I was a little drunk." Mustafa made some strange gestures.

Sjöström laughed a little.

"So I hid under the table. When she got back she grabbed my ear and said, 'Mustafa, Mustafa, you don't need to hide from me, you're so good looking'. And then she pulled me up."

Sjöström shook his head. Mustafa continued.

"One of my principles is that I respect married women."

"Good, Mustafa. So she didn't follow you home?"

"No way! Never in my life! I should have gone to the

police and reported her."
"Report her? For touching you?"
"No, for having a tiny bottom!"
Sjöström giggled.
"Can you report things like that to the police?"
"Absolutely! Sweden is multicultural nowadays."
"OK. Hey, Mustafa, about you being a bit drunk, aren't you a Muslim?"
Mustafa smiled.
"I'm a half-Muslim, I like drinking a little wine when I meet women."
"And what's the difference between a Muslim and a half-Muslim?"
Mustafa came up with his own explanation.
"Well, according to my mom, a half-Muslim goes straight to hell!"
Sjöström smiled and shook hands with Mustafa to gloss over his accusations.
"Hey, Mustafa, let's forget this whole thing, OK?"
Mustafa tried to get a little extra credit from Sjöström.
"Thanks, boss! I appreciate that you invited me to the party. I hope that you know that I respect Volvo's rules, and that I like to work hard, like the Swedes…"

Merike overhears

Merike had overheard the whole conversation from her room, and now she understood why Mustafa followed her with his eyes through the corridors at Volvo. She wanted to lure him into her room.
"You don't seem to work that hard", she said in a serious tone. "There are fluffs of dust in here!"
"Hmm, that's odd", said Mustafa and grimaced.
Sjöström's phone rang…
"An important phone call from New York, Bengt!"

said the voice from the switchboard.

Sjöström picked the phone up.

"Bengt Sjöström speaking! What can I do for you?"

Mustafa went into Merike's room.

"OK, so where are the fluffs of dust you're talking about?"

Merike sat by her desk in a most inviting position.

"In two places. There's some in the corner behind the door", she said.

Mustafa closed the door to see if there were any fluffs of dust. He reached down, dragged his forefinger around the threshold and held the finger up in the air.

"Nothing, there's nothing here! Spotless!"

Merike played along and pointed down to the floor by her desk.

"No? What about here under the desk then!" she said.

Mustafa at once understood the hint, and he got very aroused by Merike's sexual invitation. He went down on his knees and over to Merike's desk on all fours.

While on his way over to her desk, he mumbled to himself in French. "Mon Dieu, mon Dieu, ce n'est pas possible (My God, my God, this can't be true)!"

He started to think about whether Merike had a boyfriend, he had seen a lot of rings on both her hands. He suspected that it could be Sjöström.

"Has anyone famous been here under this desk before?"

"It just might have."

"Is it the boss?"

"Even higher up! Higher than the Chief Executive in Gothenburg!"

"Who can it be? Some of the guys from ABBA?"

"Better!"

"Is there anyone in the world more famous than Michael Jackson?"

"Yep! The unknown soldier!"

Mustafa laughed. Now he understood that no one had been under the desk before him. He put his head under the desk. Merike pulled up her short skirt, showed her legs and said loudly, so that Sjöström could hear...

"Can't you see the fluffs of dust here on the left?"

"No. It's quite possible there might be some, I don't know, all I can see under this table is the most beautiful legs in the world!"

Merike laughed heartily. She pulled up her skirt even more on the right side and said loudly...

"Don't you see anything here, then?"

"No, no."

"You seem to have some problems with your eyes, right?"

"No, absolutely not, but I have big problems with my ears. They're always in the way when I take off my shirt."

Merike put her foot forward and took off her shoes.

"Oh, oh, oh, oh. You're really a good-looking girl, a shame that you have such cold feet. Do all Swedish blondes have cold feet?"

"Guess you have to warm them up, then."

Mustafa kissed Merike's feet. Merike, who was ticklish, started giggling.

"Hahahaha, Mustafa, careful! Careful, I'm no camel, I'm a woman. Hahahaha."

Sjöström was still talking to New York, but at the same time he had his ear close to the door, listening to Merike's voice.

"Yes, yes!" he said on the phone.

"How could you miss me at the party, Mustafa?" said Merike.

Mustafa stopped the foot massage and looked up at Merike.

"But you weren't there!"

"Of course I was, are you blind?"

The truth is that Mustafa had missed Merike. He was

sitting at a table with some friends, drank a lot and became pretty dizzy.

"I have to apologise, how could I be so stupid and blind?"

"You must be blind. Do you know what the EU in Brussels says about the terrorist law that all immigrants should know by heart?"

Mustafa got the idea at once, he whispered and gave her a compliment.

"Yeah, absolutely! If an immigrant doesn't spot a nice looking girl like you..."

Merike talked louder so that Sjöström could hear…

"…then he must be deported immediately", she continued.

Sjöström knocked on the door and entered the room. Merike jumped up and fixed her skirt. Mustafa pretended to be cleaning.

"It's impossible to work here, with fluffs of dirt everywhere! You could be deported to the Sahara if you continue like this, then you can tread on sand as much as you want!"

"What are you saying?" Sjöström burst out. "Deporting an immigrant just because he missed some fluffs of dust?"

Mustafa played along.

"Yeah, you heard, boss. She's tough this woman."

"But things look nice here, is there really any dust?" Sjöström asked.

"Yeah, a very small fluff of dust here on the edge of the desk, it's stuck like concrete", Mustafa replied.

"Where?" Sjöström wondered and leaned forward to inspect the dust.

Mustafa pretended to clean off the dust, got up and on the way up he deliberately hit Sjöström's chin with his head. Sjöström fell back and touched his chin.

"Ouch, ouch, ouch, damn it", he mumbled.

"Oh, sorry, boss, how clumsy of me", Mustafa said apologetically.

Merike saw that Sjöström was completely groggy.

"We'd better take you to the rest room", she said.

On the other side of the corridor Ali was cleaning room number 14. He was worried and started to doubt that Mustafa would be able to get Sjöström out of the room so that he could answer the phone. Jessika, a secretary, was sitting and writing at her desk. Surprised, she looked at the big clock Ali wore around his neck.

"Ali, could you please dust off the book shelf?" she asked kindly.

Suddenly Ali's clock rang, it was two minutes to eleven.

"No", said Ali nervously. "I can't, I have to change the water."

"You don't need any water", Jessika replied impatiently.

"You have a cloth."

All Ali could think of was the phone, so he told a white lie.

"No, it's so dirty. The boss wants us to change the water when the clock rings", he said in his defence.

By now, Ali had given up hope that Mustafa would get Sjöström out for him. He decided to go with his own plan. He went out in the corridor and poured out the water and the washing powder in front of Sjöström's office.

Mustafa had just left Sjöström in the rest room and now he came running in the first corridor, but when he turned left to the second corridor to answer the phone, he slipped on the pool of water Ali had poured out and fell to the floor. All wet, he got up on his knees and started talking angrily in Italian:

- Santo Dio e tutti i Profeti di Dio nel cielo! e tutto il nobile popolo sulla terra a cui piaciono la pace e gli spaghetti italiani! Perché mio fratello è incredibilmente stupido? ("Holy God and all God's prophets in heaven! And all gentle people on earth who love peace and Italian spaghetti! Why is my brother so unbelievably stupid?")

The telephone rings

He turned to Ali and hit him with a small brush. The time was now exactly eleven o'clock, and the phone rang.

"It's ringing, it's ringing", Mustafa whispered. "Open the door, the boss is not there, idiot!"

"So, the boss is not there?" Ali repeated and ran into Sjöström's room to answer the phone.

"Hello, hello, hi, Caroline, I never thought you'd call…"

Mustafa went into the room and pulled down the shades.

"Excuse me, Caroline…" Ali said. He turned to Mustafa and held his hand over the receiver, shaking in fear of Sjöström returning to his room.

"What are you doing? Why are you pulling down the shades? What if the boss returns? We'll have pure hell here!"

Mustafa made a gesture with his forefinger and pointed under his right eye, a typical Mediterranean gesture.

"I'm pulling down the shades so that Allah can't see you lying!"

Mustafa went out and started wiping up the water in front of the door. After a while, Ali came out, sad and disappointed.

"Bad news, bro. She's very busy for some time to come."

"Sorry to hear that, bro. But you know what, Papa Mustafa always has a plan! I'll think of something. But then you have to apologise to me for pouring water and washing powder on the floor in the corridor. I got wet!"

"Sure, sorry, brother, but I got nervous, I didn't think you would be able to clear the room, so I went for my first idea. Sorry."

Just as Ali and Mustafa had finished wiping the floor in the corridor, Merike came back.

"Hello, my dear", said Mustafa. "How's the boss feeling?"

"Not so good, he went home for the day, but I'm sure it's nothing serious."

"I'll buy some flowers and bring them here tomorrow."

"How nice of you."

"By the way, have you ever been to this place at Slussen, Bux-Biou?"

"No, but I have heard about it, sounds really good."

"I'll promise you that! Why don't you come along some day, maybe this weekend?"

"Hold on, let me check my diary."

Merike went into her room and came back with her diary.

"Friday and Saturday are a bit difficult. But maybe we can go there tonight? I just got a cancellation from a friend."

"Sounds good", said Mustafa surprised.

"Shall we say ten past five in front of Volvo´s entrance?"

"Sure!"

Merike went into her room. Mustafa was overwhelmed. He jumped on one leg and danced his way down to Pedro on the fourth floor.

"Pedro, my man!"

"Mustafa, what's happening, dude?"

"I have to ask you, what do you appreciate most in life?"

"What is this? Dr Phil or something?"

Mustafa raised his fist, imitated tennis legend John

McEnroe's theatrics.

"Just answer my question! The question, jerk!"

"Ok, easy now, Mr. McEnroe. I like my mom and dad, our president Lula da Silva, Pelé and Ronaldo. Is McEnroe happy now, or do I have to go through the meaning of life too?"

"For your mom and your dad, Pelé and everyone else, lend me seven hundred crowns."

Pedro shook his head.

"Mustafa, you must be out of your mind. You owe me 1900 already, how could you possibly believe that I would lend you more?"

"Listen here, Pedro. I've just fixed up a date with the secretary, Cameron Diaz's sister! Do you get it now?"

"Damn Saharian, how do you do it? She's high society, a cleaner must be the last thing she wants in the world!"

"Apparently not. Pedro, be a comrade, give me the cash, you know I would do the same thing for you!"

Pedro laughed despondently and shook his head again.

"Damn it, Mustafa, you have more than seven thousand crowns in your bank account on the 25th every month, but they just go in and turn around. It's as if you were McEnroe and your bank account were Björn Borg. The money bounces back as certainly as Björn Borg returns every serve."

"Easy for you to be funny now, Pedro. Come on, lend me the cash, be a sport."

"OK. But on the 25th, in the morning, you're going to give me 2600, otherwise I'll strangle you!"

At ten past five Mustafa stood in front of Volvo´s entrance with his delivery bike.

Suddenly Merike showed up, dressed in a beautiful coat and fresh white boots.

"Hi, Mustafa! Let's go there, ….but how?"

"Hi, there! We're going by 'le vélo parisien', Mustafa's Rolls Royce."

Merike looked wide-eyed at the delivery bike.

"No way, I'm taking a cab."

"Bad timing, the taxi drivers are on strike today."

"There's one over there", said Merike and pointed at a taxi passing by.

"Come on, it'll be like a sightseeing tour!"

Merike looked at Mustafa and smiled.

A minute later, Mustafa started pedalling towards Bux-Biou.

Merike at Bux-Biou

They reached Bux-Biou and went into the lounge.

"Oh, it looks nice!"

"Of course!"

"So, shall we hit the bar straight away?"

"We have to get changed first! It's a pool bar you know."

"What? I don't have any bathing clothes!"

"No harm done. You see, Mustafa has resources."

Mustafa opened his jacket and pulled out a yellow mini bikini from his inner pocket.

"What's that, Pandora's box, or what?"

"Something like that. I've got most things you need in there."

Merike smiled and looked at the mini bikini.

"Is it OK?" Mustafa asked.

"I hope so, it's really cool!"

Beef Wellington à la Cameron Diaz

They went in and changed. Mustafa came out to the pool area first, Merike a moment later. Mustafa wasn't disappointed by her appearance; Merike had Cameron

Diaz's face on Jennifer Lopez's body.

"I feel really naked, it's so small!"

"No, it fits you perfectly."

"You think so? I really hate the size of my bottom."

"That's what all girls say. You look so good in this, if I had a camel's tail, I would be waving it!"

Merike laughed abashed. They found a free table and sat down.

"Mustafa, can you take care of my bag? I think I might take a swim."

"Sure, I'll wait here."

Mustafa went to the bar and ordered two Besbussa, came back and put the drinks on the table. Merike came up from the pool.

"May I treat you to a very special drink… Besbussa!"

"What do you think? Do I look like a girl who accepts drinks on the first date?"

"Absolutely! I'm convinced you are", said Mustafa with a broad smile.

Merike had a sense of humour. She didn't become upset, but instead turned on a beautiful smile.

"You must be a mind-reader! But don't expect sex on the beach, just because you treated me to a drink!"

Mustafa laughed and they toasted.

"No, no, I'm not like that. It's just that in my culture, it's a crime not to treat a cute girl to a drink. I was obliged to do it."

Merike smiled and took a sip.

"Mmm, it's so good! What's in it?"

Mustafa was a Muslim who ever since he came to Sweden had taken the distance course "Buy your own liquor and learn alcohol culture" at Systembolaget's "Wine and booze school."

"It's top secret, the recipe is locked inside a safe, hidden in a bomb shelter, 50 meters underground!"

Merike laughed, and with her laughter as a support,

he decided to attack.

"You know what? You look exactly like Cameron Diaz! The same mouth, the same eyes, same smile. Even the same hair cut!"

"Thanks, what a compliment!"

Merike drank the last of her drink. Suddenly, she started crying loud. Mustafa was completely startled by her sudden mood swing.

"Oh, what's happening? Are you OK? Has something happened?"

"I promised my mom never to accept drinks from strangers. There could be drugs in them. I've read a lot about it in the newspapers. And now I've broken my promise to mom twice!"

Mustafa looked at her with surprise.

"Twice? I've only treated you with ONE drink, and I can promise you there's no drugs in it!"

Merike suddenly burst into a beautiful smile.

"So you're going to treat me with another drink, Mustafa? This Besbussa was really good!"

Mustafa felt fooled, but in a good way. Merike had just pulled a "Beef Wellington à la Cameron Diaz" on him. He shook his head, went to the bar to get two more drinks.

"To us!"

"You scared me there", said Mustafa.

"Sorry. But it's just that it's such a current topic, there are so many girls who get drugged at bars, my friend for example."

"That's terrible, I would never make love to a drugged woman, that must be like making love to a donkey, no response, no emotions!"

"Ooh, let's talk about something completely different. Have you been painting anything these days?"

"No, not lately, now I'm obsessed with two things, comedy and buxom women with beautiful curves."

"Yeah, I've noticed that on all the notes you sent

me."

"Humour is good for stress and the best medicine against anxiety. And best of all, it makes you think more clearly", Mustafa informed her.

"How do you develop your humour?"

"Let's take a swim and I'll explain it to you."

When they jumped into the pool, salsa music started streaming out of the stereo and the bikini show started. Suddenly they had trouble hearing what the other said. They got out the pool when the bikini contest was over to see some girls and boys from "Swedish Idol" sing on the stage.

"Can I buy you a glass of wine, Merike?"

"I don't want to get drunk, Mustafa! It's so easy to get drunk on an empty stomach, and then you feel like shit the next day!"

Mustafa rolled his eyes.

"OK, I understand."

"It smells really good from the bar, what is it?" Merike asked.

"Croque Monsieur with beef meat."

"Oh. Do you think you can ask them what blood group the cows have?"

Mustafa rolled his eyes again. Who was this girl? he asked himself.

" I'll ask in the bar."

Mustafa went over to the bar.

"Tia, which blood group have the cows that you fry here?"

"What kind of a question is that? Mustafa, you've only had two drinks, are you totally losing touch?"

"I'm in good shape. But I've started to question how things are with my date, I'm actually asking on her account."

"She leaves the hard work to you, to ask moronic questions!"

Mustafa nodded and smiled. Lasse stepped into the bar.

"Lasse, listen to this…", said Tia. Lasse interrupted her when he saw Mustafa.

"Hey, Mustafa! You fool, have you found your way here again? I have to start taking rent from you soon!"

"But I buy drinks for the amount of an apartment in Gamla Stan, that should be enough as rent!"

"Your drinks would add up to the Gross National Product of a West African country! Now that you mention it… well… you alone would keep this place going!" Lasse joked.

"I should get at least a chair on the board of directors!"

Lasse laughed.

"We'll fix that, Mustafa, we'll fix that. At least you don't have to pay rent here. Anyway, how are things?"

"Good, except that my date is a little mysterious. Or what do you say, Tia?"

"Erm… yeah! This job never ceases to surprise you. Lasse, you don't, by any and I mean any chance, happen to know the blood group of the beef here?"

"The blood group of the beef?"

"Yes, the blood group of the cows whose beef the chef in our restaurant cooks."

"Is it your date wondering that? Where do you find these girls, Mustafa? Has the madhouse started some sort of dating business or what?"

Mustafa rolled his eyes.

"She's too cultural for you, Lasse, on a completely different level. You'll never understand her."

"Sure, Mustafa. Tell her that we only have camel meat here!"

Mustafa smiled and went back to the table.

"I was wrong, they only have camel meat here, no cows!"

"Oh, how exotic, I'll have two at once!" Merike giggled.

After a while, Merike had finished eating.

"Was it good?" Mustafa asked.

"It was fabulous, delicious!" Merike cheered.

"Do you want another one?" Mustafa asked gentlemanlike.

"Yeah, one or two, with camel meat", said Merike.

Mustafa went back to Tia and ordered two more Croque Monsieur for Merike.

45 minutes later, Merike had finished eating. Her cell phone rang. She looked at the display but didn't want to answer, so she let it ring until it stopped.

"Mustafa, I have to go now."

"What? Already?"

"Yeah. I have to be in bed by 21.30 if I want to be in good shape tomorrow.-

"Can I meet you Friday night?"

"I'll have a look."

Merike picked up her diary from her bag.

"Let's see… Today is December 13… hmm… this is difficult."

Merike kept browsing through her diary.

"My schedule's really full, the earliest date I'm able to get time off is January 22."

"What? That's next year! Who are you, the prime minister?"

"No, Mustafa, it's just that I love dating!"

Mustafa just yawned. He became silent and then managed to pull himself together.

"OK, and how long have you had this little hobby, then?"

"Well, it was when my boyfriend and I separated… that would have been three years ago… that was when I became interested."

"OK. And may I ask how many dates you've been on

since that?"

"Mustafa, do you think that a woman who has a bad immune defence and often has a cold counts how many handkerchiefs she uses?"

Mustafa was destroyed and his face was all red. Merike stood up from her chair and gave him a hug.

"Thanks for the evening, Mustafa, I had a nice time!"

Mustafa, at the same time sad and ruined, looked at Merike as she left the place. He mumbled silently, "Damn chick. How will I be able to pay Pedro?"

Mustafa thought that Merike came from a rich family with high position, she was always well dressed and wore nice make up. What he didn't know was that she lived in a rented two room apartment in Hagsätra, a working-class suburb south of Stockholm. Merike was self-confident, intelligent and full of charm. But she was also very greedy. And the greediness impregnated everything in her life. She was treated like a queen by men with fancy cars asking her out for dinner. Now Mustafa sat there thinking about what she said, that "a woman who has a bad immune defence and often has a cold doesn't count how many handkerchiefs she uses". That was how she walked through life.

Lasse's advice

Lasse stepped up to the brooding Mustafa.

"So, what have we got here? She left like she had fire in her ass!"

"Yeah, I can't believe this. Lasse, you're Swedish. Can you see on a woman if she's good or just a swindler?"

Lasse laughed.

"With chicks, it´s a bloody lottery. If you don't draw a winner you risk a life in poverty! Experience, my good Mustafa, experience! Tell me, how long have you been here in Sweden?"

"Three and a half years, soon four."

"Man, that's nothing! You have a lot to learn, Mustafa. Listen to Papa Lasse here, I've been out in the Stockholm nightlife for many years. I can give you a fresh story directly from the bar over there. There were two girls, one of them ordered the most expensive champagne we have. I heard that the other girl was shocked. 'How can you afford that, your boyfriend doesn't make that much'? 'No', said the other. 'But I have a lover who gives me eight thousand a month'. 'My God, that's good', said her friend. 'I don't know any guy who can give me that much'. 'Get two then', said the first girl, 'and let them pay you four grand each! Or four that pay you two thousand each. Or eight that pay you a thousand each!' The other girl laughed like hell, and started to yell at me for some snacks. I closed my eyes and said 'Wake me up when you're down to a hundred each, then I can serve you snacks!"

"What kind of style is that, swindling guys for money like that."

"Style? It's a job, Mustafa, a job! They should pay tax and be entitled to a pension. They're black market workers"

Mustafa looked thoughtful.

"Well, Lasse, I guess I just got in the way of one of those black market workers."

"Guaranteed, Mustafa. Trial and error, brother, trial and error! You have to practise to get the sense for who pays tax and who doesn't. But don't hesitate to consult Doctor Lasse if you're here at Bux-Biou and meet some girl that looks suspicious, I'd be glad to help out."

The day after, Mustafa told Pedro what happened on the date. He also asked Pedro to move him back to his old floor so that he wouldn't have to meet Merike at work.

An appointment with Caroline

Mustafa booked an appointment for Ali with Caroline at Liljeholmen's health care centre. The next day, Ali sat in the centre's waiting room with a bouquet of flowers in his hands. A nurse handed over a form to Caroline.

"Ali Babuba!" Caroline shouted loudly. "But hey, is that you, Ali?"

Ali nodded and gave her the bouquet.

"Here you go", he said and blushed on.

"Thanks, what beautiful flowers!"

They went into Caroline's room.

"Now you have to tell me about what problem you have", said Caroline.

Ali looked down to the floor, as if he wanted to say something that bothered him.

"I have a heart problem", he said thoughtfully."I want you to listen to my heart when I tell you this story."

"Then I have to ask you to take off your shirt, please!"

Ali took a step back.

"No, no, no", he said, worried. "I'm afraid of all those hospital instruments and machines.

Caroline placed her stethoscope on the table and put her head against Ali's heart.

"OK! Then we do it the old way. Now tell me!"

Ali's heart kept pounding, and his pressure rose.

"Caroline! That thing I said about my job when we met at Kafferepet, it wasn't true. But the union is going to help me with an education."

"The union? But your brother told me you're an economist."

Ali got nervous and started moving his head like a camel.

"No, no, no, I'm no economist! I'm scared that if I

tell the truth, everything between us will be ruined. OK, I'm a cleaner, I'm so sorry."

Caroline moved her head back from Ali's heart.

"I already knew that", she said with a smile. "Extension number 666 belongs to Bengt Sjöström, he's my cousin."

Ali fell back onto the floor, kicking with his feet like a small child.

"Oh, my heart can't take another heart attack! I feel so ashamed, I can't look you in the eyes!"

Caroline's daughter Kim, a ten year old girl, came into the room.

"Oh, how cool, he does just as I do when I am angry. Are you the one who sent me chocolate cakes?"

Ali sat up on the floor and nodded.

"Yes, little girl, it was I."

"Thank you! Where do you come from?"

"Tunisia."

"Do you have camels at home in Tunisia?"

"No, but our family has our very own donkey! She's sweet, obedient and her name is Besbussa!"

"Besbussa! What a strange name."

Caroline nodded and smiled.

"We have her in our apartment a couple of hours every day, she likes that."

"Is that really true, can you have a donkey in your apartment?"

"Of course you can! We have to get used to it in stages, as the Frenchmen say, 'peu à peu'!"

"You speak strange, what do you mean?"

"How old are you, Kim?"

"Ten and a half."

"You know, in thirty years we'll be out of oil, so when you are 45, you won't be able to drive a car anymore, then you either have to ride a bike or a donkey!"

"Oh, is it true? Then I'll take the donkey!"

Ali and Caroline laughed.

"What a strange name, Besbussa", said Kim. "Can I come and look at it?"

"Of course you can, you're welcome, you and your mother!"

"Please, mom", Kim begged. "We have to visit him so that we can see Besbussa the donkey!"

Ali became hopeful.

"It would be an honour to have you over for some couscous on Saturday."

"Couscous! Do you read the Koran before you eat couscous?" Kim asked. "I have some classmates from the Middle East, and they always read the Koran before they eat."

"No, we don't, my mom cooks such a good tasting couscous, so we don't need to read the Koran!"

A broad smile spread across Caroline's face.

"Please, mom", Kim begged. "I want to eat couscous and meet the donkey this Saturday!"

"But that's impossible", said Caroline. "It's your birthday on Saturday! Your friends will come to our home. And Anna, too!"

"But please, mom, it will be the best birthday ever, with couscous and Besbussa the donkey! And Anna and the boys can come too?"

"But we're not sure if Anna and the boys want to come."

"But they like foreign food! Don't you remember when we were at their place and they cooked that strong stew?"

Kim turned to Ali, who was still sitting on the floor.

"Do you know Anna Lindh, the Swedish foreign minister?"

"Eh... yeah?"

"Can she come to your home too?"

Ali fell down on the floor again, shocked. He turned

to Caroline.

"Ouch, ouch, my heart, I can't take another heart attack today! Do you really know Anna Lindh?"

"Yeah, she's my friend. And our kids are friends."

"Please mom", Kim interrupted, "can't we visit them and bring Anna and the boys with us? It would be the best birthday ever!"

Caroline smiled.

"I have to think about it, I'll call Anna and check if she can come along."

Ali said thank you and left. He took the underground home to Skärholmen and told the family about Anna Lindh's supposed visit. He couldn't believe it was true: Anna Lindh for dinner at their place, in Skärholmen!

A party for Caroline

Two days later, when the family was having coffee, Caroline called Ali and confirmed that they could come on Saturday at five, together with Anna Lindh and her sons.

"That's amazing, do you really mean THAT Anna Lindh?" Merjam nearly spit out her coffee when Ali told her.

"Then I guess we have to cook something really good", she said.

"I promised it'd be something with couscous, Kim likes that."

"OK, let's do that. But…"

"What is it, mom?"

"I just realised… it's the 'Humour without borders' party on Saturday night."

"Oh no, I totally forgot that."

Merjam remained seated and pondered it all for a while.

"You know what, Ali? I can skip the party. I think it'll work out fine without me, they're starting to come to grips with things now, and Claudia is so clever. I mean, it's not every day the Swedish foreign minister comes visiting. I can at least call Claudia and ask?"

"Are you sure?"

"Yes, don't worry, Ali, there'll be more 'Humour without borders' parties."

Ali while his mother is away

Merjam, Bibbi, Fatima and Mustafa were going to Falun in Dalarna, a province northwest of Stockholm, to celebrate Bibbi's grandmother's birthday on Thursday. Ali stayed in Stockholm. He had trouble sleeping and thought about Caroline all the time. He decided to take three days of compensatory leave from work.

On Wednesday, he went to IKEA and bought a bunch of green plants, both big and small. Then he bought a synthetic grass carpet the size of the living room floor from a shop in the city.

On Thursday he got help from Pedro and another friend to rip out the old living room floor and put the synthetic grass carpet there instead. Then they put all the plants Ali had bought in the living room.

On Friday afternoon Fatima was supposed to come home from Falun. She was responsible for planning the Saturday dinner together with Ali. Merjam and Bibbi stayed an extra day to see some more of Dalarna - Mora, Leksand and Rättvik.

Mustafa went to Borlänge, another town in Dalarna, to see his old love Eva.

When Fatima came home she couldn't believe her eyes. But she decided not to complain, she left that to her mom instead.

Beef Wellington à la Mel Gibson

Saturday just before noon, Fatima's neighbour Yvonne and Yvonne's daughter Madelene sat in the Babuba living room.

Ali came home with his friends. He had a black ghirba, a twenty litre water container made out of goat skin, hanging over his shoulder.

It was a souvenir that Merjam had inherited from her grandfather, who used the ghirba when he sold water in the market of Matmata. Her grandfather had worn a traditional Moroccan costume with a big leather belt over it. He had attached hooks in the leather belt, on which he had hung aluminium cups for his customers to drink water from.

Ali's friends had brought a wheel barrow, vases with plants in them and green pepper. Besbussa had company: a sheep, a goat, a rooster and chickens. All of a sudden, the Babuba flat had turned into a zoo.

"Hurry up, boys", said Ali. "We don't have much time."

Fatima jumped out of the couch.

"What are you doing?" she yelled.

"We're going to make a hole in every corner of the room, and then put vases filled with green pepper in the holes", said Ali.

"But how are you going to make holes? The floor is made of concrete."

Ali lifted up a sledge hammer from the wheel barrow.

"With this , of course!"

"Are you out of your mind, Ali? This is reinforced concrete!"

"We are three strong men, we can do it!"

"What? Are you mad, removing the parquet floor without mom's approval? And now you want to cause us more trouble! The landlord is going to throw us out!"

"I don't think so."

"Listen, Ali. You can NOT dig up the floor!"

Ali now got mad at Fatima.

Besbussa got in between them, hindering them from hurting each other. The donkey protected Fatima like a mother protects her daughter, and started to bray so loud that half of Skärholmen heard her.

"Watch out, watch out", Ali screamed to the donkey, "or I'll get really mad!"

Fatima took shelter behind the donkey, screaming, "Besbussa, Besbussa..."

The donkey moved, to the left, to the right, following every move Ali was making, stopping him from getting close to Fatima.

Yvonne and her daughter watched the drama with open wide eyes. They had never seen anything like it before.

Ali yelled at the donkey, which kept on braying louder and louder.

"Shut up, Besbussa, shut up!"

"Ali, you give us immigrants a bad reputation. Immigrants will have problems finding places to stay, the word will be spread all over Europe that immigrants are ripping up the parquet floor and growing vegetables in the living room..."

"I don't think so."

Then Mustafa came home, with flowers in his hands. He looked surprised and smiled. The donkey continued to bray loudly.

"For the last time, Besbussa. Shut up", said Ali in despair. "Please, Fatima, I'm going to grow spices, Swedes like that stuff!"

Fatima looked at the vase with the plants in them. "You're going to grow spices from green pepper seeds? You think I'm stupid? You need sun for that!"

"Dear sister, evolution is moving forward", Ali

answered charmingly. "You don't need sun, you just tell under-the-belt jokes, and the peppers start blushing in no time!"

Merjam comes back from Dalarna

Merjam came home and put her travelling bag on the floor. She looked at the chaotic living room with surprised eyes. The donkey was screaming so that the whole neighbourhood could hear, the sheep bleated and the goat too, the rooster crowed, the chicken cackled - a cacophony. Ali stood with his back to Merjam. so he hadn't noticed that she had come home.

"Enough is enough!" Fatima shouted. "First you took away the parquet and now you want to make holes in the floor!"

"It's my party!" said Ali cockily.

Merjam went into the living room and saw the green grass carpet. She lifted it and discovered that Ali had taken away the parquet. She was furious.

"It's my apartment, you fool!" she shouted. "I call the shots here. Who has given you permission to take away the parquet?"

"Please, mom…", Ali started.

"SHUT UP! We're thankful that with a little help from Bibbi we have the opportunity to have the donkey with us here in the apartment, at least for a couple of hours a day. But apparently, that's not enough for you, you want sheep, goats, all kinds of animals! And who has given you permission to ruin grandfather's ghirba, the best memory of our culture?"

"Please, mom", said Ali. "Why are the Swedes allowed to have up to four big dogs, and cats, in their apartments? What's the difference between a little dog and a little pig? Animals are animals! I want to create a little green Tunisian farmstead, with animals, and…"

"Listen up, Ali. There's a saying: 'When in Rome, do as the Romans do'. First of all, cats and dogs are pets..."

"But mom..."

"Shut up! The Swedes have nice green homes, they have their plants in their windows, but they don't tear up the parquet floor! Why have you taken it away? WHY?"

"I was inspired by Mel Gibson."

"What?"??

"I saw his film, 'What Women Want'. I was inspired by his way of picking up chicks."

"So Monsieur Gibson tears up the parquet and grows potatoes and carrots in the apartment in this movie or what?"

"Not exactly, but in women's magazines, they always talk about variation in your home. Taking away the parquet is one way to create variation, and variation brings excitement and warmth."

"Are you stupid?"

"Why does no one understand me, my worries and my emotions? I have so much trouble finding a girl... Girls are like fish nowadays; hard to catch!"

"No, Ali, you're wrong! There are plenty of fish in the sea! You just lack the right hook, what we call the Mel Gibson hook!"

"You're cruel, mom! How can you say that to your own son?"

Merjam waved aside Ali's criticism.

"I'm angry! You bring animals here, rip up the floor, walk around like a clown carrying water on your shoulder, and..."

Mustafa interrupted Merjam.

"Water, dear mom! It's the most important thing we have! We have to be careful with the water."

"What? In a country like Sweden there's water for all of us!"

"Mum dear, do try to understand why Ali wants to

walk around with his ghirba. It's like a film about a mobile bar."

"What? Is it some comic act?"

"Mum, comedy often tells the truth. There's an important truth in what Ali is doing, carrying water."

"What kind of good sense is that?"

"Well, the truth is", Mustafa explained and used the al-Jazeera argument, "that within twenty years, millions of people will be short of water, there's going to be a water war! Ali here wants to emphasise the water question, simple as that!"

"What do you mean?"

"The demand for water is going to be higher than the supply. In 2016 the Arab world and Africa won't have enough water."

"Are you drunk or are you pretending to be a prophet?"

"You know, mum, people come from different cultures: Americans, Arabs, Europeans… but they all have one thing in common - they have the same enemy."

"And which enemy is that?"

"People who don't want to hear the truth! Ali here is a visionary, he wants us to find solutions, start a debate. Right, Ali?"

"What are you talking about, Mustafa? I don't have any water in this", said Ali and pointed at the ghirba.

"Yes, you have!" Mustafa replied.

"No, you fool!"

"What are you carrying then?"

"My savings, 30 000 kronor, which I changed into one-kronor coins. It's all in this bag!"

"You're mad, you just look ridiculous", said Merjam.

"Wait, wait", said Ali. "Newspapers like Dagens Nyheter and Svenska Dagbladet, Le Monde, New York Times, Washington Post, in the culture section they say that it doesn't matter how you look, as long as you have a warm and generous heart behind the Usama bin Laden wallet. Mom, have you ever heard the sweet Las Vegas-music?"

Ali had sewed a zipper at the bottom end of his great grandfather's ghirba. The old treasure was around a meter long and half a meter in diameter.

He walked up to a basin which he had placed on the floor, leaned forward and opened the zipper on the ghirba, so that all the one-kronor coins could drop out.

It rattled like when hitting the jackpot on a slot machine.

"Voila – this is what women want to hear! You see mom, there are two things that women like: variation and money."

Merjam looked at Ali. She calmed down, and although she was furious at her son, she started to grasp just what a nerd he was, and how he had completely misunderstood "what women want."

Her heart ached as she looked at her confused son and the rebuilt living room around him.

"There won't be any party here tonight!" she commanded him. "And you have to get a new parquet floor from IKEA tomorrow! If not, you have to move out!"

Merjam went into her room and slammed the door. Mustafa stepped up to Ali.

"Now you have to stop arguing with mom, Ali. Pick up your coins and return the animals to their owners."

Yvonne and her daughter were silent; They felt embarrassed.

"Maybe we should go now", they said. "Bye."

The ghirba was valuable to Mother. Mustafa understood that Ali was brave to put a zipper in it. Mustafa stared into space for a moment. He had thought on many occasions about filling the ghirba with wine and walking around in Stockholm on Midsummer Eve and New Year's Eve and offering people wine from 'Hollywood's mobile bar'.

Ali collected the animals and went out. When Merjam heard the door slam, she went to the living room, where Mustafa was sitting. She was still irritated.

"How could Ali do this behind my back? Did you know about his plan, Mustafa?"

"No, mom, I swear, I didn't know anything, I was with you in Dalarna!"

Bibbi came into the apartment without ringing the doorbell, she had her own key. She was going to return an umbrella that Merjam had forgotten in the trunk of her car. When Bibbi came into the living room, she was met by Merjam's screams.

"Damn this family, causing so much trouble", she yelled. "As soon as you turn your back on it, some shit happens!"

"What has happened?" Bibbi wondered.

Merjam lifted up the synthetic grass carpet and showed Bibbi.

"Ali has ripped out the parquet floor in order to grow potatoes, pepper, and carrots."

Bibbi laughed.

"Why?"

"He's inspired by Mel Gibson, how to pick up women."

"What?"

"It's insane, I feel like running away from Sweden."

Bibbi smiled, but she decided not to butt in. That was one of her principles, not to do that, despite knowing the Babubas so well.

"Here's your umbrella, you left it in my car."

"Thanks."

Beef Wellington à la Parkinson

Mustafa knew how much Merjam liked the British talk show host Michael Parkinson, who knew his interviewees inside out, just as he and Merjam knew each other inside out. To save his brother's skin, he tried to cook up a "Beef Wellington à la Parkinson."

"I agree with you, mom. Ali should have asked you first. But maybe fate has settled things for Besbussa."

"And exactly what do you mean by that?" Merjam muttered.

"Mom, remember how bravely you fought for all the donkeys who were carrying heavy loads and were struggling in Tunisia. And then you came to Sweden, where people take care of animals. And all of a sudden, you're letting our own donkey slip around on the parquet floor!"

"What are you talking about?"

"Please, mom, this is really dangerous for Besbussa, walking around on the parquet floor. That's why she's all tense, she's afraid of slipping!"

"I, sure as hell, haven't noticed that!"

"Oh yeah, she does that all the time! And that's not good for her! It's just like asking an Arab woman who has walked barefoot in the Sahara all her life suddenly to move to Sweden and there force her to walk on ice wearing high heeled shoes."

Mustafa walked over to the other side of the living room and cried.

"Besbussa, Besbussa!"

Besbussa started walking towards Mustafa with steady steps, relaxed.

"You see, mom, what a difference! And by the way, mom, you know that it's forbidden according to the Swedish social board to have a donkey that walks on the parquet floor in your apartment, we must thank Bibbi who made a little exception for us!"

Merjam was getting insecure and had trouble finding words.

"Oh, it's nothing", Bibbi interrupted her.

"You, Mother, who have fought evil people who treat their animals badly, should be pleased that Ali has removed the parquet floor. I remember when I was twelve in Tunisia. There were all these kids by the big garbage dump, throwing stones at cats and dogs. And you ran after them, mom, you took off your shoes and threw them at the kids, and you ended up hitting that English charmer with one shoe, you know, the one who looked like Parkinson, he lived at the hotel where you were working! Do you remember that?"

"Sure, I remember that. I thought that he would be mad but he only laughed and said that violence never pays off. You have to keep cool, like the English."

Bibbi laughed. "Yes, the English are happy when they go abroad, the sun shines and the beer is half the price compared to in England", she said.

"I'll explain to you, Bibbi", said Mustafa excitedly. "Once, when I was out shopping at the market with mom, we saw a couple of young boys throwing sones at cats. Mom had learned from the English charmer how to handle people who are cruel to animals. She asked them, 'Why are you doing that? You can make big money from cats'! Do you remember, mom?"

"Sure."

"And then you told them that you had raised a cat which became your loyal friend. It became so loyal that later when you sold it to some tourists, it always came back to you. You sold it five times and it came running back every time! You made 200 dinars off that cat! A month's salary for a Tunisian worker!"

"Well done, Merjam!" Bibbi burst out. Merjam nodded and smiled reluctantly.

"One of the boys wondered how you could make a cat become so loyal that it came back to you five times", Mustafa continued. And mom answered, 'By not throwing stones at it, and being kind to it. Animals need love and warmth too'."

"Stylish! English gentlemen are too diplomatic to start throwing stones." said Bibbi and turned to Mustafa, who added:

"Yes indeed, over there the Society for the Protection of Animals is a Royal Society."

"What did the boys do afterwards? asked Bibbi. "Did they make friends with the cats?"

"To be sure they did! Mum really taught them how to behave. If the prime minister had seen her, he would have made her minister of education."

"Now I know why you always change channels from al-Jazeera to Swedish Television when they show Parkinson!"

Merjam shook her head.

"Are you going to start fooling around too?" Merjam asked.

"Absolutely not! I was genuinely glad when I heard Mustafa's story. You're a real animal lover, Merjam."

Merjam looked despondent.

"An animal lover with people problems! Imagine if the landlord discovers what Ali has done. He'll probably tell the media that immigrants take away the parquet and grow potatoes and pepper. What a scandal!"

Mustafa charmed her and made a little joke.

"Oh dear! If that happened, I think the integration minister would rather run away from Sweden than face the Swedish media."

Bibbi laughed. Mustafa hugged Merjam.

"I hope we can still have this party", he said.

Merjam nodded.

"I have to go now", said Bibbi. "See you!"

Tidying the apartment

Fatima and Mustafa started to tidy the apartment. Mustafa went out with the empty boxes and threw them into the container outside the house.

Then he received a phone call from a sad and disappointed Ali.

"Please, Mustafa, call Caroline and tell her that there won't be any party. Here's her phone number…"

"No, no", Mustafa interrupted. "The party is on! We're so happy to see Caroline and the Swedish foreign minister!"

Ali was overwhelmed.

"What? Just how have you managed to persuade mom? I mean, she's an Arab feminist of colossal proportions!"

"Difficult feminists like mom need something digestible, like a 'Beef Wellington à la Parkinson'. It is served with intelligence and charm."

"Thanks, you really saved my day!"

"I had to do something, didn't I? But damn you if you try to play Arab farmstead in our home again. We live in an apartment."

"Yes, but you know, it's in every newspaper, every magazine these days. Women want variation."

"Moron! Idiot! Peasant! Were you born under the kitchen table or what? Women want variation, yes, but in bed! Different positions and stuff. It has nothing to do with potatoes and carrots!"

Merjam was in the kitchen cooking food. Mustafa, who had just returned, was busy dusting the bookshelf.

"What are you doing?" said Mustafa harshly. "Here I am, cleaning, and you're just destroying. Where did you find those books?"

"In a box under my bed."

"Are you mad, those are full of dust and shit, throw them away!"

"Our apartment is a typical immigrant home – full of decorations but we don't have a single book in the living room."

"That's enough! Your room is full of books."

"We have to show that we're cultural people!"

"I want to ask journalists from all over the world: what is a cultural person? Is it someone who understands his fellow citizens, like Mustafa? Or is it a person who hides his egoism and frustration behind words and phrases?"

Merjam, who had listened to the discussion, interrupted.

"Mustafa! Stop arguing! Go and greet the guests by the garage!"

Ali came home and Merjam greeted him in the vestibule.

"Hi, mom."

"Hi, Ali."

"I'm so sorry, mom, it was really stupid what I did."

"You should have spoken to me first, I could have explained a thing or two about variation for you. Variation avoids monotony in a couple's life. You go to the movies, theatre, restaurant, you travel, you do things together!"

Ali looked at Merjam, astonished at a sudden understanding.

"So that's what they mean?"

Merjam nodded.

"Yes! I want to apologise too. For what I said about the Mel Gibson hook, that was really stupid of me. You have the best hook, you are a kind, gentle and funny guy, there's nothing girls like better, I promise you!"

"Ah, stop it, mom."

"Come here."

Merjam gave Ali a long, warm hug. Then he went to

take a shower and in the shower, he thought about Mustafa's and Merjam's ideas about variation. He wished that Mel Gibson could send him an e-mail with tips about how to become "what women want."

Caroline and Anna Lindh

At five o'clock, Caroline, Kim, Anna Lindh and her sons stood outside the entrance door with their bicycles. Caroline shouted.

"Ali, Ali…"

Ali, who was in his room, freshening himself up in front of the mirror, heard the shouting and walked to the balcony.

"Hi!" he said and smiled delightedly. "I'll be there in a sec!"

Ali continued to the kitchen, excited.

"Mom! Caroline, the kids and the Swedish foreign minister have come here on their bikes!"

"Ce n'est pas possible. The Swedish foreign minister going by bike! Mustafa is waiting for them by the garage, we thought they'd be coming here in a limo. Hurry up, get the camera, Fatima! I have to take a picture and send it to al-Jazeera, show them how Swedish democracy works!"

Fatima smiled a weary smile.

"Forget about al-Jazeera, there's no film in the camera!"

Merjam and Fatima greeted the guests with cries of joy while repeatedly hitting their mouths with one hand… RRA, RRA, RRA…

"Welcome, merhaba!"

Kim was fascinated by the somewhat unusual greeting.

"More, more", she begged. "It sounds so beautiful when you do RRA, RRA, RRA…"

Merjam and Fatima made their sound of joy once

again: RRA… RRA…

"Choukran, thank you very much", said Anna Lindh and Caroline in.unison.

"Come on in to the living room", said Merjam.

The kids, Kim and Anna Lindh's two sons, walked up to the donkey and started patting it.

"Oh, such a cute donkey", said Kim happily. "Oh, and she smells so good! And such a cosy place!"

No limousine

Fatima went down to pick up Mustafa, who stood by the garage with flowers in his hands. He had cordoned off a space for three cars with a rope. Mustafa thought that a minister in Sweden would move around just like the ministers in Arab countries. Their neighbour Nikos drove up in his Volvo.

"Hi, Mustafa! Are these spots booked or what?" he asked.

"Yes, they are", said Mustafa cockily. "For a very important person."

Nikos looked curiously at Mustafa.

"And who is this very important person?" he asked.

"Guess who's coming to dinner at the Babubas'!"

"Guess… impossible! Who can it be?"

"Look, mate, it's the Swedish foreign minister, Anna Lindh!"

"Jesus Christ! I'll be damned! Can you ask her to fix work a permit for my cousin?"

"Business! Just give me that envelope with sweet smelling banknotes in it,and I'll ask her to fix work permits for your whole family, including your grandmother! The Babuba family has struck it rich in a big way."

Nikos laughed. A Saab came up behind him, passed by and stopped some distance in front of Nikos. It was another neighbour, Lars, who had come home from his job as a garbage collector. He stepped out of the car, dressed in blue working clothes and looked at Nikos and Mustafa.

"Mustafa, do you need all those spaces?" he asked.

"Ah oui, we're expecting a limo, it's going to be parked there in the middle, and on each side of the limo there are going to be cars from the police and the security company."

"So, Mr Arafat is finally coming to Skärholmen, right?"

"No, but Mrs Anna Lindh is!"

"I'll be damned! Is there some sort of political meeting here in Skärholmen today? I didn't know that."

Lars didn't wait for an answer from Mustafa, he just jumped back into his Saab and drove a bit further away. Then Fatima came running to the garage.

"Mustafa, come with me, the guests have already arrived!"

Mustafa looked at Fatima, surprised.

"What? Have they landed somewhere with a helicopter?"

"No, they've taken their bikes! Come on now!"

"Fantastic, here we have immigrants driving Volvos, and Swedish workers driving Saabs, while the foreign minister rides a bike. Sweden is a strange country. Are the Swedish politicians ashamed of driving cars, or what?" asked Mustafa.

"No, I don't think so", said Fatima. "Sweden is an open society and the ministers like being among people. This proves that we have a democracy! I wish that all ministers in the whole world would imitate Anna Lindh."

Couscous

They went into the apartment. Fatima introduced Mustafa to the guests.

"This is my brother, Mustafa."

Mustafa shook hands with the guests, one after another. When he had come to Kim, she wouldn't let go of his hand.

"Such a funny moustache", she said. "The colours of the Swedish flag!"

"Thanks! A new trend I started."

"Why have you started a new trend?"

"Well, you see, men also want to have accessories."

Everyone laughed and looked at Mustafa. He became nervous.

Merjam was serving juice. Mustafa's hand started shaking, and he accidentally spilled out his glass.

"Are you nervous, Mustafa?"

"No, mom"

"I sure hope not, because if you are, you could be causing trouble for Anna here. She's going to meet the American Foreign Minister Colin Powell soon, I read it in the newspaper!"

Anna Lindh was surprised and looked at Merjam.

"What sort of problem do you mean?" asked Mustafa.

"Haven't you heard what the Americans are saying?"

Mustafa shook his head.

"They say that every time a nervous Scandinavian spills something, on the other side of the Atlantic an American dies of fear."

Anna Lindh smiled and put her arm around Merjam.

Mustafa, Ali, Merjam, Fatima, Caroline, Anna Lindh and her sons sat down to have dinner in the living room. Kim sat down on the donkey instead.

Merjam had cooked couscous, goulash and mokli. A friend of Mustafa's, who just had come back to Sweden from Tunisia, had brought sun-ripe tomatoes and pepper so that they could make mokli, which was Mustafa's favourite dish. But they started off with couscous.

"Oh, this is good, I really like couscous!" said the

foreign minister. "How do you cook couscous like this?"
"You can do it in two ways", said Merjam.
"In two ways? How do you mean?"
"Well, it depends on if you want your guests back a second time or not…"
Anna Lindh smiled.
"It's so good", said Caroline. "It melts in my mouth… come and eat, Kim!"
"No, thanks. Not now! I'll be there later."

Mokli

Mokli is a special Tunisian dish, simple to cook. Some people call it "poor man's food." The Babuba family broke the bread into little pieces. Then they dipped the pieces in tomato sauce and took fried pepper and French fries by hand.

Anna Lindh and Caroline studied how the Babubas ate mokli and tried to do the same.

"I haven't tasted anything this good", said Caroline. "How do you make this mokli?"

"It's so simple", said Merjam. "You fry pepper in olive oil, and then you fry potato wedges. Remember! You cannot do the potatoes first. Then you fry tomatoes with garlic and different Tunisian spices."

"Come and eat mokli, Kim!" said Caroline. "It melts in your mouth!"

Kim, who was still sitting on the donkey, started to get curious when she saw her mom and the rest eating with their hands. She had never seen that before. She jumped off the donkey and walked over to the table.

"Yummy, yummy", she said.

Minutes passed, everyone enjoyed the food. All of a sudden, the phone rang in Fatima's room. She went to her room to answer.

Merjam started gathering the plates.

Kim jumped up on the donkey again and discovered the bookshelf. She took out a book from the shelf.

"Look, mom!" she said. "Astrid Lindgren's books, do you like Astrid Lindgren, Ali?"

Ali had never heard of Astrid Lindgren. He had never studied Swedish in his new home country, and neither had Mustafa. The Babuba family had learned Swedish from Bibbi, on her visits to Tunisia in the summers. They had come to Sweden on a Friday and on the following Monday Mustafa and Ali had started working at "Keep Stockholm Clean," a job which Bibbi had arranged for them. But now Ali tried to be a cultural person and took a wild guess.

"Astrid Lindgren, you mean that happy TV chef who sleeps with her big glasses on to see all the spices in the world while sleeping?"

Kim laughed. She was curious about the Babubas and decided to test Mustafa too.

Merjam ran back and forth to the kitchen, fetching food.

"And you, Mustafa. Who's Astrid Lindgren?"

"Madame Astrid Lindgren is a big celebrity who can capture an audience... children, young and old, she really has an aura. I can tell you that I have shaken hands with her, at Åhléns,(a chain of department stores)!"

Kim got more curious.

"But Mustafa, Astrid Lindgren is dead!"

"Really? No, that can't be, I got her autograph last Saturday. When did she die?"

Kim giggled, she didn't know what to say...

"One year ago...", said Anna Lindh

"I'll be damned", said Mustafa. "I have to start reading Aftonbladet and Expressen, so I can keep up with what's going on in society."

Merjam called for Mustafa from the kitchen...

"Monsieur Aftonbladet and Expressen. Come here and get the salad!"

Mustafa came into the kitchen. Merjam pinched him on the cheek.

"Ouch, ouch, ouch! Fatima is insane, taking books from the container!" said Mustafa. "Who is Astrid Lindgren? How should I know!"

"You should keep quiet when you don't have any idea! Understood?" said Merjam.

Mustafa came out to the living room with the salad bowl. He pretended that it was really hot, so that none of the guests might have thought that his "ouches" came from Merjam pinching his cheeks.

"Ouch, ouch, ouch, it's so hot!"

"The salad?" said Caroline inquiringly.

"No, the bowl comes straight from the dishwasher." Caroline lifted the salad bowl and smiled. It was cold. "Speaking of Astrid Lindgren, do you have her autograph here somewhere?" she asked.

"Ah oui!"

Mustafa had never seen Astrid Lindgren, neither in a picture nor in reality. He took the photo out of his breast-pocket and gave it to Caroline. She looked at the photo, surprised.

"This isn't Astrid Lindgren, this is Victoria Silvstedt (a Swedish supermodel)!"

"Ah, this is what happens when you don't manage the Swedish language properly", said Mustafa. "You mix up Astrid with Madrid, and Silvstedt with Siljan (a lake in Dalarna). It's terrible!"

Mustafa tried to come up with something funny. He turned to Caroline.

"Why does this happen, I mix up one thing with another?" he wondered.

"Well, monsieur, maybe it's like when you eat so fast that your stomach can't keep up and you get an ache, for example."

"He's not got an ache", said Merjam. "He's a real

good-for-nothing! You should see his room! He's the laziest man on earth, and as soon as I ask him to help out at home, he lies down under his bed for several hours and wails, 'My head is aching, my head is aching'!"

"Why do you lie down under the bed, Mustafa?" Anna Lindh asked.

"I want to study our donkey's behaviour and prove to mom that in fact our donkey is the laziest creature on the planet and not I!"

Caroline smiled and applauded.

Fatima came back into the living room, and Kim asked again, to test Fatima: "Fatima, which Astrid Lindgren book do you like the best?"

Fatima had studied Swedish for immigrants and she had already read several Astrid Lindgren books in class.

"Oh, Astrid Lindgren is my favourite author, she's written so many great books, I can't decide! I guess 'Mio, my Mio' and 'Ronia the Robber's Daughter' are my favourites. And don't forget all the good films that are based on her books!"

Kim started applauding, and everyone else in the living room joined in a big applause for Fatima.

Anna and Merjam

Anna's sons started playing with Besbussa, Caroline remained seated, talking to Ali, Mustafa and Fatima. Anna Lindh went into the kitchen, where Merjam was working on the dessert, a chocolate cake.

"And you're just standing here working and working!"

"To me it's not a job, it's only fun to treat you with our specialities! But I'm a bit annoyed that I forgot to buy wine."

Anna tried to say that she liked Merjam, a fantastic mother of three.

"No, no, we don't need wine. I'm already moved by your hospitality, your warmth and your humour. I wished that all immigrants here in Sweden would feel so content as you seem to."

Merjam nodded and gave Anna Lindh a hug.

"Thank you very much, Anna!"

"I was so curious about you before I came here", said Anna.

"You were curious?"

"Yes I was, and I still am. I want to know how immigrants like it here in Sweden. I wish I had more time, then I would ride around Stockholm on my bike, meet immigrants, and see how they are."

"And I wish politicians across the globe were infected by the Anna Lindh disease! Then they would leave their castles and go out biking among ordinary people."

Anna Lindh smiled.

"I really hope it's no disease. It's a politician's duty to go out and meet people, to see how they're doing. You learn so much from that. Like when I was in Sarajevo and had dinner with a Bosnian family. You get a completely different understanding when you do such things."

"Yeah, that is how all politicians should think! That's how they did it in the Middle East in the 8th century. Back in those days, the Arab emperors couldn't eat or sleep before they knew for sure that everybody had enough food for the day. But it's a different mentality these days, it's as if most politicians mainly cared about their bank accounts."

"I can agree with you on that, partly. It's a shame, but remember, all politicians aren't like that!"

"No, and you're one of the best ones. But hey, now I'm going to invite you to something delicious!"

Merjam handed over a spoon of chocolate mousse to Anna Lindh. She tasted it.

"Oh, this is good! What is it?"
"Home-made chocolate mousse with fried pears."
"What do you do for living, Merjam, are you a chef, perhaps?"
"Thanks for compliment, but no, I work as a factotum at the Stockholm University library. And on the weekends, I work as a volunteer for a non-profit organisation, called 'Help Africa'. And I'm a member of 'Humour sans frontières', humour without borders, here in Skärholmen."
"That sounds fun, what is that?"
"We've started a parents' organisation for our kids in Skärholmen. Multicultural dance and humour are our specialities. Together with our children we arrange dance competitions, stand-up comedy competitions and lots of other stuff. We feel that we come closer to our children this way, we look after them, we know where they are and we and do something meaningful together with them."
"That really sounds fantastic! But how do you have time for all that, work, kids, donkey, volunteer work, organisations..."
"I'm happily unmarried, no man, I have time for everything, it feels good..."
Fatima came in and took the chocolate mousse and the pears, Merjam continued with the chocolate cake.

The neighbours

The rumour about Anna Lindh's visit had now spread in Skärholmen. Suddenly, the doorbell rang. Fatima opened the door and it turned out that half the neighbourhood stood outside in the stairwell.
The neighbours Dorota and Clara were standing at the front. Behind them, you could hear the sound of drums. Fatima invited her neighbours to the kitchen where Merjam was.

"What are you doing, Merjam?" said Clara. "You've caused economic trouble for us here in Skärholmen!"

Merjam, with chocolate on her hands, looked at Clara.

"What have I done?"

"Don't you see what it means to invite Anna Lindh? Now the rents will skyrocket here in Skärholmen!"

Anna Lindh laughed.

"Do you think so?" said Merjam.

"Absolutely, we have brought a box full of rent subsidy forms", Clara replied.

"I don't need any rent subsidy, I've got a job."

"Well, we all work", said Dorota. "But when the rents go up to over half of what we earn, we can't afford to stay here. And it's all because of you!"

"Please, minister", Clara begged, "help her fill this form out. Her fingers are all soggy."

Anna smiled and opened the box. In it was a big cake with something written on it: "Anna Lindh, we love you! Skärholmen 2002" Everyone cheered.

"Welcome to Skärholmen, Anna!" everyone said in unison.

For the second time that evening, Anna Lindh was touched by the welcome.

"Oh, thank you! You're all wonderful!"

"Welcome in, everyone", said Merjam.

"Have a seat in the living room, I have chocolate mousse with fried pears for you!"

"We don't have time", said Dorota, "we're on our way to the sports hall! Mustafa! Monsieur belly dance expert! Are you coming tonight?"

"I'm afraid of the dark, I won't go without my mom!"

Big laughs. Mustafa turned to Caroline and Anna Lindh.

"Do you want to see something exceptional?" he asked.

Multicultural dance

"Absolutely", said Caroline. I like exceptional events.. What is it?"

"A multicultural dance contest! The contestants mix the dances of their own cultures with modern disco dance. And then there's a contest called 'Humour without borders'."

Merjam was a little annoyed by Mustafa suggesting that they guests should go somewhere else, before she even had served them dessert. After all, they had declined this party tonight because of their visitors.

Anna Lindh became even more curious.

"It would be fun to go there and have a look - if you don't have anything against it, that is?" she said and turned to Merjam.

"What are we going to do with the cake? It's ready now!"

"It's a long night here in Skärholmen! We can come back and eat it later, and quite frankly, I'm rather full now!"

"Ok, then, off we go!"

Everyone went together to the sports hall, except for Ali and Kim, who made a detour to the stable and left the donkey there. Then they went to the sports hall too.

The Skärholmen sports hall was packed with people. The walls were filled with posters: "Dear friends: we will give away a holiday to whomever knows the funniest story or can do the grooviest dance." There was a mixed audience, Swedish, immigrant, young, old, side by side. Every time the organisation had these meetings in the sports hall, one different nationality took care of the pastries. This time it was the Turks' turn to show their specialities. Claudia was tonight's hostess.

"Hello, everybody", she shouted. "I feel so happy when I look out in the hall and see that so many people have come! When Merjam started this organisation three months ago, there were about 20 people here. How many are here tonight? Two hundred? Three hundred? Amazing! We're going to start in a minute, but first I have to present a very special guest that we have here tonight. It's an honour for me to tell you, that with us here tonight is foreign minister Anna Lindh!"

Big cheers, and big applause, everybody stood up to look for Anna Lindh. Where was she? After a while, Anna stood up and waved a little. When people noticed her, the cheers and applause grew louder.

"OK, shall we get started?" shouted Claudia.
"YEAAHHHHH!" from the audience.

Mamadou

"Our first candidate in the competition 'Humour without borders' is Mamadou Camara! He's 45 years old, works as a postman and at his job he has earned the nickname 'Sweden's funniest postman'! Mamadou's son Abdoulaye will be competing in the dance contest later tonight, so we'll see, maybe the Camara family will hit the jackpot tonight! Big applauds for... Mamadou!"

The whole sports hall applauded and whistled. Mamadou was a known figure in Skärholmen.

"Thanks, thanks", started Mamadou. "They use to say that a good laugh prolongs your life. But I also want to say that laughter makes it easier for kids to learn new languages. I have a son who takes French in school, and for a long time, he thought it was really difficult. I told this to Merjam, and she gave me some advice; 'humour... it's the best way to learn a new language. Get him some easy and funny books in French, and you'll see, your luck will turn when he has fun and a zest for learning.' Said and done, I went to the bookstore and bought some humorous books for the boy, and you know what: our luck really has turned! He will soon speak French like Zinedine Zidane!"

Loud laughter in the audience.

"So, humour, my friends, is not just fun and jokes, it can be used for other stuff too, for language, for the body and for the soul, for health. And, it can also be used AGAINST things: like violence, for example."

Applause again.

"OK, that's all from me, thanks!"

Mamadou ran off the stage, to the audience's confusion. Was that all? A moment passed, then Mamadou came up on the stage again.

"That's right, I forgot, I had a story to tell too. OK, are you ready?"

"YEAAAAH!"

"There was this girl from Senegal, Esther, who was working illegally in Stockholm at a dry cleaner's. Esther was shy, and she desperately needed a work permit in Sweden. Her employer, a Swedish woman, suggested that she go to the Hilton Hotel by Slussen, where the possibility of meeting middle-aged gentlemen seeking a life partner was high. She said to Esther, 'Put on something beautiful and go there, before the night has passed you should have found someone who wants to marry you, and then you get your work permit'. Said and done, Esther went there. The day after, she didn't show up at work. Her Swedish boss of course started to worry a bit, and since the Hilton Hotel lies just by the ferry harbour, she thought that Esther perhaps had taken a ferry, maybe to Finland, or to Estonia. At one o'clock, Esther suddenly showed up at the dry cleaner's. She was very pale, but still looked happy. 'So, you came after all! But we're closing in two hours, it's Saturday, you know. You look pale, what has happened'? (Here,

Mamadou spoke with a French accent). 'Well, it's not that bad today' said Esther. 'But you should have seen me yesterday, I was so sea sick'. 'Sea sick? I knew it! You took the ferry to Mariehamn and back, right'? 'No, I've just been out dancing, at that Hilton hotel you recommended. 'Do you get sea sick from dancing'? asked the boss. 'No, but I followed a Swedish man home, and he had a gigantic waterbed'!"

The audience laughed and applauded.

"We thank Mamadou for that", said Claudia.

Zaineb

"Next man in line is a woman! Her name is Zaineb Ben Hadj, she's 52, comes from Morocco and looks after old peoåple. I have to congratulate Zaineb, she had been unemployed for a year, and after working as a stand-in at Björkgården old people's home, she captured everyone's heart in such a strong way that the boss now has offered her a steady position! Cheers to that!"

Cheers and applause again. Zaineb was moved by the audience's reaction.

"How does it feel, Zaineb?" Claudia asked.

"Oh, my eyes get all wet, a thousand thanks to all of you, you're so wonderful!"

"What made it possible to get a steady job?" Claudia asked

"Dear Claudia, humour, humour! With humour you can get a steady job. I want to thank Merjam. Yes, I also call her Merjam. Maybe I shouldn't, I'm even older than you, Merjam! But to me, and I think that I can speak for all in Skärholmen here. you are mother Merjam to all of us, such an immense power can only come from a real mother! So, I suggest we give Merjam a big applause!"

"Merjam, you've helped me so much. Without your humour and your warmth, I don't think I would have made it. To go unemployed is to die slowly but surely, you wither away, you feel so low, everything looks black. But thanks to your humour and warmth I made it through tough times. And now my luck has changed, I have a steady job and it's so wonderful! This organisation has been like a miracle cure for me, I joke, I laugh, I have fun. And all because of you, Merjam!"

The audience applauded again. Merjam looked embarrassed by all the complimentary words.

"OK, now we all know", said Claudia. "Applause to Zaineb!"

"Yes, my friends. I used to work in geriatric care before, too, in a place near a forest. An older man and an older woman got a crush on one another. Every day they went to the forest, and they always brought a mushroom basket, because there were plenty of chanterelles in the forest. But there were never any chanterelles in the basket when they came home. So, one Saturday when the weather was nice, they came back from the forest and the basket was suddenly filled with nice yellow chanterelles. 'Oh, good job today, so many chanterelles', I said when I saw the filled basket. 'Well', said the old man, 'there were so many people in the forest today, we had to pick chanterelles'!"

Zaineb threw kisses at the audience.

"Thanks, Zaineb! OK, let's move on... there's going to be tons of things happening here tonight, we have a dance contest, 'Humour without borders' continues, we have a band coming on later... but first I'd like to present a fantastic person, a person who's like a newspaper coming out every day, but with only good news in it! It's a great honour for me to present to you... 'Madame Volunteer', Elisabeth Holmberg!"

Elisabeth

"Thanks, Claudia. Great presentation, I must say. And the thing is, this newspaper… which is me… it has some good news today, too. I happen to work for a charity organisation called 'Help Africa'. At the moment, we're working on a new project. I'm sure you all know that many children have a tough time in school. The staff working in the schools does a good job, but it's not always enough. I'm sure all parents do their best to help out too, but sometimes that's not enough either. We want our children to be able to pass school and get an education for the future.

So we at 'Help Africa' have started this project, we call it 'The knowledge bank'. We've recruited senior citizens with an academic degree who volunteer to help school kids with their homework after school. We've already had a successful get-together in Skärholmens gård, we were 40 school kids and five seniors, and everyone was really satisfied with the outcome, young as well as old. Now, we will continue with this project, to start with two afternoons a week, that would be on Mondays and Thursdays at 4 in Skärholmens gård. I encourage all of you, young and old, parents or kids, teachers or students, to come by and say hello, to see what we're doing. We're having a really good time together and we hope that this will grow and become a tradition here in Skärholmen. That was all I had to say, there's going to be a showcase by the exit doors for those interested in more information. Thanks, everyone!"

"Thanks, Elisabeth! Stay here on stage a moment, I have a question for you."

"OK."

"How did you become a volunteer worker, how did it all start?"

"It was my mother, she's had some trouble with men

over the years. She went through psychological difficulties for a few years. She saw a lot of doctors and psychologists. It was what you might call a 'rich man's disease'. But then at a party she met Abdoulaye from Senegal, who was a volunteer worker for the Red Cross, and he brought my mom there. Soon enough, mom started working for the Red Cross, and after a while, she was feeling much better! Now she lives in Casablanca in Morocco together with Abdoulaye, and she's very happy. When I saw how good my mom was feeling just from helping others, I wanted to do some volunteering myself. And here I am!"

"Amazing, what a story", said Claudia.

The audience cheered.

"I have to ask you just one more question, too" Claudia continued. "One thing I've always wondered. How did you get the nickname 'Madame Volunteer'?"

Elisabeth lit up.

"I knew you would ask that question! It's my good friend Merjam who's given me that nickname, you have to ask her!"

"OK, how appropriate that Merjam is here tonight, then! Let's hear a really large applause for Merjam."

Merjam came up on the stage.

"Elisabeth, my dear", said Merjam. I'm not going to tell this until you've told your famous 'white wine' story."

"Oh no, you're not going to make me tell that one again", said Elisabeth and started to walk off the stage, but Merjam blocked her way down.

"You can't run or hide, Elisabeth."

"OK, oh my, you're causing problems for me, Merjam." Elisabeth smiled.

"Beautiful!" Claudia cheered. "OK, then we're going to let Elisabeth tell a story, and I ask you in the audience who want to learn the Lidingö accent (Lidingö is an affluent suburb of Stockholm) to listen closely now! Hands up for 'The Pearl of Lidingö', 'Madame Volunteer'…

Elisabeth!"

"Thanks, thanks. OK, there was this English boy, trying to pick up girls on the Internet." Elisabeth talked with an exaggerated Lidingö-accent. "One day he picked up this Swedish girl. He fell in love and decided to go to Sweden and meet her. He came here and met her, and he just fell in love with her even more. And best of all, she fell in love with him too! He decided to move to Stockholm, where she lived, and move in with her. That's what happened, and he found himself at home immediately. He had no job, so to spend his day, he sat home drinking white wine. After a while when he became a little drunk, he used to call her up and talk about all the great sex they had the night before, and the great sex they were going to have the night to come. The girl was really embarrassed, was that the way all Englishmen spoke on the phone? She asked him to stop making those dirty phone calls to her work place. 'The girl in the telephone exchange can hear it' she said. 'No, honey, why? You don't need to feel ashamed about our love, it's wonderful', said the boy. 'No, I don't', said the girl. 'But the way you say it, you make it sound so nice that I'm afraid the girl in the telephone exchange is going to steal you away from me'!"

The whole sports hall cheered.

"Thanks, Elisabeth, that was brilliant", said Claudia. "May I ask you to remain on stage? Is there anyone in the audience who can say 'vitt vin' (white wine) with a Lidingö accent?"

Buzz in the audience, Elisabeth just laughed.

"I don't think that everybody heard, can you say it again, Elisabeth?"

"Sure!"

"And now you in the audience have to remember to repeat after Elisabeth. OK, may I ask you for silence…"

"Vitt vin! Vitt vin!"

"VITT VIN, VITT VIN", the audience shouted.

"No, no, no, not good, not good", said Claudia. "Let's take it one more time. Rock It, Elisabeth!"
"Vitt vin!"
"VITT VIN! VITT VIN!"
"Almost! Brilliant!" said Claudia.
Elisabeth walked off the stage to the audience's cheers and applause.

Merjam on stage

"Well, Merjam", said Claudia. "Now you have to tell me, how did you come up with that wonderful nickname, 'Madame Volunteer'?"
"It's a long story, but I'll give you the short version."
"Shoot!"
"Elisabeth has a heart the size of a continent, and that continent is not Europe! It's bigger than that! She's always there for you, helping other people without wanting anything in return. I just thought it was a good nickname for her, simple as that!"
"Who gets a pet name like that - Volunteer?" Claudia asked.
"Everyone that helps out; Anna Lindh is Madame Volunteer."
Loud applause from the audience.
"Everyone that helps out, for example if they call lonely and sad girls to cheer them up, take elderly people out for a cup of coffee and a chat, I call 'Madame or Monsieur Volunteer'. You, Claudia, you are Mademoiselle Volunteer, you're also helping out.".
"I sure am! But Merjam, since you're here, we didn't think that you were going to come here tonight, you had asked for the night off but you showed up anyway."
"We had a slight change of plans", said Merjam abashed.
"Well, then you're going to have to work a little. You

can present the next point on the programme tonight. Here you are, Merjam!"

Claudia handed over a list with the names of the dancers who were going to participate in the dance contest.

"Thanks, Claudia! I'm more than happy to work a little here tonight, it's an honour. So, next point… multicultural dance!"

More cheering.

"Our first six couples competing all come from different countries. From Argentina… Carlos and Esmeralda! From Nigeria… Ekon and Adeola! From Russia we have Sergej and Tatjana! From Malaysia… Farid and Aishah! From Thailand… Aroon and Kulap! And finally, from Tunisia… Mustafa and Susan!"

Cheering and massive applause from the audience.

"Multicultural dance is about dancing to a famous western pop song, for example something with Michael Jackson or Justin Timberlake, and mixing in a dance from your home country, for example Arab belly dance, Finnish tango, Polish mazurka, Greek zorba, African dance, and so on. One minute, the couples dance disco, and the next they do some dance from their own cultureo.

"Before we start, I'd just like to say that I think that all the competing couples are so good at dancing disco dance."

All the dancing couples smiled and blushed.

" We have to thank MTV and all the European TV companies for that! But…when it comes to their own cultural dance it's a disaster! It's a shame! I was very disappointed last time. The Greeks, the Turks, the South Americans... All of you! You have to practise the dances of your own cultures more! We have big plans for this multicultural dance project, we're planning on starting competitions in the whole of Sweden, and maybe in the future abroad too! Our goal is that Skärholmen will be leading in this. We want young people from different parts of the world to meet, dance and have fun together and build bridges."

Applause from the crowd.

Prime Time Girls

"But before the dancing contest begins, we're going to present a new, hot group from here in Skärholmen! It's four young, talented girls, and they have just released their first demo with fresh, groovy songs! And from that demo, we're going to hear a song called 'Sweden is fantastic'. Let's hear ... 'Prime Time Girls'!"

A group of girls came up on stage, two of them with African background, two of them European blondes. They started singing 'Sweden is Fantastic' and combined the singing with cool choreographed dancing. The audience started dancing and singing along. When the song was finished and the audience had applauded 'Prime Time Girls', Merjam presented the dancing couples, two by two.

Then she walked off the stage and went back to her friends in the audience.

Anna Lindh turned to Merjam.

"What a cultural meeting", she said. "What a great atmosphere it is in here! Do you get support from the municipality for this?"

"No, we don't need to, we borrow the sports hall, and the money we get from the entrance fee, we use to purchase the winning prize. We give it to the best storyteller and the best dancer. "

"Very good!" Anna Lindh said.

"This party prevents isolation, frustration and segregation. We have fun together, parents and kids. That's what's important!"

"Good to hear that! I get so glad when I see all this happiness and warmth; this is stuff that makes a Swedish

politician sleep well at night."
"Thank you, Anna!"

When the party was over, everybody felt happy and content. The Babuba family and their guests for the evening, Anna Lindh and Caroline with their kids, had all eaten so many Turkish pastries that they didn't have room in their bellies for more desserts at the Babubas.
"So, how did you like our little party?" Merjam asked Anna Lindh.
"I loved it, it was wonderful to watch everything. Do you really know what you've created, Merjam?"
"No, what do you mean?"
"You've helped immigrants out here in the suburbs to find a place in Swedish society, it's called integration!"
"Oh, thanks. That's my goal, actually. To make people from different countries and cultures meet and have fun together."
"Seems like you've succeeded", said Caroline. "Great concept, this 'Humour without borders' . A great way of bonding, making friends and getting closer to one another."
"Yes, and creating a better world", said Anna Lindh.

Caroline's daughter Kim

The romance between Ali and Caroline fizzled out, but Caroline still wanted to be friends with Ali. She appreciated his honesty. By now, Caroline had understood that it was Mustafa who was the brains behind the pick-up technique at Kafferepet. But she had also found warmth and compassion, and new friends, Merjam and Fatima. And her daughter Kim was in love with the donkey Besbussa.

Exactly two weeks after the dinner at the Babubas,

Caroline was going to work the night shift at Huddinge hospital, and so they decided that Kim should sleep over at the Babubas in Skärholmen.

The doorbell rang, and Mustafa, who was home alone, opened the door.

"Hi and welcome!"

"Thanks", said Caroline and Kim in unison.

Kim rushed into the living room and started shouting, "Besbussa, Besbussa, where is Besbussa?"

Mustafa calmed her down. "Fatima and mom has taken Besbussa to the veterinarian, they'll be back any second now."

"Sure?"

"One hundred and ten per cent", said Mustafa, and turned to Caroline.

"Do you want anything to drink?"

"A cup of coffee would be fine, thanks."

"And how about you, Kim?"

"I want Besbussa!"

"OK, Besbussa will come. I'll give you an exotic drink with mixed fruits which is called 'Besbussa'."

"Oh", said Kim. "You can drink Besbussa as well?"

"Oh yes", said Mustafa smiling. He went out in the kitchen, put on the coffee machine and started mixing a non-alcoholic Besbussa. After a while he came into the living room.

"Here you go", he said.

Kim tasted the drink. "Mmm...good. What's in it?"

"I can't tell you, it's a secret recipe. If I told, you wouldn't come back here, right?" he said and dabbed Kim on the head.

Caroline took a sip of coffee and opened her bag.

"Mustafa, you know French, what does this letter say?"

Caroline dug up a letter from her bag and handed it to Mustafa. It was from an Algerian woman, who had been on holiday in Stockholm together with her husband a couple of months earlier. On the second day of the holiday, the Algerian woman had passed out in Gamla stan. Caroline had been nearby and helped her get to the hospital. She had now received a thank you letter from the Algerian woman. In French.

Mustafa looked at the letter, cleared his throat, opened his mouth…

"Eh, erm, hrm…"

A thousand thoughts went through his head in a few seconds. He had already lied to Caroline once, should he do it again? Improvise a new "Beef Wellington?" It would be dead easy, but the risk was, Fatima and mom could be home any minute, would he be able to make it in time?" He looked down on the floor and told the truth.

"Excuse me… but the thing is… I'm an illiterate, I can neither read nor write."

Caroline and Kim were astonished.

"Really?" said Caroline. "You? Who can hypnotise people, you, who express yourself so well?"

"Well", said Mustafa without looking her in the eyes.

Suddenly, his cell phone rang. Saved by the ringtone.

"Hi, it's mom. Are Caroline and Kim there yet?"

"Yeah."

"May I speak to Caroline?"

Mustafa gave the phone to Caroline.

"Hi, Caroline", said Merjam. "Sorry for being a bit late, but we´ll be there in an hour, at the latest. Can you stay that late?"

"Sure", said Caroline. "If you ask Mustafa to do me a favour."

"Sure! What favour?"

"It's a secret", said Caroline and smiled delightfully.

"I see", said Merjam. "Let me talk to Mustafa, please!"

Caroline gave the phone back to Mustafa.

"You heard, Mustafa?"

"Sure, no problem!"

"I count on that! Oh, seems to be our turn here, bye Mustafa!"

Mustafa hung up.

"What kind of a favour?"

"I was just so curious, how is it possible that you're an illiterate? It's the first time that I have met one in Sweden, so it's sort of special. Didn't you go to school when you were a kid? Tell me about your childhood! That's the favour I'm asking you."

Mustafa shook his head.

"When something is tough to talk about, I use to do what my mom does: get help from a Tunisian psychologist."

"Tunisian psychologist"

"The water pipe, of course! If I'm going to tell the whole story about my childhood in Tunisia, I need one."

"Do they call the water pipe "a psychologist" in Tunisia?"

"No, it's just I who call it that, but it does help me talk."

"I also want a water pipe", said Kim.

Mustafa smiled. "I'll order a small kid's pipe from Tunisia for you, but tonight you have to settle for Besbussa."

Mustafa's childhood

"I grew up on a small island called Djerba, off the Tunisian east coast. In many ways, it was paradise. It was almost unbearably beautiful and the weather was always good, all year around. But our family had to scrape by. Mom and dad divorced when I was only three years old, dad left and mom was stuck with three kids to support alone. When I was little, there were three things I hated: school, macaronis, and couscous. I had a schoolteacher who was very strict, and at the same time nervous and weird. He beat me more than once, even though it was forbidden. I liked playing the clown and making my fellow students laugh. My biggest dream was to become a comedian. The first year at school, I went there for a few months, but then I didn't want to go any more. It was so bad at school and we were having a tough time at home too. We had so little money that mom could only give us couscous or macaroni. Fatima and Ali loved couscous and macaroni, but not I. So I, who really like the Tunisian dish mokli…"

"The thing we ate at your dinner that melts in your mouth?" Caroline said.

"Exactly! I've always loved mokli, and I just couldn't stand macaroni and couscous every day. So when I went into town, you know, you could sense the smell of my favourite dish from far away.

There was this little Arab restaurant next to the bike shop in town, they always fried pepper in oil with black pepper and fried potato, and fried tomatoes with lots of garlic and spices… mmm… mix all those things on a plate, add an egg to it, and a warm crispy baguette… that's just top notch! And our Tunisian tomatoes are so sweet and tasty thanks to the sun. One day I was standing there, stone broke, I was only eight years old, and I was dreaming about having a few dimes to buy mokli. Suddenly I was offered work in the bike shop, just next to the restaurant. An offer that just came falling down from the sky, hitting little me. It was perfect, I was able to get out of school, I would get money to buy mokli, it was just like your kids here in Sweden who only want to go to McDonalds. The difference is, here the parents can afford it. Mom never could. I started skipping school and worked for the bike shop owner instead. He was a real joker, repairing and renting out bikes. I worked with all kinds of stuff, I was an errand boy, I cleaned the shop, went out buying things for the boss, and when he went home for lunch and siesta, I stayed and took care of the shop. From the little I earned, I bought mokli every day, for me and for my siblings, they often came running to the shop from school during the lunch break. The poor guys, all they had for lunch was a small slice of bread with olive oil and pieces of tomato on it, and for dessert, a couple of dates. And they had a long walk home from school too. I gave them some chocolate and candy, that way I could bribe them into not telling mom I was out of school. Back then, mom worked for slave wages down at Hotel Abounawas. She cleaned the rooms. Got up at half past five in the mornings, went to work and came home at six in the evenings. She must have had one and a half hour's trip from home to work. My biggest fear was that mom would lose her job, so I thought that it was good that I had a job too and could helpt her. But I was never in school, and after a while, people started wondering where that Mustafa kid had gone. My employer solved the problem. A friend of the bike shop owner went to my school and presented himself to my teacher as my father. He reported that I had moved to another school. Then they faked my school grades every year. I had decent grades during those years, at least for a guy who was never in school.

  The owner of the bike shop was, like so many other Tunisians, a big fan of James Brown. All day long, he would play music and videos with James Brown and other pop artists, like Michael Jackson and Prince. When the boss went for lunch or siesta, I took the time to try out some dance moves. I tried imitating James Brown, but I just couldn't pull it off. I thought that James Brown had little wheels under his shoes, how could he slide on the floor that easy with normal shoes?

  I tried Michael Jackson's way of walking and moving, and after a few weeks I was able to do the 'moon walk'. It was my happiest day. I used to call Michael

Jackson 'le grand Maestro'. The world will never forget Michael Jackson and James Brown! I wanted to be able to slide like James Brown, so one day I went to the shoemaker and asked him to put a couple of small wheels under each of my two shoes. And voilà! I was James Brown. I had bought a plastic carpet, perhaps one by two meters big. Sometimes when my boss went to take his siesta, the owner of the restaurant next door put on James Brown's 'I feel good' and shouted: 'Mustafa, come here and dance'! So I put down my plastic carpet and started dancing and sliding like James Brown. I had a stick in my hand, it served as a microphone. I often got coins from the restaurant guests as a reward. A couple of minutes dancing would often give me more money than a day's work in the bike shop. I especially remember a man named Josef, he would give me a whole dinar, that was a lot of money in those days. I dreamt about being a clown and an artist, an entertainer like James Brown or Michael Jackson.

I didn't want my mom to notice that I bought extra food, so I told her a kind of semi-truth, that I worked in the bike shop two hours after school to get a little extra money. I started to buy proper food: groceries, butter, oil, bread, and a special cheese which Fatima and Ali loved, 'La vache qui rit'. Mom was so happy that we had enough food. She was always joyful around the house, and I was a funny clown. We were happy.

The jasmine seller

One summer, when there was no job in the bike shop, I came in touch with a jasmine salesman. I started working from home, stringing small jasmine flowers on a thread, making beautiful necklaces or bouquets. You stuck about twenty jasmine flowers on twenty straws, one jasmine flower for every straw, then you gave them to the salesmen and they sold them everywhere on Djerba.

One summer day when mom came home, she got a surprise. She found me sitting under an olive tree, on a white sheet in a mountain of jasmine, I had been sitting there making jasmine bouquets. She hugged me and said, 'What a good son I have! So young, yet taking so much responsibility. I'm so proud of you, you're an angel'. I gave mom ten dinars which I had got from the jasmine salesman. She then continued, 'It's fantastic that you want to help me, and not just play around all day'. After about a month I asked mom if it was possible for me to start selling jasmine on my own, because my salesman had offered me that opportunity. You could make much more money from that. She objected at first, saying I was too young, only nine years old, plus it was too far from our house to the hotel and the centre of Djerba. It would have also been hard for me to meet the competition, there were already so many people selling jasmine on Djerba. Secondly, the jasmine salesmen weren't allowed to go into the hotels and bother tourists by selling jasmine. Thirdly, tourists weren't used to carrying flower chains or bouquets of jasmine. I thought, if I only moved like Michael Jackson, did a little 'moon walk' then I would sell more jasmine than them all! I knew mom was smart, and you had to persuade her the right way. So I said, 'Mom, give me a hug and everything is going to be all right''.

Mom answered, 'Just wait until you're a little older, bigger and stronger, you're only nine years old. There are many hotels on Djerba, and they are far apart. Just walking on the beach is tough for you, and then carrying a tray with jasmines on the head, it's heavy, you should know that'.

But I refused to give up. I tried to persuade her that you have to take the opportunity and make some money during the high season when there are lots of tourists. I tried intimidation tactics: 'You don't know if you still have a job when the low season comes, and besides, walking on the beach between the hotels is going to give me strong legs, that must be good, right? Please mom, perhaps I could do like your idol, James Brown!' After a few days of begging, I got my mom's permission, on one condition. I had to be home before dark every day, otherwise I would have to stop. I felt like the happiest nine year old on the planet. I bought a traditional Arab suit, with Arab pants and a fez. Already back then, it was unusual for kids to wear that kind of clothes, most kids ran around in t-shirts and shorts. My goal was to draw the tourists' attention and to be able to sell more jasmine."

"So you became an entrepreneur, only nine years old?" asked Caroline.

"You might say that", said Mustafa smiling. "Of course I didn't understand it then. I had two big dreams in my life: the first one was to help my mom at home, having enough food. The other one was to buy her a scooter, so that she could get to work easier. As I have already told you it was far rom home. I started selling jasmine, charming the tourists at the hotels. Some of them were very generous, sometimes I got twice the price for a bouquet. They were always playing music in the hotels, in the bars, by the pool, on the terraces. So there was always music around me and I took advantage of it. I moved like Michael Jackson, on my head I had a bucket with jasmine, and in my right hand I held a couple of jasmine necklaces. I did like a juggler. The tourists gathered around me, fascinated.

Some days, I sold out in half an hour, no jasmine left. I made four times as much as mom, I started stockpiling groceries, and…"

"Hold on a sec, was there a war going on in Tunisia?" Caroline wondered.

"You could say that to live in poverty and insecurity is like living in a war."

Caroline had never followed what was happening in other countries. Mustafa had been living in another world.

"Aha, now I see…"

"So I was worried about mom, she wasn't a steady employee at the hotel, and during low season they used to cut down on the staff. I thought she might have to leave. So, every Monday during high season, Ali and I took the donkey and the wagon and went to a grocery store. We bought oil, cans of tomatoes, spaghetti and flour, so that mom could bake bread. Another week it could be other groceries, like tea, sugar and coffee. We stored everything under our beds and in the donkey's room. That was a high point for me, seeing the happiness in mom's eyes when she saw how much food we had managed to store. She used to hug me, and every time it felt as if I was flying to the moon. The hug was my reward."

"Fantastic", said Caroline. "and you were only nine? So clever and so caring!"

"Well, I don't know. Life was hard, you did what you had to do. And I loved seeing mom happy."

"Mustafa", said Kim all of a sudden. "didn't you play with your friends?"

"No, but my siblings and I had the best game!"

"What game, hide and seek?"

"No, it was much more advanced. Since I was an illiterate, I asked Ali and Fatima to help me calculate how much food we'd need, for example how much oil mom would need if she used six spoons a day. Ali and Fatima took a litre of oil and started counting how many 'six spoons' there is in a litre, and how many sugar lumps we needed per month if we used 15 a day. Fatima poured out one kilo of sugar lumps on the table and started counting, to see how long a kilo would last. And then we did that with all the other groceries."

"Strange game", said Kim. Mustafa and Caroline laughed.

"It was the best game we had", said Mustafa. "We felt safe, all of us, if we knew that we had all we needed during the low season, from October to April. We used to say, 'Welcome autumn, welcome winter, welcome spring! We're ready'! You see, Kim, in Tunisia, there were the rich, the middle class and the poor. We were "the poor". But we fought. At last, I managed to get enough money to buy mom a second-hand scooter. During the low season I pretended to go to school, but in reality I worked at the bike shop. I didn't make that much money. I bought school material for Ali and Fatima. Mom didn't miss dad and there was plenty of joy in the family, especially when mom came home. I continued to work in the bike shop during the low season, and sell jasmine during the high season. By the way, when I was nine, Bibbi came to Tunisia for the first time."

Bibbi in Tunisia

"Bibbi, right, your mom told me about her", said Caroline.

"My sister Fatima became best friends with Bibbi. Since our entire family liked Bibbi, and wanted to talk to her, we started to learn Swedish, all of us. Bibbi used to bring language courses on tapes, "Swedish for immigrants". She used to stay for two months every summer. She would gather Ali and Fatima under an olive tree and teach them. Bibbi used to hang pictures on the branch of an olive tree. Ali and Fatima listened to her, and wrote down words at a Tunisian tea table, Besbussa lay on the ground and listened. Bibbi loved the smell of olive trees and the ocean and the blue sky. So, Fatima recorded a couple of words for me every day. When I went to work in the morning I listened to the words on my Walkman, repeating the new words in my head. When mom came home in the evening, Bibbi had a class with her, too. Fatima was the one in the family who was most thorough and passionate about learning Swedish, and when she was

17, she spoke more or less fluently. The dream about perhaps moving to Sweden started to take shape in our heads. So all the year round, we had Swedish Thursdays when we ate pancakes with butter, and pea soup, and just spoke Swedish to one another."

"What language do you speak in Tunisia?" asked Kim.

"We speak Tunisian, an Arabic dialect, and French."

"When do you speak Swedish, then?"

"When we want to say bad things about other people!"

"Hey, Mustafa, what bad stuff are you teaching my daughter?" said Caroline, who had trouble keeping herself from laughing. "OK, go on!"

"When I was twelve I was sent to a brother of the bike shop owner. The brother's name was Moncef. He ran a second hand shop nearby. Moncef bought and sold old furniture, porcelain, all kinds of stuff you need in the house like pans, stoves and so on.

I was sent there to help polish old aluminium saucepans with lemon juice and a traditional arab cleaner so that they shone like new. Moncef was a 50-year old man who always smelled bad and who abused poor women in trouble. Ethics wasn't his thing. The shop was divided into two rooms, a big one and a smaller one with a bed. Sometimes poor women came to sell a saucepot or some chair or whatever, just to be able to buy food for themselves and their kids. Moncef could see the situation they were in, how desperate they were, and he used it to his own advantage.

He used to say, 'Well, I can't sell this, but I can give you a little coin'. And then he took them to that other room and used them. It happened many times that I was alone in the big room, while he was in the other room doing his thing. It turned out I was a good salesman, even better than Moncef.

The brothers, the bike shop owner and Moncef kicked me between their stores like a football. I didn't enjoy the work, the salary was low, and I didn't feel good about knowing what the women coming to the second hand store went through. So when Hedi, whose father owned the best pottery shop in Djerba, one day came to repair his bike in the bike shop, I asked him to find out if could I go over to their shop as an apprentice and make a little money. They gave me a job. The best job I ever had, very artistic, I learned to paint, and a whole lot about art.

"Interesting!" Caroline said.

The ceramicist

At the ceramicist, they made big bowls, vases, jars, beautiful Arab plates and wall trays.

I started off as an apprentice. The place was owned by Bechir whose family had made ceramics for generations. He was 65. Bechir was both an artist and a craftsman and he was into history, big time. When the products were made, they were painted, often with his favourite motif, Elisabeth Taylor.

Hedi had trained to become a teacher, he had studied French literature at the Sorbonne in Paris, but he was also an artistic person. He wanted to work with his hands, to paint, rather than to stand in front of tough students in some school. Hedi loved literature. His favourite author was Molière. When I started off at Bechir's I went to work with almost no clothes, bare feet and with short pants, because it was so hot on Djerba. Bechir thought that I was a very funny person, and he called me 'little Diogenes'. I asked him 'who is Diogenes'? 'When you've made your first couscous plate I'll tell you', said Bechir. After a few months I managed to make one. Bechir was very satisfied, and he told me about the Greek philosopher Diogenes, who lived in a barrel. I was touched by the story about Diogenes and Alexander the Great, and I felt very proud when Bechir called me 'little Diogenes'.

I opened my heart to Hedi and told him about my dream, to become a clown and an entertainer. I loved playing the clown and imitate the Egyptian comedian Ismail Yassin, Chaplin, and the French comedian Louis de Funès, among others. Hedi told me, 'You have to learn the comedies of Molière; they will give you a good platform'. 'Who's Molière?' I asked.

In Tunisia, the craftsmen loved to talk while they worked, and I was a good listener. I sucked everything in like a sponge. Hedi was glad to pass on his knowledge, especially about Molière. So after work I didn't take the bike home, instead I walked slowly, repeating what I learned about Molière. I did what Bechir, the owner of the pottery, used to do when he had seen Elisabeth Taylor at the cinema. He went around the whole island repeating the film script in French. In Tunisia, all of the Western movies were dubbed into French. I wanted to paint and Bechir allowed me to paint and decorate plates, and the result was perfect. Apparently, I had a talent for painting. But after a while, I started thinking about what I was going to do with my life. I felt attracted to comedy and being a clown.

I started thinking more and more about how to shape my life.

I had two obstacles, one that I was illiterate and the other that there was no drama school on Djerba. Even if I had been able to read, I would have had to go to big cities like Sousse, Sfax, or the capital city, Tunis, to study comedy and theatre. And who would have then helped mom with the household and making money?

It was impossible in every way. But I found other things to occupy my mind with. I found out that there was a video store on Djerba, and it became a dream of mine to work in that store. There were all kinds of films there, the

Marx brothers, Chaplin, the French comedians Louis de Funès and Smain, Arab comedians and so on. I wanted to learn acting techniques by watching and imitating, to see how the pros moved and acted. I saw it as my only chance of becoming a comedian. One day when I was free from work, I took a walk on the beach. Close to our house I found a wallet with a driver's licence, one dinar and the receipt from a hotel. I took the donkey and walked to the hotel. I saw this as a sign of luck, I was going to pursue my dream, to learn comedy. At the hotel, I met the wallet's owner who gave me 20 dinars as a thank you. I went straight and rented my first movie with the Egyptian comedian Ismail Yassin. I didn't have a video player at home so my goal was to get to know the owner of the video shop. Then I continued to rent movies, one at a time with my 20 dinars. I charmed the owner of the video shop, I joked with him and tried to build up confidence between us. The next time I brought a small bouquet of jasmine to the shop owner and thanked him for having such good comedies. In reality, I hadn't been able to read a single title or name on the video cassettes. The same month there was the Muslim feast 'laid'. I asked Bechir if I could make a big plate with the words 'Good laid' on it, and give it to mom, but instead I gave it to the video shop owner.

A couple of days before laid, I went to give him a couscous plate as a laid gift and rent a video with what I had left of the 20 dinars. I would come back after laid and return the video. I was thinking intensively about how to get a job at the video store. Then it happened. The owner of the video store, his wife, his mom and dad were so delighted by the plate that they decided to invite me to eat couscous with them. Before going to the dinner at the video store owner's, I lubricated my hands with ointment and bought rubber gloves. Then I went to the dinner, brought a little jasmine with me, and explained to them that I had troubles with itching in the evenings. I was going to see a skin therapist in Gabes, who regarded as the best in south Tunisia. The video store owner, who's name was Imed, felt sorry for me and said, 'If you want you can help out in the store when I go to lunch or take siesta, or do errands. I said to him that I could only work there in the winter time, in the summers I sold jasmine. It was OK. I was going to start two weeks later.

I wore rubber gloves and I played my role every day at Bechir's.

I said that I was going to see this skin therapist, but Bechir told me to take a break for a few weeks instead, maybe it was the material, something with the ceramics. That was exactly what I wanted. Everything went my way! I started in the video store two weeks later. The best thing about the store was that they had a copy machine to copy ID cards from customers. That meant I could manage the job without any reading or writing. I did fine even when Imed wasn't in the store. I really liked being on my own in the store. I used to put on a tape and study famous actors, see how they worked.

Mustafa's theatre school

Two months later, I got the key to my own private theatre school."

"The key?" Caroline asked.

"Yep! An old locker with a mirror, my theatre school wasn't bigger than that. One of the regular customers at the store was Josef, I got to know him. He gave me that locker, he really liked me. I took off the door with the mirror on it, and sold the rest of the locker."

"Do you pronounce 'Josef' the same way in Tunisia?" Caroline asked.

"Yeah, Josef was Jewish, so it's the Jewish pronunciation.

Really good guy, he introduced me to the comedian

Michel Boujnah and to the movie 'The Man From the Riviera' with Danny Kaye. Josef told me, 'If you want to entertain people with dance and music and comedy, watch videos like these'. Have you seen 'The Man From the Riviera' by the way?"

"No. I must admit, I hardly know who Danny Kaye is", said Caroline.

"I'll be damned! Those who haven't seen Danny Kaye, don't know what real comedy is. He has made me crazy since I was twelve years old. My dream is to become a comedian as good as him."

"OK, I'll take a look at his films", said Caroline. "But what did you do with that mirror?"

"I hung it up on the branch of an olive tree outside our house. There it stood with the mirror, with the blue sky above, with the beautiful sand and with the blue water of the south Mediterranean behind me, and behind the mirror, the olive trees and my only audience, the donkey Besbussa. Since I started working at the video store at eleven, I used to leave home together with my siblings. They went to their school, and I went to the edge of the olive grove, and that is where I started my own drama school. I screamed, laughed and trained my mimicry, so that my face would become like rubber and I could express whatever I wanted."

"I have the picture in my imagination" said Caroline and smiled. "What a great sight. And such inventiveness."

"Yes, and what a beautiful view!"

"When you were standing in front of the mirror, did you repeat the expressions in French that you had heard on the video?"

"No, I don't understand French. I mimed and said everything in Arabic."

"Mustafa, did you do this every day?" Kim asked.

"Yes, absolutely! I always started with the multiplication table."

Chaplin's multiplication table

"We do that in school too! Do you start with five times or six times?"

"No, my friend, it's called Chaplin's multiplication table, it's with him that you learn how to mime."

"Cool!" Caroline said.

"I wanted to be like the big comedians and have perfect facial expressions. If you want, you can do it", said Mustafa. "So, at a quarter to eleven I took my bike and went to work, I always brought my Walkman, rehearsing Swedish. I discovered so many great comedians by working in the video store, and I practised all day, as soon as my boss was out. I didn't get it straight away, but I studied the pros, how they raised their voices, screamed and laughed at the right places, and after a while, I started to practise those techniques on my customers. When I spoke Tunisian I used mimicry, facial expressions, practised my comical skills. The customers laughed and laughed, I got such a great response. Imed was happy, I attracted customers. I wanted to play the clown, my dream was to travel the world and learn from the best comedians in every country. I wanted to find my own style and profile.

I couldn't wait to turn 14, because then you didn't have to go to school anymore. In Tunisia, almost everyone goes to school for six years to qualify for secondary school or vocational school. Those who don't qualify have to get by on their own and try to become an apprentice for some craftsman. I continued to fake my grades. Just before I turned 14, Imed, the owner of the video shop, came home to our house. He presented himself to mom and said that he wanted to offer me a job in the store. Mom was delighted by the offer. That day was like New Year's Eve for me. I didn't have to lie to mom anymore. I loved her more than anything."

"Did you still sell jasmine during the high season?" Caroline asked.

"Sure! There was much more money in that, I made more by selling jasmine for four months than eight months of working in the video store. But there was a higher value in the video store job, it wasn't just about money."

"You mean learning to act?"

"Voilà! Money's not everything, and the jasmine job made us live through the winter more than well. I used to surprise my mom, can you guess what I did then, Kim?"

"Maybe you dressed up as a clown?"

"I was a clown 24 hours a day. I didn't need to dress up for that. No, I found another way of making her happy. When I had sold a lot of jasmine, I used to put the money I had earned under the sheets in mom's bed, in a row, a long row of banknotes. So when she went to sleep, she got herself a real surprise! I continued to do that until she got used to it. Then I changed places, like putting some money in a saucepan, so when she was going to cook dinner... yeah, you know. You might say I played hide and seek with money! Mom was always happy when she found it."

"Mom, can't you play that game with me too?" said Kim.

"You'd like that, wouldn't you?" said Caroline and hugged Kim.

Mustafa smiled.

Mustafa's film school

"So, Mustafa, tell us more", said Caroline. "For how long did you work in the video store?"

"Until I was 18."

"And then?"

"I started at the 'Arab film school'!"

"What? Without knowing how to read or write?"

"Yes! It's not like a school, all you need to do is be kind and charming."

"How do you mean?"

"I'll tell you. It was a summer day and I was standing outside an Arab café trying to sell jasmine. I had my selling tricks as you know, I was inspired by Danny Kaye, Louis de Funès, and Michel Boujnah but by this time, I had my own act. A young waiter, who happened to be cousin of the café owner, came up to me. 'You should try and get in at the film school in Tunis', he said. 'You're a real clown! If I write you a good script, would you play in it'? I asked him if he was a script writer. 'No', he said, 'not yet, but I'm in my second year at the film school in Tunis'. I asked him what he was doing in this café then. Turned out he was only here working during the summers. 'The cafés', he said, 'are the best school for learning how to write a dialogue. You can listen to how real people talk, how they express themselves'. I wondered if that worked for someone who wanted to write comedy too. It did, he said. 'All day long you listen to funny stories and jokes. One piece of advice: record everything on a tape recorder, you'll have some fantastic material'! That guy really started something for me, suddenly I had fire in my butt. He went on, 'Many great comedians have started as stand up comedians, they have used things that they've heard, and then they've been discovered by producers, they've got parts in TV series and comedies'. I couldn't wait with my question, 'Can I take your job when you go back to Tunis again'? I took a chance of course, he was just a waiter - it was not as though he owned the place. He gave me the expected answer, saying that I should try and get into the film school, and then maybe work at the café in the summers instead. He couldn't have known that I was an illiterate. I told him the truth, that I had to work to support my family, and that I couldn't read.

I got a job at the café at the beginning of October and

I quit the video store with mom's approval. Every other day I started at one o'clock, and before work I practised in front of the mirror with the donkey as my only audience. After some time, the practice became more and more oriented towards telling stories I had heard at the café, with mimicry and gestures of course. At the café I came in touch with Tunisian tourist guides who helped me translate my sketches into German and English. Then came the summer, and the tourists were coming. I started selling jasmines again, I sold jasmine with humour! The tourists liked me, especially when I told funny stories in their language. I had the customers in my hand.

Move to Sweden

This was the best time in my life, between the ages of eighteen and twenty-one. My family - and I, for that matter - started hoping that we could maybe move to Sweden."

Kim interrupted: "Here's to Sweden!"

Mustafa and Bibbi raised their glasses. "To Sweden!"

"So Bibbi had promised that she could help us get work permits. I thought that if I came to Sweden, she would help me go further in my career and become recognised. And who knows, I could have met someone who wanted to risk some money on me and produce my comedy."

"What's the name of your comedy then?" Kim asked.

"Beef Wellington à la Mustafa!"

Caroline laughed. She immediately came to think about the incident at Kafferepet. She understood the technique that Mustafa had used with "Volvo Respect".

"Mustafa, you're a genius!"

"Anyway, I remember it so well, we came to Sweden on a Friday, Ali and I, and on Monday we started working at 'Keep Stockholm Clean'. Bibbi had already set us up with a job."

"Bravo! You are brave and assiduous."

Mustafa was proud of the fact that he had been working ever since he came to Sweden. Suddenly the doorbell rang. He went to open it and there stood a girl dressed in postman's clothes.

"Hi, there, I have a parcel for you", she said. "Just sign here."

Mustafa spit on his thumb and pressed it to the paper.

The girl started to laugh loudly.

"Is this really your signature?"

"Absolutely", said Mustafa smiling. "Bye and thanks."

The girl looked stunned. Mustafa closed the door and went back to Caroline and Kim in the living room. He opened the package.

"In this package lies the master's course for those obsessed with comedy", said Mustafa.

The package contained a bunch of DVD films from Italy which Fatima had ordered online for Mustafa.

"Look here, the best stand up comedians in Italy! Great guys."

Caroline and Kim looked at him, surprised.

"Do you speak Italian?" Caroline asked.

"A couple of words."

"Someone gave you a tip about these guys?"

"No, I've watched different talk shows on RAI, like Carlo Conti's show, there used to be lots of comedians on that one. I watched different talk shows from different European countries. They always have different comedians as guests. Thanks mom, for buying such a big satellite dish! So, when I meet Spaniards, Germans or Greeks, then I always ask about the name of the biggest talk show in their particular country, and the best comedians. It's like a drug for me, I always have to find something new, something more."

"But what are you looking for when you search for

new comedians" Caroline asked. "Is there any difference between a Swedish and an Italian comedian?"

"There's a big difference! No, I don't understand Italian, but the acting, the body language, they have a different style down there."

Caroline looked at the DVDs.

"Do you have any Swedish comedians?" she asked.

"Absolutely, like Robert Gustavsson, Lasse Brandeby and many others."

"Do you have Mr Bean?" Kim asked.

"Of course! What would life be without Mr Bean and John Cleese?

"Come, I want to show you something!"

Mustafa took Caroline and Kim to his and Ali's room. One of the walls was packed with posters of comedians from every corner of the world.

"Not bad, huh?" he said proudly.

"Wow!" Caroline bust out.

"Wow, wow, wow!" said Kim. "Here you have my idols."

"Pick one comedian, and I'll imitate him", Mustafa said.

Kim pointed at a picture of Mr Bean.

Mustafa immediately started his imitation, Kim started laughing almost as immediately.

"How do you do it?" Caroline asked.

"First and foremost, I have big ears", Mustafa joked.

"And then it's about practice, practice, practice. I've been practising since I was your age, nine, Kim."

"But why aren't you going to school here in Sweden?" Caroline asked. "Are you a member of the union?"

"Sure", said Mustafa.

"Then you have the right to get paid for learning to read and write in Swedish, for the same salary as you make by cleaning."

"Why would I do that? I have a job, and I don't want to use Swedish society for my own sake. I'm poor and I'm proud!"

"But please, Mustafa, these are your rights!"

"But please, Caroline! There are thousands of immigrants and Swedes who know how to read and write perfectly, but have they got anything from that? Yeah, 300 000 kronor in study debts and no job. As things look today, anyone who has a job can jump on one leg and dance happily!"

Caroline became silent. She looked at Mustafa.

"I just wonder one thing… how can you be such a good storyteller, and how can you be so up to date on everything happening in the world? You almost sound like an intellectual cultural celebrity when you speak. Yet you don't know how to read or write. How does it hang together? Yesterday I read in DN (a morning newspaper) about the problems with ethanol, causing starvation for people in the third world. You talked about that three weeks ago! I don't understand."

"al-Jazeera, al-Jazeera, I go to the al-Jazeera University", said Mustafa with a smile.

"But, Mustafa, don't you want to go to school here in Sweden?" said Kim.

"No, you see, Kim, a man can't do two things at once, only women can do that. Right now I'm focusing on learning 'the meaning of life' at Stureplan!"

"What's that?"

"It's a place for grown ups, you're too young to be there, you have to be 18 first!"

"I don't believe you."

"It's the truth, ask you mother."

Caroline nodded.

"It's true what Mustafa says. But, Mustafa, how long will you look for the meaning of life at Stureplan? Do you really believe that you'll find it there?"

"Yes, I'm certain! It will take me a couple of years to prove it, but when I've done that, I'll put up a tent there on Stureplan and help young men and women finding the meaning of life!"

Caroline shook her head and smiled.

"I have understood that you have worked selling jasmine flower on the beach, worked in a bicycle shop, in a second-hand shop, in a pottery shop, a video shop and as a waiter. Is there something you have done that you regret?"

"No. They were useful experiences, all of them."

"But you said that you felt bad when you worked in the second-hand shop and the bicycle shop, they were just bluffing and lying and ripping people off."

"Yes, I felt bad then, but it was the school of reality. Today I don't see any difference between a second-hand shop in Tunisia that is bluffing and someone who rides a Rolls-Royce in London. It's the same technique."

"But this second-hand dealer used women."

"Yes, he did it on purpose. He tells the women who come to him that what they want to sell isn't worth much, so that he can make a lot of money. President Bush did the same thing, he scared the American people by saying that Saddam had weapons of mass destruction and persuaded the American taxpayers to start a war that they didn't want. It's the same thing here in the West - they use rhetoric for bluffing."

Suddenly the outer door was opened, and in came Merjam, Fatima and Besbussa.

"Finally", said Kim. "Here comes the donkey!"

IN MEMORY OF ANNA LINDH; 1957-2003

My novel is divided into three parts under the overall title: *Beef Wellington à la Mustafa – the Babuba Family in Stockholm*. Each part is an independent story, a chain of adventures confronting the Babuba family in their new homeland Sweden.

Mustafa is one of the thousands of millions in this world who can neither read nor write. His life in Stockholm goes up and down like a trigonometric curve; he never quite reaches his goal.

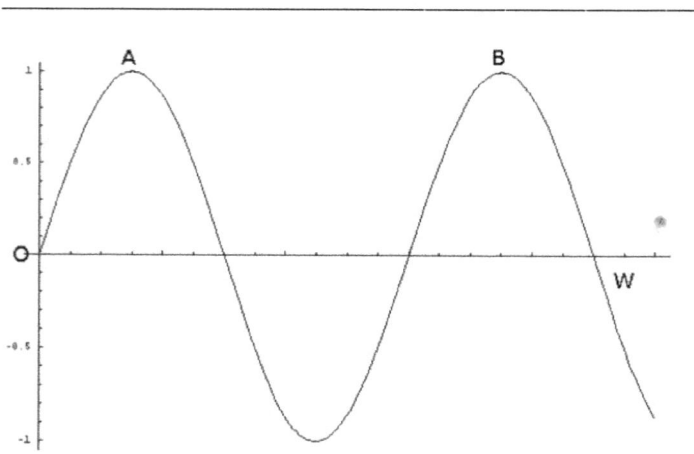

Sometimes he comes as far as A on the way up, but then he tumbles back to his cleaning job with bucket and mop. He makes a new start and climbs to B, only to collapse again.

This is a comedy that says something serious about how we live.

My project is to find people in different parts of the world who understand humour and comedy and can develop the story as a novel and as a TV series (sitcom). How would the Babuba family fare in London, Paris, New York, Los Angeles, Moscow and so on? Humour and comedy can help us understand how one culture can adapt to another.

If you are interested in participating in this project, contact me in any language through: lesitcomologue@comhem.se

www.ingramcontent.com/pod-product-compliance
Lightning Source LLC
Chambersburg PA
CBHW062147080426
42734CB00010B/1588